Stories of a Lifetime

from Ballyearl to Mossley, Abbots Cross and Ballyclare

A Memoir

Jack McKinney

Other Books by Jack McKinney

Facts Figures and Fractions (First Edition) 1980
Facts Figures and Fractions (Second Edition) 1983
They Came in Cars and Carts 1989
Published by The North Eastern Education & Library Board Area Resources Centre Antrim

Ulster Images: A Cultural Heritage Miscellany (With Cahal Dallat) 1992
Published by Educational Company, Belfast

Where the Six Mile Water Flows 1990
Published by Friar's Bush Press, Belfast

The Kennedys of Skilganaban, A Family Memoir 2018
Published by Shanway Press, Belfast

Printed in 2021 by Shanway Press,
15 Crumlin Road, Belfast BT14 6AA

Cover design: Rita Pimenta

ISBN: 978-1-910044-30-8

Acknowledgements

I must first thank my wife, Joan, and recognise the encouragement and practical help she has given me over the past years on this project. This applies particularly to her recent editing pages of text to bring the work to a conclusion.

Similarly I am indebted to my sons, Ronan and Eoin, daughter Emma and daughter-in-law Kira for their ideas, suggestions and prompt responses to my frequent appeals for answers to questions arising from my primitive operation of digital technology. In this family category I appreciated the assistance of Olga and Ken McKinney and Ina Dundee who helped name faces in photographs. Samuel Kennedy and Andrew McKinney edited text and from an early stage offered support for the project.

I owe a special debt to Tom Adair, former colleague in Abbots Cross School, who did much by his positive comments to encourage me not to give up and continue with the writing when my spirits and flagging energy had reached a low point.

Peter Davison and Rodney McMichael, former pupils, shared with me interesting memories of life at Abbots Cross School. I found this helpful. Peter provided a link with his mother following her retirement as Vice-Principal of the school. The Abbots Cross chapters were the first text to be written and followed a lengthy correspondence with Elsie Davison as she eagerly recounted incidents and episodes I have recorded here. Peter, I know, had to listen to his mother's frequent recital of her days at Abbots Cross. His patience in this chore and oversight of these sections of the book are appreciated.

I gained information and heard useful comments from Herbie Martin and John Strange on Ballyearl; from Tommy Kernohan, Stanley Dubois and David Hunter on Mossley and George Brown, Nan Moore and Tom Andrew, on my years at Ballyclare High School and teaching career in Ballyclare. I offer them, and many others in these areas I have neglected to name, my thanks and appreciation.
I received welcome assistance from Elaine McCracken (nee McAuley) in identifying those in the Abbots Cross PS photographs.

I am grateful to old friends from Abbots Cross School for the impressions of their time at the school – Tom Adair, Guy Warner and Donna Kells (nee Eaton). I also thank Frank Martin for his contribution relating to study and extra-curricular experiences of students at Stranmillis Training College in the late 1950s. He and fellow student Regggie Patterson proved invaluable in helping to identify students in the photographs of the College groups.

I need to outline some background to the photographs appearing in the book. These are taken mainly from family albums, especially those of my mother and aunts Agnes Hall (nee McKinney), Mary Kennedy and May Cranston (nee McKinney). With such collections it is virtually impossible to source and credit the photographers or photographic businesses responsible for producing the prints. Among those, over the years, who allowed me to copy and publish photographs in their possession were: Wesley Houston, Stanley Dubois, David Cooper, Tommy Kernohan, Olga and Ken McKinney, Wesley and Edwin McKinney and Timothy Dundee.

Some years ago I was fortunate to have been given an album of photographs by Sadie Seaton of Ballyearl. Belonging to her late husband James, a manager in the mill, these date from the 1930s and are of Mossley Mill, Mossley Hockey and Bowling teams, the Recreation Grounds at Mossley and various scenes of the Mossley district. I have used a number of these in the book.

Finally I gladly acknowledge how interesting and useful I found the book *A Well-Spun Thread – Memoirs from Mossley Mill* compiled by Jim Johnston and produced by Newtownabbey Borough Council. The fascinating accounts in this book of those who lived in Mossley and worked in the mill certainly complemented my own memories of Mossley – albeit of a much later period.

Introduction

Around the year 2000, I began to draft a few notes about my family background and my early years growing up in Ballyearl and Mossley. This was in response to a comment from my son, Ronan, who told me that he knew very little about my childhood and was curious to know more. I jotted down a few paragraphs and, illustrated with some photographs from my mother's tattered family album, I presented it to him at Christmas.

By then I was steeped in nostalgia and, before long, was well into the process of exploring and describing all the fun I had enjoyed with my brothers and young friends in the fields and laneways of Ballyearl. Eventually I remembered and recorded incidents and happy times, in Mossley Primary School and Ballyclare High School. From here it was logical to continue and outline my student life at Stranmillis Training College and teaching career in Abbots Cross and Ballyclare.

What I have set out to record in this book is a picture of everyday life in the communities where I lived, went to school and began my teaching career. I describe the incidents and, above all, the characters who made a distinct contribution to my development from a raw village youth to a mature adult.

Life in Ballyearl and Mossley in the 1950s centred on many door-to-door, daily conversations, neighbour-to-neighbour, concerning news and gossip shared in droll or witty style, but rarely unkind or unpleasant. Such exchanges surged through the life blood of village living. I dare say the 21st century equivalent of such customs is the internet and social media.

There were the unusual incidents, tragedies, the traditional, annual celebrations and exciting excursions on the train to exotic corners of Ulster such as Bangor or Portrush. Other opportunities for exploring the horizon beyond Ballyearl arose from occasional bus trips to Belfast and Ballyclare or a bike ride up the Carnmoney brae to the post office or dispensary.

I have also tried to highlight the banter and witty, spontaneous humour of the colourful characters who, in those days, continually seemed to appear and disappear, often as vagrants, beggars or travelling traders doing the rounds of the houses in Ballyearl. Their regular appearance and eccentric behaviour added a bit of spice to what could otherwise have been the humdrum monotony of our isolated existence.

I should explain that this book is the second edition covering my lifetime experiences. In the Spring of 2018 a younger cousin and I arranged a get-together for members of our Kennedy relations. In time for the event I produced a slim volume of anecdotes and photographs based on my memories and those of my Kennedy relatives. The book was entitled *The Kennedys of Skilganaban*. I believe the material it contained proved popular and added to the success of the family reunion. The appearance of this previous publication has consequently limited the selection of photographs, text and stories included here from my mother's Kennedy background.

It would give me pleasure to think that the following pages evoke readers' own memories of similar experiences, episodes or emotions in their lives mirroring, perhaps, what I encountered on my long but interesting journey from Ballyearl to Ballyclare.

Contents

Chapter 1: Ballyearl

I grew up in Ballyearl and Mossley. The name, Ballyearl, was that of a townland but it was used to refer to what was no more than a number of semi-detached houses and bungalows which straddled the Doagh Road and a terrace of twelve dwellings owned by William James Girvan, a local farmer. The farm was known as Ashley House and the terrace Ashley Park.

My family consisted of mum, dad, my three brothers and myself. I was the eldest. I was born on 26 August 1940 in the Samaritan Hospital in Belfast. The others were born at home – Iona, Ballyearl, Carnmoney, County Antrim. Although there were four boys, our ages meant that we were really two twos. Ken and I, separated by two years, were close and Edwin and Wesley, the younger boys, born respectively in 1947 and 1950, grew up together as a pair.

The McKinney Home at Ballyearl

The name Iona was originally on a plaque attached to the front wall midway between our semi-detached house and that of our next door neighbours – the Higgins family. My dad was proud of this mark of distinction and when it fell off the wall, as it did quite often, he put it back up. Contrary to my dad's opinion I didn't think the Higgins family worried too much about its presence. After his death it was the least of our worries and it disappeared for good. We still used it on our address, mind you, before eventually, the house acquired the dull anonymity of 605 Doagh Road, Newtownabbey.

Our house was semi-detached and situated beside Springtown lane or loney as we called it. This led to a cluster of cottages built, I believe, for the farm workers at Ashley Farm. There was also a larger detached house here and in our time it was occupied by the only labourer on the farm, Mr Ben Ross and his large and diverse family. The name came from a little well beside the lane and surrounded by a stone wall like the one pussy fell down in the nursery rhyme. My mum often took us up here for a walk and, from her account, I liked to throw pebbles into the well. For some reason I called this 'dashing in the obbit'.

About a hundred yards up Springtown loney there was an entrance to a field beside a stream and it was here that the Ballyearl residents took refuge from possible air raids during the Belfast Blitz. This spot had no cover from above and I never could understand why they felt safer from Hitler's bombs here than in their back gardens. Perhaps it was the group therapy which gave them all comfort. I was born in 1940 so I must have been there with the neighbours but I have no memory of any of these evacuations. The house was one of four which had been built, I think, at the end of the 1930s by a builder called Greer and I think he lived in one, possibly ours, for a time. It had the reputation, at least in our family, of having been built with shoddy, second hand materials and this was certainly borne out by our experience. It had serious patches of damp, especially under the windows and an alarming infestation of woodworm. There were parts which were so badly holed that they were unsafe.

Downstairs we had a parlour with a bay window. We used it very seldom, only when special visitors such as the minister came on his annual visitation of the neighbourhood. Our main room was called the kitchen and here we relaxed and ate our meals. It was our general purpose room and in spite of its name no cooking was ever done here. This was done in the scullery. In my early days we had a range – a black monstrosity which my mum hated as she was obliged to black lead it every week. Later we got a Devon grate. These were very popular then and I remember Joe Ryan, a fireplace supplier from Ballyclare, installing it. It had the disadvantage for my dad that he could only put on modest blocks of wood or reasonably sized shovels of coal, it was certainly not railway sleeper friendly – my dad's fuel of choice. This suited us boys because we hated sawing up the sleepers.

The scullery had a hand pump for drawing water from a well in the Higgins' garden and a jaw box sink where mum did the washing up and the weekly laundry. Dad preferred this sink for his evening ablutions, we others used the bathroom. The toilet cubicle was outside with an entry door round a right- angled runway. The space for it had really come out of the scullery rectangle.

Upstairs was our bathroom of which we were very proud; not too many houses in Ballyearl had separate bathrooms then. At least that's what my dad said. We also had two bedrooms on the first floor, the back room for Ken and myself while Dad and Mum shared the big front room with Eddie and Wesley who had a small bed behind the door. When my dad died Wesley had just turned eight years old and with Eddie ten their removal to a separate room was imminent. I don't know what plans my parents had to accommodate them. After my dad's death in 1958, other changes occurred to alleviate the problem, notably Ken's frequent spells living with Aunt Sylvia and Uncle Alfie Davis in Belfast.

Outside we had a grand little shed built by a neighbour, Tommy Strange, unusually from new timber and corrugated iron sheets. I vaguely remember this work being done on Tommy's week-ends. He lived in a cottage up Springtown lane. This was a well built shed unlike the later banty house assembled by my dad from discarded railway cattle wagons. The shed became a repository for his tools and all the odds and ends he regularly brought home or had delivered from redundant transport supplies.

It was our play space on wet days and even in later times when the banty house extension obscured its only window, it formed a sanctuary for bad tempered boys to cool off and for those in a huff to come to their senses.

The shed became the centre of an episode of great hilarity to all our family. This story, unbelievable but true, was not so funny at the time for my mother and brother Eddie. It happened just before Ken got married and left home. These were happy times and we always found something to laugh about especially at my mum's expense. She was a good sport and took the ragging she got from her sons in good heart.

For some time the shed door had been falling off its hinges and mum got fed up asking Ken and me to fix it. One Sunday she began the job herself and after some coaxing, Edwin was enlisted to help her. Edwin would admit that he was not handy with tools, rather like our uncle George whom he resembled in looks and temperament. He was not the best choice as mother's assistant.
My mother was never very good with tools either though she had had plenty of practice over the years. She was particularly ingenious in her improvisation of tools. A poker or a hatchet was used as a hammer while a range of blunt knives, all our knives were blunt, served as screwdrivers and if pliers were needed then a pair of old scissors proved useful. Considering the poor implements she employed it must be admitted that sometimes she made out quite well.

On this particular day she had found a heavy hammer of my dad's in the shed and she and Eddie set about driving six inch nails into the screw holes in the hinges. There was a considerable amount of noise – not unusual with this type of operation – and, as we listened from the comfort of our seats in front of the television, we judged that progress was being made.

However, after about an hour and a half we became aware that the hammering had stopped and that the noise we were hearing was more a kind of muffled shouting. Had they fallen out, not that unusual on my mum's projects? One of us ventured out and discovered that they had managed to imprison themselves in the shed.

 It seemed that they had inverted the hinges so it became impossible for the door to open or close. The six inch nails had been clinched over the hinges and the scissors were useless for pulling them out. We had an on site conference about the best course of action to extricate them. Ken was all for prising a sheet of tin from the roof to allow the pair, as he put it, to pop up like two slices of toast. Mother took exception to the laughter coming from our end of the operation. Eddie had resigned himself to waiting patiently for rescue.

Eventually we managed to get the door open using a spade to prise it off its hinges, six inch nails and all. Afterwards there was less talk from mother about repairing the shed door.

Another time after Ken and I bought our first car we decided to add an extension to the shed to allow it to be used as a garage. I was clerk of works. No plans were drawn up, indeed no proper measurements were taken. We just assumed that it would work even though it was obvious there wouldn't be a great deal of room to spare. One end was taken out of the shed and a set of double doors made from the corrugated sheets of the original end were fitted.

When the doors were opened they came very close to the garden hedge. The first attempt to put the car inside was tricky to say the least. It was just possible but very difficult. We had to make about ten steering cuts to enter and, once inside the shed , there was precious little room to disembark – a job not to be undertaken in a rush. Eventually the project was aborted and the sides were quietly nailed back on to the shed. We rather futilely hoped the neighbours had not noticed our failure.

We rented the house from Mr David Boyd of Boyd's Quarry at Carnmoney and it was virtually impossible to get repairs carried out promptly. The rent man, a pleasant gentleman, Mr McVicar, acted for the agents, Ferguson and Son, and called regularly to collect the rent. I remember his soft trilby hat, which he always doffed to ladies, and his chalk striped three-piece suit. Then, such a suit was the mark of a real gentleman. The rent was about ten shillings a week. A neighbour considered she paid too much rent for the condition of her house. Asked if her house was damp she curtly replied: 'Aye, it's damp and dammed dear!'

There was no mains water when I was a boy, the supply came from a well in the yard of the Higgins' house next door. We had to employ a hand pump to fill the storage tank in the roof space for the hot water system. I think the drinking water was hand pumped straight from the well. The pump, like many other appliances in our home, was temperamental and had to be primed before use; this was called giving it a drink! Occasionally James Higgins emptied a bag of lime into the well to keep the water sweet. Pumping water to fill the upstairs tank was one of our regular chores. 'Pump pump' was on a list of jobs written out by my dad for my brother Ken and me to do on Saturday mornings. The list was usually quite long and one autumn day Ken added 'Dig Snow'. Dad was mystified stating that there was no snow to dig but Ken told him that there certainly would be by the time we had got through the other jobs. He was not amused.

The biggest difficulty I remember with the landlord was getting him to arrange for the septic tank to be emptied. This was a brick lined pit covered by thick concrete slabs at the top of the garden and was not really a proper septic tank, more of a cess pool. At least it didn't work very efficiently. Mind you, we were unusual in having a water closet then but there were snags. The Higgins' toilet was piped into the tank in our garden and we always seemed to have the responsibility of contacting the landlord to have it emptied. We certainly knew when this was needed because the sewage backed up and I remember regular plunging taking place to make it serviceable. It was unpleasant. Mind you other houses around only had a bucket and dry ash pit which also had to be emptied regularly by Girvan's farm cart. The day this took place in the neighbourhood was always a good time to go off somewhere for a breath of fresh air.

Our septic tank was emptied by farm hands from Boyd's farm using a tractor and a trailer with a number of empty oil drums. The men used what can only be called large ladles to scoop out the black gunge from the tank into the barrels. We never enquired what became of this but, judging from the smell, it must have done wonders for someone's grass.

My mother gathered us all into the house with the doors and windows closed to await the completion of this delicate operation. She was amazed that often the men sat down in the yard and enjoyed their sandwiches at lunchtime not bothering to wash their hands first. Even when it was not blocked the toilet was temperamental. Its position was unusual. A corner of the scullery had been bricked up and access to the toilet was from outside. A path led from the back door round a corner to the closet entrance. My mum called this the runway and often the speed of desperate users proved it was an appropriate term. It was private if not entirely soundproof and the ventilation relied on the cracks and holes in the badly built door. I remember when, in a fit of DIY enthusiasm, I made a more closely fitting door, I was compelled to knock out a couple of bricks in the outside wall to fit a ventilator. If I hadn't done this someone would have been suffocated.

The cast iron cistern bore a trade name The Deluge and no piece of equipment was less appropriately named. To get it to release any significant volume of water one had to learn from experience the correct combination of long and short tugs on the chain. To this day I'm sure I could reproduce the right combination; we all learned this in the same way we learned other washing and toilet routines. The main problem arose when visitors, and they had to be very desperate, used the facilities. I can still recall the embarrassment of listening to continuous, fruitless chugs of the chain as various combinations were tried. I suppose we should really have had the correct sequence posted in Morse Code on the wall.

The Higgins family lived next door. There was the old mother whom we called Granny Higgins, two sons, James and Edward and a daughter, Kathleen.

Of these only Edward had been married. I think he moved back in with his mother after his wife died. They all seemed very old to us and, except for the mother who indeed was old, they were probably no more than 50.

Edward had a pigeon loft in the garden and we listened to him whistling to his birds in the evenings. Granny Higgins had her moments but the others were quiet and rather gentle folk who kept themselves to themselves. With a sallow complexion and grey hair the old lady was always dressed in black and with a shawl and a pinny. She reminded me of a 'shawlie' from a William Conor painting.

She loathed football and was annoyed when our ball went into her front or back garden as it often did two or three times a day. We sometimes did sneak through a hole in the back hedge to retrieve it but she was usually on constant guard at the front.

When we played on the road using our wall as a goal she took up position behind the curtains in the parlour and rushed out to wave her fist at us if we dared to tiptoe into her garden for a stray ball. The games were thus brought to an end as we hadn't the courage to face her down. Our parents were always afraid that we would annoy our quiet neighbours.

When she became senile in her advanced years Granny Higgins would wander down the Mossley Road and Kathleen, her daughter, had to go after her. She prepared meals for the 'weans' as she remembered her family of long ago. The old woman was not without humour and she always greeted Hamilton McConnell the Ballyclare undertaker, on a visit in his taxi to the neighbourhood, with the remark 'I'm not ready for you yet, Hamilton dear!'

She did live to a ripe old age slipping more and more into her dotage as the years passed.

Kathleen worked in Mossley Mill canteen and I remember her walking up the road from work at about two-thirty each weekday. I once went into the canteen in the dinner break from Mossley school and I recall Kathleen in charge of spreading margarine on the large baps on sale there.

It was sad to see Kathleen eventually afflicted in the same way as her mother in her old age. Indeed she developed the habit of sitting on the stairs and shouting vile abuse through the single brick wall at my mother. This always started about bedtime even though she had been quite civil the rest of the day. She also harangued the neighbour on the other side by shouting through the garden fence. Like her mother she lived well into her eighties in sheltered accommodation.

Brother James had been a painter in Ballyclare Paper Mill and he seemed to spend much of his time touching up the woodwork in their house. The smell of the paint is one I've not forgotten nor indeed the pungent odour of his pipe tobacco. We even smelt this as it drifted through the wall from their toilet to ours. He must have been banned from smoking inside the house.

The Higgins had a meat safe in their yard, a wooden box with sides and a door of chicken wire. There was no electricity then so there were no refrigerators. I had never seen such a contraption before and it intrigued me.

We children related better to Edward than to any others of the Higgins family. He was gentle and always spoke to us across the hedge, often telling us about his pigeons and where they had flown from before fluttering down to the loft. This was kept spotless and it was painted regularly by James. From the steps of the loft he overlooked our back garden and we often heard him whistling and chuck-chucking to attract the birds on their way home from a race. The constant cooing from the loft was one of the distinctive sounds of summer in our back garden.

The Higgins had a dog called Diamond and we were afraid enough of him to be discouraged from going into their property very often. It was a small, black Pomeranian and bad tempered. In temperament it perfectly resembled old Granny Higgins.

We were always on good terms with the Higgins family but there was one little aspect in which they differed from us. It was rumoured that Granny and the family sometimes had a little sup of whiskey. In a neighbourhood where the presence of any form of alcohol was rarely a household item this marked them out as different. I'm sure that there were other households where there was an occasional tipple but whiskey was in a different league. Unless it was used for strict medicinal purposes whiskey drinking was uncommon.

The centre of Ballyearl was the bus stop. Here, throughout my boyhood, the 156 Belfast via Mossley and the Ballyclare via Mossley UTA bus services took us all to and from work, shopping and school. The frequent green buses told us the time of day, kept us supplied with newspapers and gave us some feeling of connection with the rest of the world. In the 1950s Ballyearl was a backwater where life was often not very exciting.

Mossley, a mile away, had its mill and school, Carnmoney boasted churches, a graveyard and a big quarry. Ballyearl simply had Samuel Tweedie's grocer's store and Willie Forsythe's confectionery shop.

Mind you, Tweedie's shop was an enterprising concern. The pride and joy of Mr Tweedie, nobody called him Sam, was a red, chromium Berkeley bacon slicer which gleamed on the wooden counter. Unlike some of his competitors around the district Mr Tweedie kept this magnificent machine spotless and it fairly peeled off the thin slices for which Sam was renowned.

There were tall tales told by his young assistants of bits of fingers shorn off in times past and delivered in parcels of bacon. In these times you had to serve your time to the grocer's trade and a succession of local lads, on very low wages, spent a lot their time weighing out tea and sugar into paper bags from chests in Sam's back store.

Sometimes at lunch time three of the assistants had a game of hockey on the road outside the shop front. One day a shot was struck a bit too energetically and the ball flew straight through one of the small windows at the side of the shop. The culprit was Bobby Lough, a school friend of ours, and he told us that Sam deducted every penny it cost for a replacement out of his meagre wages. The Tweedies had earned a reputation in the district for being just a wee bit 'near'. I remember my mum being quite overcome on one occasion when Mrs Tweedie actually deducted a sixpence from her account.

Samuel Tweedie probably never realised how he fell foul of the boys in Ballyearl. Our football pitch was on a part of a field opposite Ashley Park which never seemed to be used by the Girvans. We presumed that they owned it as they did most of the surrounding land. It was almost waste land but flat enough for football. Mr William James Girvan senior certainly did not chase us off it as he did regularly from his other fields. He had, as our headmaster in Mossley would have put it, a great command of the English language and employed words to hound us off his land that we knew not to repeat in front of our parents. This never happened at 'Ashley Stadium' so we reckoned that there was something different about this field.

Disaster struck in the 1950s when Samuel Tweedie was extending his premises and used the pitch as a dump for the spoil from the excavations. The large mounds restricted but did not end football games and these continued in a smaller area. Often, especially on summer evenings, these involved others from Ballyearl, parents and older lads who were at work in Mossley Mill during the daytime. We boys played there for hours on end and returned to our homes when it got dark, sweating profusely and often upset by altercations which had broken out during play. With no referees this was hardly surprising.

Here I made two big discoveries. My quick temper and love of football usually got me into fights and my short sight was a serious handicap. Possibly the latter aggravated the former and I grew up with the dilemma of wearing my glasses and being able to see the ball or discarding them in the interests of safety and aiming my kicks a bit more wildly. Sometimes I even scored a goal but it was more often than not hit and miss.

Perhaps it was such frustration that got me into trouble with Mr Tweedie. He was a respected elder in our church in Carnmoney and a Sunday school teacher in Monkstown. One day when I was in his shop doing a message for my mum he took me aside and asked me if I realised the kind of language I used on the football field. This proved to be one of the biggest surprises of my young life. I was totally unaware of this and was immediately terrified that he would tell my dad. If he had done so I would have been punished, but he generously said that if the colourful language stopped there would be no more heard of it. I thought this very decent of him especially from someone whose actions had threatened the continuation of football in Ballyearl. I must have cooled down after this incident because I had no more lectures from Samuel though I have to say that even when I was older and got to know him better I never lost that feeling of discomfort in his presence.

There might have been echoes of this incident later when one day I was helping my mother by writing out from her dictation a list of shopping items she needed from Tweedie's shop. Before I gave her the final list to hand to Mr Tweedie that I knew was her usual procedure, I added a postscript in capital letters 'B'oul Sam you're a dacent spud'. I thought mum would have seen the addendum and removed it before it reached Sam's eyes. Unfortunately not! I could imagine the horror on her face as he read the comment. Apparently she knew from his broad smile – he seldom laughed – that there was something amiss.

To my mother Mr Tweedie was a figure of respect second only to Mr Hamilton the headmaster of Mossley school or Rev. S.H. Nicholson our minister in Carnmoney Presbyterian Church. One did not joke with such dignitaries. Later my mother was able to laugh at this little prank but at the time I probably got a clip on the ear for my cheek.

My dad's relationship with the Tweedies remained a bit less deferential but was still very formal. I remember going down with him to see Mr Tweedie after shop hours to discuss buying some timber he had left over from the work on his extension. We had never been around the back of the premises before and my dad knocked on the first of the two doors there. He knocked again and again with no answer and we were just about to leave when there was the sound of flushing and the door opened and Mr Tweedie, looking a bit sheepish, emerged from the toilet. My dad was not easily flustered but on this occasion he did redden a bit. Mind you we got the timber at a good price, and Samuel was not renowned for bargains.

There were few public or community buildings in the district when I was a boy and other than the public elementary school in Mossley village and the church in Carnmoney, Mossley Orange Hall was the one that made an impression on my young life. It continued to do this well beyond my teenage years.

First I went to Sunday school there, probably from the age of four. At that time my grandfather was the superintendent and my aunt May taught the younger children. I therefore had no escape, not that I would have wanted it. I enjoyed the Sunday afternoon classes and especially the Christmas party and annual excursion, always to Portrush on a Saturday in June.

I had been called John, though my family called me Jackie, for my paternal grandfather. He, too, was known as Johnny but not often in the presence of younger relatives. He was very devout, cleaning his boots on a Saturday night rather than desecrate the Sabbath, and Ken and I were terrified of the stern disapproval we detected of most of the antics we got up to down on his farm.

One Sunday I was asked by Aunt May to go down to the farm, about half a mile from the Orange Hall, to fetch his spectacles that he had uncharacteristically forgotten. I met a few senior scholars, as we were called, on the way back and they asked me light heartedly if I had been down to get 'Johnny's windows'. The news of his oversight had got around but more significantly I learnt his nickname. In my daydreams, and I can assure you it went no further than that, Ken and I hailed him casually – 'Hello there, Johnny!'

At Sunday school every week we got a small coloured transfer with a biblical text and illustration to put in our bibles or catechisms. I remember wearing Moses sandals, ankle socks and short grey flannel pants with a Fairisle patterned pullover. The teachers were really kind, gentle and pleasant.

I do remember one Sunday being very upset and weeping because of some gloomy references made, I think, to death and the torments of hell by an overly zealous male teacher. My grandfather had gone by this time and I think my dad had just had his first heart attack and the mood in our house was sombre. The teacher quickly realised why I was upset and he was then very pleasant and comforting. At this time the main influence on the Sunday school was the Monkstown Baptist church and it had gone very revivalist. The title of the school was Mossley United Sabbath School to emphasise its non-denominational teaching and usually the doctrine was very moderate. Anyway the parties and excursions were as good as ever.

The attendance at the Sunday School was high and most of my friends went too. There was always a long line of kids trooping down the road from Ballyearl to Mossley just before three o'clock every Sunday afternoon. I think the parents were only too glad then to get an opportunity for a bit of peace and quiet for the afternoon. The music was always rousing. We sang from a little red book titled Alexanders Hymns and most of these hymns and choruses were meant to be belted out with vigour. Only one or two were dreary. One I still remember dealt with lighthouses and ships wrecked far from home. This was a bit strange for youngsters most of whom only saw the sea once a year at Portrush. Our family had an aunt living in Whitehead where there was a large lighthouse so we could appreciate the lines:

> *Brightly beams our father's mercy, from his lighthouse evermore*
> *But to us he gives the keeping of the lights along the shore.*

Nothing pleased my mother more on a Sunday night than to gather us all around the sitting room fire and sing hymns from the wee red book. She sometimes read to us from a sacred book called The Peep of Day. My dad escaped as Sunday night usually found him down at his mother's or sleeping on the sofa.

For a very long time I was confused about the writer of these hymns. My grandfather's right hand man, his eventual successor as superintendent of the Sunday school, was Mr Alex McIlwaine. He was a gentle and friendly soul and a perfect counter to Granda Johnny's stern image. He took the senior bible class and in later life as a teacher I wondered how he had effortlessly kept control and gained the respect of these lively teenagers. His whole family taught or attended the Sabbath school and John the youngest was a talented musician and expert pianist. It was because of his lively playing that the Alexander's hymns went with such a swing. With a different background he could have succeeded as a jazz pianist.

This musical connection with the McIlwaine family probably strengthened my belief that Alex McIlwaine was the Alexander from the hymn book. To me this conclusion was perfectly natural and was not undermined when I discovered that there were two editions of the book. I knew that Alex worked in Mossley Mill because from the school playground we saw him making his way home to Sunnyside Terrace for his dinner. I never doubted that this quiet, wee man spent his nights and weekends, when he wasn't at the Sunday school, writing his hymns and choruses with John playing the piano at his side. Much later when I learnt that the Alexander hymnbook had a global circulation and that Alex was not that Alexander, I was bitterly disappointed.

The bit I remember best about the Annual Sunday school party happened for an all too brief spell right at the start before the organised games began. Perhaps more by default than for any other reason we were allowed to run wild about the small hall, whooping and aeroplaning in any open space. It was rare freedom and a great contrast to the formality of Sunday's huddles in classes. 'Down on the Carpet' and 'Round goes the Bun' never had the same attraction as this noisy overture.

The summer excursions were anticipated months beforehand and not just by the children. In the austere aftermath to the war they provided the only opportunity for many families to get away from Mossley, never mind off to the seaside. My grandmother planned for this as for a military expedition. There were endless bags of buns and sandwiches assembled and often a churn of milk from the farm was taken on the train to accompany the teas. She went with my grandfather and she had additional supplies just for the train journey and the minor tea breaks during the long day.

The main food for the scholars and their families came in paper bags, a few sandwiches and a pastry or two- usually fruit squares or Paris buns. These were eaten in a hall hired for the purpose. It also served as a rallying point for the day trippers. My grandparents, spurning the ordinary fare in the hall, had their dinner in Bamford's grand restaurant on Portrush Main Street. Our family accompanied them at least once and this was certainly the first time in our lives that we had eaten out. I remember the silver dinner service, the china plates and the black and frilly white uniforms of the waitresses. I'm sure my grandfather paid for this annual treat. I can still recall the excitement on the station platform at Mossley as we all awaited the train. The first puff of smoke in the distance beyond Monkstown heralded the train's approach and before long the platform was vibrating and the rails singing as the huge engine and carriages hissed to a halt beside us.

I know that my dad judged this to be a crucial moment. From one or two bad experiences in the past he realised that it was a long journey to Portrush if you were shut in with certain notorious persons. They were always non-corridor type carriages so you had to be careful. We boys were impatient to board but he kept an eye out for a certain lady and her large family to get on before he made his move. I think the family's attempts to eat egg sandwiches with runny noses had disturbed him on a previous excursion.

Mossley Sunday School excursion had a good record for fine weather just as it often rained on the excursion of our other Sunday school in Carnmoney. On one occasion we had the dreadful experience of being shunted into a siding in Ballymena station following the breakdown of the engine. We arrived in Portrush with only an hour or two for the sandcastles and Barry's Amusements. That's what you call a real disaster for children.

Often a band was hired to accompany the excursion and it led a parade to the hall for the two meals and to escort everyone to the station for the train home. There were always stragglers and, as the train set off, the cry would go up that so-and-so had been left behind. Usually this was either wishful thinking, because seven o'clock came early on a sunny day, or a false alarm.

My grandmother and grandfather set up their base camp on the sands at the West Strand. She wore her best black hat and coat and he tolerated his starched collar and tie perhaps taking off his waistcoat and rolling up his sleeves if the day was sunny. It often was not! Conversation with passing excursionists never flagged and was a highlight of the day.

Mossley Orange Hall was also the venue for different types of entertainment. Here, with my dad, I saw my first Hopalong Cassidy film. An entrepreneur in a small van travelled round the local halls showing 'pictures' to locals utterly mesmerised at this new entertainment. Afterwards toy revolvers were popular Christmas presents, some even with percussion caps to add proper sound effects. There was also a toy bomb which was simply a piece of painted metal on a string. A cap was inserted in a slot and the bomb dropped to detonate the device. The results were impressive but not always successful especially if the caps got damp. On one occasion mine succeeded brilliantly but got me into serious trouble with my dad.

My grandmother had a chronic heart condition, she often took weak turns as she called them. Often she dozed off beside the big, open fire in her armchair, her glasses slipping off her nose and the newspaper falling to the floor. One evening when she was asleep I crept up behind her and dropped the bomb on the stone flags of the floor, the best possible surface for maximum effect. She awoke startled and her paleness worried me. I will draw a veil over the scene that followed when my dad was told the news. It is sufficient to say that the bomb ended up on the dunghill where all unwanted items on a farm were discarded.

Granda and Granny McKinney at Portrush with Aunt Annie Kerr and daughters Joan and Mary

The films were popular but we didn't go too often. In those days, going to 'the pictures' was regarded as sinful and I'm pretty sure that knowledge of our visits would have been kept from my grandfather. The hall was often filled to overflowing and even the aisles and entrances were jammed with patrons. My uncle George told me how one time high spirited young farmers had sneaked in at the back when the show had begun and let loose a number of squealing piglets to run among the feet of the audience. It is not hard to picture the subsequent pandemonium in the darkness of the auditorium especially among the women and young girls.

Concert parties also made regular visits to the Orange Hall and these were great fun. Usually it was a variety bill with tap dancers, virtuosos on the accordion, banjo and harmonica and always a comedian. I remember an elderly artist called Billy Reynolds and can still recount some of his funny stories. He was an excellent mimic and his daughter Marjorie Rea and son Tom Raymond achieved local fame in the late 1950s. I also admired the pianists. We had no television then and it was unusual to hear the piano being played with such gusto. The old instrument almost bounced on the floor as the pianist struck the keys with force and skill. The shows seemed, at least to our inexperienced eyes, very professional and everyone there enjoyed them immensely.

There were plays performed by various dramatic societies often Straid or Ballycraigy Young Farmers Club players. The comedies of George Shiels were a regular standby and the standard was good.

My dad was a member of the Orange Lodge that met here LOL 134 and my brother and I had the privilege of carrying the strings of the banner on the march to the field demonstration each twelfth of July. This was really exciting for small boys. We set off from the hall and marched to the railway halt at Mossley or Ballyclare Junction to board the train for Larne, Antrim or Randalstown. There were always spectators along the roadside and we were even accompanied by a few of the more enthusiastic women followers. My mother was not among their number. We had a band in front, perhaps the Mossley Pipe Band with Drum Major Willie Forsythe, our greengrocer, leading the parade. The train journeys alone seemed endless. Everyone was excited and happy. For many country people this was perhaps their only outing of the year.

I remember how windy weather brought the best out of the stalwarts who struggled with the poles of the heavy banner. Very rarely did they give in to the elements and dismantle the banner. On return to Mossley there was a peculiar ceremony when members of LOL 134 lined up on either side of the road and allowed the neighbouring lodge LOL 795 to march through on their way to their hall in Carntall. This was done to the strains of 'Abide with Me' from the band. For some strange reason my uncle George was a member of 795 while my dad was in 134 and if the weather was particularly good and the hay season in full swing uncle George was forced to miss the Twelfth and work in the hayfield. My heart bled for him then.

The best bit was when we came home to the hall after a tiring day. The Worshipful Master set a crate or two of Kinahan's appleades on trestle tables. These were for the string bearers and the members – it was a temperance lodge – and we ate sandwiches. We were also given some pocket money for our day's work.

My dad was never a fervent Orangeman and I knew because, before taking his place in the ranks each Twelfth morning, he had to pay his annual dues. He did not attend many monthly lodge meetings.

Every year there was an evening meeting of the lodge when family members could attend. This was known as the Installation and there were formal speeches and sometimes an entertainer. I went with my dad once or twice. He never missed the big occasions. There was a three course meal and afterwards came the toasts to the Queen and other dignitaries and Orange bodies. One lady of a simple disposition and, unfamiliar with the formalities, was told by her neighbour not to drink all her orange juice but to leave some for the toast. She replied: 'Where in the name of glory will we put toast after all this spread?' After repartee such as this the entertainer's jokes at the concerts could seem rather dull.

I have hazy memories of going to other social functions in the works canteen of Mossley Mill. One such event might have been connected with VE Day in 1945. I would have been five years old then. There were crowds of people there but, sadly, details of other big nights in Mossley have completely disappeared from my memory.

Chapter 2: Eddie and Martha

The parents of both my mum and my dad were farmers, the Kennedys at Skilganaban near Ballyclare and the McKinneys at Mossley. My mother and father were married in Ballynure Presbyterian Church in 1939. Looking back through the family tree of the McKinneys and Kennedys I discovered that this was not the first time that an Edward McKinney had married a Martha Kennedy.

Both families were originally from the Irish Hill district not far from the village of Straid. My parents had told me that both had been born within a mile of each other. Indeed, passing through this area one day my dad had shown me the exact farmhouse of his birth place situated not far off the Straid-Mossley road. When we acquired a car in the 1960s mum loved a Sunday evening jaunt up to the Irish Hill to visit our Kennedy relations and on the way she proudly pointed out the farm where she had been born. It was occupied then by a family called Henderson and mum claimed that we were distantly related to them. This was not surprising to me and my brothers because from her previous references we reckoned that we had had family connections in the past with at least half the families from this neighbourhood. One afternoon about thirty years ago I took a telephone call from a complete stranger called Terence Bowman. After a bit of preliminary chat he asked me about the common Christian names of my McKinney ancestors. I was a little puzzled but he seemed genuine and I told him those names I could immediately remember. There were a number of Johns – my own proper name - and Georges, Edwards and of the women – Agnes, Martha, He stopped me there and surprised me by stating excitedly 'I think you and I might be related!'

It appeared that he had recently been researching the McKinney side of his family connection – the name had disappeared from his family through marriages in the female line – and realised that our McKinney side were all he now had left. He was delighted to discover that his McKinney connections had not all disappeared. Incredibly in the following months he proceded to compile a lengthy treatise based

Edward McKinney and Martha Kennedy's Marriage, 1939

on his research setting out clearly the development of our McKinney clan. He was able to tell us that the first McKinneys in our line arrived in Ulster in the !7th century. From the Downshire Estate records he found that in 1686 a John McKinney had rented a holding in what today is the Victoria district of Carrickfergus. Later his family moved to a farm on the Irish Hill and, from an estate map of the period, he found that they settled there next to, I could not believe it, a family of Kennedys. Now while it must be admitted that from those days to the present time, the Irish Hill, Straid district abounds in Kennedys. Terence, however, was able to assure me that the Kennedys farming next door to the McKinneys in this period were the same connection as that of my father and mother.

At the time of their marriage my mother lived with her father, mother and seven brothers and sisters in a farm at Skilganaban between Ballyclare and Ballynure. My father travelled to court her in Skilganaban riding on his bicycle from the farm at Ballyduff, Mossley where he lived with his mother, father, brother and three sisters. The whole thing is most mysterious but what I have never been unable to discover is what mutual connection or perhaps random meeting brought my mother and father together in the first place. Skilganaban and Mossley are certainly more than a field's distance apart and, sadly, this is one area where my good friend, relative and expert geneaologist, Terence Bowman, could not apply his remarkable abilities to solve the puzzle.

There was never a chance that my dad would stay on the family farm. He had a weak chest, was badly mollycoddled by my grandmother and he hated farm work. Once in a while, maybe, he did some work with the horses in the hay season but my uncle George, his brother, was the more natural farmer and did succeed my grandfather on the family farm. He had a milk round in Mossley and Carntall.

Eddie McKinney as a young man

Eddie McKinney with some workmates

My dad's name was Edward but in the County Down Railway and other transport holdings where he worked as an electrician, he was known as 'Ned.' He served his apprenticeship in the Belfast and County Down Railway after a false start with a local builder – Mr Hugh Kirkpatrick, known to my dad as Huddy Duddy. Dad became disillusioned with him after he was asked to carry a bag of cement to a job on the bus. I still have a copy of his apprentice electrician indentures signed by his father in 1931.

I have held on to a T-square of his with BCDR (Belfast and County Down Railway) on the handle. He was popular at work as we found out from the friends who visited our house and wrote to us after his death in 1958. He was also a good electrician but strangely reluctant to do odd jobs at home. He did lots of electrical work for relatives and he alone wired our house for electricity when a supply became available in our area early in the 1950s. I helped him with this job.

I remember crawling around the very sooty, roof space pulling up wires to link the connections. He had an elaborate system of bits of paper tied to the different wires to code them. Tidying up as usual, I threw them away and held up the work. He was good natured about this, I remember. This and other experiences helping him at home and in other jobs for friends, gave me a liking for working with my hands and I did consider becoming an apprentice electrician at one point. Fate dictated otherwise and it was brother Ken who followed in his footsteps.

At one point dad thought about supplementing his income by taking on repair work and went so far as to get a board printed up with the legend 'Electrical Repairs and Alterations Carried Out.' A friend in his work made it. It was planned for a space beside 'Iona' on the front gable wall but my mother's pride intervened and the plan was aborted. The redundant sign lay about the house for ages.

My dad tended to go into things on impulse and my mother saw her role as that of keeping his feet on firm ground. She failed to prevent him buying a set of volumes on Electrical Enginéering from a travelling salesman. They were never used to any great extent, except on occasions when they served to prop up the folding table in our kitchen. They lay in a cupboard in pristine condition for years. I have kept one as a souvenir. These were published by George Newnes & Co and this name became a joke in our house. When we needed an answer to some knotty problem the cry would go up ' Why not try George Newnes?'

I'll never forget the day my dad arrived home with a gramophone. It was black, rather smart in appearance and I believe he had bought it from some colleague who was hard up for cash. He had also acquired a bundle of records. I must have been about ten at this time and such items were difficult and expensive to buy from the big Belfast stores. The gramophone had to be wound up of course, we had no electricity at the time, and occasionally, in the middle of a piece, the motor ran down and the music tailed off in a series of groans and squawks.

Few later acquisitions gave me more pleasure. I sat in the parlour for hours winding up the apparatus and discovering how the needles were changed. These didn't last long but you could buy a boxful for a small sum. The records were of the large eight- inch variety made from Bakelite and very brittle. The selection of music included some ballads from Harry Lauder, the Scots comedian, and some mournful hymns. I had to restrict myself to these on Sundays as anything else was considered sacrilegious, indeed my granda McKinney would not have approved listening to Harry Lauder at any time. One song captivated me and I repeated it continuously, trying my mum's patience to the limit. I have forgotten the name of the singer but the song had the distinctive line:

'And he played his ukulele as the ship went down.'

I'm sure that my dad wasn't interested in sport or in any strenuous physical exercise except a little bit of cycling and walking. In those days these were the main ways one could travel about so it was a necessity rather than choice. I know in his younger days he rode the bicycle from Mossley to Skilganaban to court my mother. Jackie Blair, a friend of my uncle Sammy Kennedy and one of the many 'ever presents' at the Skilganaban farm, told me often how he used to commandeer this machine and ride it around the roads beside Skilganaban whenever my dad's mind was on other things. It was a splendid new machine and my dad was very proud of it, perhaps he had bought it with his first wages as a fully qualified electrician. The bicycle ride would have been around ten miles but young men then were well used to some regular exercise in the pursuit of romance.

One of dad's temporary obsessions at Ballyearl was trying to rear bantam chickens or "banties" as we called them. He prepared for this by building a wooden house in the garden beside our shed. As usual he acquired the materials from his work, they were bits of disused railway cattle wagons. Some still had traces of manure hardened on the boards. He got these to hold together, more or less. The banty house was extremely well ventilated and this proved a serious fault later.

My dad could get most things from work and he made arrangements for a pal to bring him in about five banties to start the breeding process. According to him these frightened birds were released at lunchtime by someone and took refuge in the rafters of the Duncrue Street works. All hands were recruited and eventually they were persuaded to fly down within reach and captured. The episode apparently provided amusement for all and for years afterwards his mates laughed over the affair of Ned's Banties.

My mother and I were in Belfast with him one Saturday shopping when we heard the sound of 'cock-a-doodle- do' coming from a bus stop. My dad exclaimed 'That blighter McNeill must be about here somewhere!' My mum was not amused.

14

The banty project came to grief when rats entered their house through the ventilation holes and picked them off one by one. It was a sad occasion for us all. I can picture my dad dressed with the top button of his trousers undone to give him breathing space and almost always, even at work, wearing a white shirt. He had an obsession about having his shoes shining. He polished them most nights. Saturday night was a big night for shoe cleaning; this habit of preparing for the Sabbath was no doubt learned from his father. He always seemed to wear good Oxfords to work. I remember him wearing bicycle clips on his trousers, wide bottomed as fashion dictated at the time. He wore trouser braces or 'galluses' as he called them. These were used to tuck in his shirt, when he shaved in the scullery every night.

I often went to Belfast with my dad on the bus to do shopping. I'm sure he did this on his own rather than with my mum. She preferred to stay at home, content to leave the decisions on what I should have up to him. It always seemed to be for shoes or clothes. There was then a shop, Hyam's, in North Street near the old Alhambra Cinema, where he bought me a ready-made suit, probably my first. I think it was a blue checked pattern and, of course, it came with short trousers. I must have been around ten at this time. Long trousers were not considered appropriate for boys until they reached fourteen. It was said that boys had to slide down the banisters to fit into their first pair of long trousers, or so this first stage of approaching adolescence was called.

Like most folk from the country areas, when we went shopping in Belfast we never ventured far from Smithfield Bus Station. My dad always finished off his visits to the city with a call at Andy Crowe's butcher's shop at the corner of Upper North Street and Garfield Street for a pound or two of his famous sausages.

Later when I was about 15, he went with me to see an optician in Belfast. This was a bit of a crisis for me. After a long time struggling to decipher the destinations on buses I finally admitted defeat and told my dad about my difficulties. Dr Wilson, our GP from Whiteabbey made a quick examination and said we needed to consult an optician. After a few queries, there were no Yellow Pages then, my dad got a recommendation for Harold Allen BSc of Duncairn Gardens in Belfast. Crucially his business was convenient to the Mossley bus route and close to Duncrue Street where dad was working for the Ulster Transport Authority.

I vividly recall old Mr Allen, he was probably about fifty then, peering into my eyes while brandishing a little light. As he did so he screwed up his face and narrowed his eyes. I could not see the letters on his test board but could clearly pick out every single hair in his moustache and smell his slightly sour breath. I needed glasses and at this period there were certainly no designer frames on offer even if my dad's budget could have stretched thus far. Instead he fitted me with the standard issue wire National Health glasses. Oddly enough they became quite fashionable in the 1960s.

Mr Allen's taste, like my dad's, was conservative and in later years I remained loyal to him despite having to choose my frames from the meagre selection he produced from a shoe box in his cupboard. I had to wear my glasses at all times. Sometimes I even wore them in bed. We never called them spectacles, only Mr Harold Allen did so. They improved my vision and I stepped on the Mossley bus thereafter with more confidence but otherwise they had a disastrous effect on my ego.

I got off to a bad start when I wore them for the first time. An insensitive teacher in Ballyclare High School asked 'Who is the 'owl' in the back row?' Previously I had always been first into the front row to be able to see the blackboard. If I hadn't already been nicknamed Jake I might have been stuck with The Owl throughout my high school career. I could easily have lived with a teacher's snide remark but what I found impossible to get over was the blow the glasses made to my two adolescent passions.

In those days wearing glasses did not have the allure of the present and I had the perception that they had seriously affected my prospects with girls. All the advantages of my natural curly hair had gone with the glasses and I reckoned that I was doomed to be attractive only to plain Janes at the Christmas parties. Anyone can understand the effect of such a realisation on a sadly mixed- up adolescent.

To make matters worse I could not wear them safely while playing football. At one stage I had thought that the glasses would at last have improved my game by allowing me to see not only the whereabouts of the other members of my team but the distinct outline of the goalposts. I wore them anyway for practice matches at the Samuel Tweedie Stadium in Ballyearl and in no time the glasses became flattened so that I was forced to wind them round my ears to keep them from constantly falling off. I also became expert in repairing them with fuse wire and elastoplast. This certainly did not add to my attraction with the young girls but football then was always the more important of my passions.

Our family doctor was Dr Kenneth Wilson of Whiteabbey and, to visit his surgery, we caught the Belfast bus to Cloughfern Corner and walked to Whiteabbey village from there. I must have been about eight or nine when I developed swollen glands in my neck. I went with my dad to the surgery for several treatments. I always liked going out with him. He was good fun and made jokes frequently but this trip was unpleasant because after the first time there I knew what it involved. We caught the five past seven bus down and came back on the eight thirty or if we missed this one the last service at ten o'clock. I can still repeat the times of all the bus services to and from Ballyclare and Belfast via Mossley.

The waiting room usually was crowded but there was quite a bit of conversation and I remember thinking that my dad enjoyed this sense of a social occasion. He was good at initiating casual conversation. I sat petrified dreading the moment when Dr Kenneth would open the door and we would be ushered in. The procedure was simple if painful. He prepared a sterile syringe then pushed it gently into the lump in my neck. He drew out a horrible pussy substance and the tears came to my eyes. On the way back to the bus my dad did his best to cheer me up by recounting amusing episodes from that day's jobs at work.

Although my dad was generally good natured, at times he could become very single minded, even headstrong. He wasn't the only member of the McKinney connection to exhibit this trait. One morning about 1954 my youngest brother, Wesley, was getting off the bus on his way to Mossley School and dashed across the road without looking out for traffic. He was struck by a car and sustained a badly broken leg. He endured a long spell in hospital. He spent a number of weeks at Lissue House hospital near Lisburn. It was a terribly awkward place to reach entailing two bus journeys and, with no motor car, my parents found it difficult to visit him as regularly as they would have liked. I remember going on the bus with them and it seemed like an expedition.

The teachers at Mossley School and the neighbours were most concerned for Wesley's progress. These were the days before crossing patrols at schools and I remember there was pressure from the community to have a zebra crossing created beside the bus stop.

The driver of the car involved was a trader from Ballyclare and he came to our house to enquire about Wesley's condition. He was a kind, well-meaning gentleman and it was accepted that no blame for the accident could have been attributed to him. Nevertheless my dad remained very surly in his presence and I remember my mum chiding him for his unreasonable attitude. It didn't make a bit of difference. Somebody had hurt one of his children and no amount of persuading could make him be civil to such a person. I was surprised at his stance and indeed at how the passing of time and Wesley's complete recovery didn't change his attitude.

My parents often involved us boys, at least the older two, in their fun telling over and over again family episodes which had amused them. One incident I recall occurred on a Sunday afternoon at dinnertime when a small Corgi dog appeared in our yard and my dad, annoyed that it was a stray and heading for his vegetable garden, rushed out to frighten it off using 'lively' language to encourage it to move along. He was in full flow when the dignified figure of Mr Samuel Tweedie, our grocer appeared around the corner full of apologies for his corgi's presence. He had indeed come up to visit us on some church business and he had the dog with him. As you would expect from Mr Tweedie's dog it was always well behaved and my dad became thoroughly embarrassed at his hasty reaction. My mother had difficulty in restraining her laughter.

Edwin and Wesley McKinney, c.1957

Although never in the same class as his brother George for quick witted replies he did have his moments. He excelled himself on one occasion when, in our presence, Mr William James Girvan, Senior, or "The Boss" as he was commonly known on the farm and in the area, accused my dad of taking a large boulder out of his field hedge beside our house. The Boss was often testy and feared by most people in Ballyearl. He had a wonderful command of the Queen's English, most of it peppered with mild expletives.

My dad found this feudal attitude to tenants strongly opposed to his Labour party principles and, not being one of his tenants, was never intimidated. I'm pretty sure that dad had taken the boulder but he was not dismayed and shouted over the hedge to William James 'What stone are you talking about – the stone outside Dan Murphy's Door?' referring to the popular Irish song. Such simple events retold repeatedly kept us all amused.

My dad was very good at acquiring various odds and ends from his work. He had an eye for a bargain but quite often he had difficulty in finding a purpose for many of these items. The process of lifting railway track was in full swing in the 1950s so wooden sleepers were easily obtained. He could always persuade some colleague on the Ulster Transport Authority lorries to transport them out to our garden. My mother's two brothers, John and Jimmy, were then freight managers in Antrim and Carrickfergus UTA depots and they were often able to assist him.

My brothers and I hated the sleepers because it became our job to saw them up for fuel. This was no easy task because we only had a terribly blunt hand saw and the sleepers had been steeped in creosote and had many knots which were nearly impossible to cut.

I think there was only ever one item that he got delivered to our garden for which even he could not find a suitable use. This was a large rectangular metal tank used, I believe, in the railway depot for steeping sleepers in creosote. It was much too big to go into the shed and it stayed in the garden where we had to bail the rainwater from it every so often. It was nothing more than a nuisance and eventually, many years later, my uncle John found the perfect use for it as a meal bin on his farm. He said it was the only thing he had ever owned that the rats could not chew through to reach the feedstuff.

Before this it gave my mother the surprise of her life early one summer morning. She heard, as she described it, an odd noise coming from the vicinity of the tank. She approached it cautiously and, I thought afterwards rather bravely, to find to her amazement a large white goat lying on the bottom of the tank and chewing its cud. A stray dog or a cat would not have been out of the ordinary but it had to be admitted that stray goats were a touch unusual. Eventually the owner was found in the Ashley Park terrace over the back field and the goat was escorted to its home.

My dad loved a good fire. When he worked with the railway company there was never any shortage of coal and the fires at work were always well stoked. He put the coal on our fire at home by the bucketful.

I remember dad shoving logs or sections of sleepers, too long to go on the fire any other way, up the chimney to burn down gradually over the course of an evening. It is a wonder that the chimney did not go on fire more often. Mind you it did burn when, usually early on a Sunday morning, dad 'cleaned' the chimney by shoving sheets of newspaper up the flue and setting them alight. They went up with a roar but, apart from producing dense smoke over the neighbourhood, no harm resulted. I'm sure the neighbours were not too pleased but they never complained.

Our coal supplies came from The Northern Coal Company in Belfast and we got, I think, a quarter or half a ton at each delivery. My grandfather McKinney often bought us a delivery of coal for a Christmas present – perhaps the cows were milking well at this particular time. It was a difficult operation but the coalman was expert at entering our kitchen with a sack on his back, turning first sharp right then immediately left, before tipping the sack into the coal house beneath the stairs. Thinking back now I realise this must have caused an enormous amount of dust to be spread around the house. My mum, like all housewives at this time, could only accept this as a necessary nuisance – a wee bit of coal dust would never have upset my mum.

In my early years there was a range in our kitchen fireplace. It had to be polished every week with Ebo black leading. My mum could cook on the range but I remember her using an oil stove in the scullery much more often. I also vividly remember the day when the range was dismantled and the bits thrown out into the yard through the big open window in the kitchen. A neighbour, Frank Rea, did this job, it must have happened around 1952. Frank was a big, strong man and did work regularly on farms and for my grandmother McKinney after she came to live at Pansy Cottage in Ballyearl. He was expert at trimming her boxwood hedges with dead straight edges.

The house at Ballyearl was infested with mice. We tried various methods of catching them but the many badly fitting doors and the poor quality of much of the wood meant that it remained a recurring problem. Usually we set spring traps baited with cheese but my dad once decided to experiment with a new method. This was an extremely sticky green substance called Dek. It was spread on a piece of cardboard with the bait in the middle and placed in a prominent position to attract the mice. They were meant to paddle onto the Dek and become stuck. It worked well for a while until one morning at half past six my dad struggled into the kitchen from his bedroom, half asleep as usual, and plodded straight into the Dek. He got the most of the substance off eventually but I believe for a week he found it hard to take off his socks at night. That was the end of the Dek experiment.

Although never too keen on 'Do It Yourself', dad sometimes took on interesting projects. One time he decided to repaint the bath. It was made from cast iron and age had led to streaks of rust dimpled over its surface. He must have read about this procedure somewhere or, more likely, a painter in his work had offered advice on the way it should be applied.

At first the painting went well and seemed a success with just the final treatment to be completed. This involved filling the bathtub with cold water and leaving it untouched for a time. Whatever the period was, it proved insufficient because when my dad, probably too impatient to wait any longer, took a bath there was a single but not insignificant complication. He found on emerging that, not only was the paint a bit sticky, but some had stuck to his bulky figure. We laughed at this occurrence but my mother was not amused and the bath had to be taken out of commission for a long time before the paint finally hardened.

Dad had a bath once a week so the inconvenience was minimal. He often washed and shaved in the scullery in the evenings. I can picture him with his woollen inside shirt tucked under his trouser braces, lathering his face with a wobbling brush before stroking a safety razor with a '7 o'clock' blade over the stubble. The blades came in individual waxed packets and they were used also to pare corns, both his and my mother's, a delicate and dangerous operation people often carried out in those days. Like his father he was very diligent at polishing shoes, quite often taking on those of all the family. With better health he would have made a good soldier.

Pansy Cottage, Ballyearl

He acquired a set of big hand brushes, previously used for polishing rail coaches. He had quite small feet and I remember how his shoes were always shining and his brown overalls spotlessly clean. He liked to dress up to go visiting or to attend church and he regularly used a tie pin which made his tie bellow out from his suit waistcoat. These were the days of separate collars for shirts and they were starched and ironed up for him before outings. I remember he had difficulty attaching his shirt studs to the collars and they often cut painfully into his neck leaving red marks.

One day stands out very clearly in my memory of childhood. This was in March 1951. My grandfather McKinney had recently retired from his farm and my uncle George took over there. My grandparents bought Pansy Cottage just a matter of yards from our house in Ballyearl.

They intended to have some renovations done to the house. My grandfather would then spend his time keeping some hens and cycling to the farm at Mossley to help uncle George with the farm work. On this day in March my dad arrived home early from work and I saw he was distressed. We were playing football in the garden and I can still visalise him rushing through the gate with his overcoat over his arm. I soon learned the reason for his early return.

My grandfather had been cycling down the Doagh Road near Cloughfern to see a builder about the renovation plans and, crossing the road, he was knocked down by a van and seriously injured. When I think about his accident I realise how unfortunate he was. At the time there must have been little traffic on this road. Apparently he was turning right, across the line of traffic and perhaps his hearing was not too good. He had never been ill, unlike my grandmother who was the invalid of the family. He was always concerned for her health and his plans for the Ballyearl cottage, were mainly to install a bathroom, to make her life easier. He had bought her one of the first mechanical washing machines seen in the district. We eventually inherited it and it sat in our shed unused because my mother preferred using the washboard and big bars of Sunlight soap. We did use the wringer attached to the machine for many years. My grandfather died soon after arrival in hospital. Dad got a copy of his injuries and the report of the inquest. I still have this today. Most of all, I remember my dad weeping and the gloom which surrounded our whole family following this tragic death. My grandfather was a fit man in excellent health and his death was a great shock to everyone.

The funeral was held at Ballyearl. The cottage and our house nearby were completely filled with relatives. After the interment the mourners came back to my grandmother's house for a meal and, because there were so many attending the funeral, a sitting was held in the house of Mrs May Scott, the next door neighbour. Brother Ken and I were assigned to have our broth in her house and I still remember, perhaps because it made such a contrast to the general air of gloom, sitting opposite one obscure relative with a large drooping moustache and watching him slurping his broth noisily from his plate. I was a notorious giggler throughout my childhood, indeed far beyond it, and this sight was too much for me. I had to keep my eye away from Ken otherwise my giggles would have become an object of shame to the family.

My dad always seemed to spend a lot of his time in the evenings sleeping on the living room sofa. He had no interest in sports or recreation, a man indeed of simple pursuits mostly connected with his family. My memories though, tend to concentrate on the years following his first heart attack in 1952 when he was 38 years old.

We children liked my dad immensely. He was warm hearted and jolly, very good fun when he was in good form and, while he could be firm when we transgressed, he got on with us really well. In church Ken and I often got a fit of the giggles and my dad was expert in reaching over unobtrusively and squeezing our knées in what was known as a 'donkey's bite'. This sufficed until we got home when he could give us a lecture about giggling in inappropriate places.

One Sunday morning even my dad struggled to suppress a giggle or two. It happened that a regular worshipper had the not unusual habit of dropping off to sleep during the sermon. On this occasion as sleep overcame him the old man's bald head jerked forward and struck the front of the pew with considerable force. The sound of the collision reverberated round the silent church gallery like a cannon shot! Fortunately we were not the only ones in the gallery that morning to have our hankies stuffed in our mouths to control our sniggers!

I use the word 'liked' rather than 'loved' in relation to my dad because in our family love was not a word that figured highly except in a religious context. I think this was general then in rural communities. Country folk did not generally display emotion readily, indeed it could be regarded as simple soppiness or even weakness. My mum and dad were devoted to each other even to the extent that, following my dad's death, my mum found it difficult to carry on without his love and support.

We were a very close and loving family but we hardly ever kissed each other. I have few memories of kissing my mother. Kissing tended to make us uncomfortable with each other. Some relatives were different. My dad's Aunt Essie (short for Esther and pronounced Acie) was a great one for kissing, much to my dad and uncle George's embarrassment.

She was a large, severe lady with a keen sense of her senior position in the family. My aunts and uncles had been brought up to revere her and, when she got within range, she dashed over to kiss them affectionately, especially the men. We were children, to be seen and not heard, and therefore did not come within her notice or indeed within kissing range very often.

It was the highlight of the Christmas gathering at our grandparents' farm in Mossley when my dad and uncle George dutifully lined up to give Aunt Essie her farewell kiss. Often George pleaded farm business in the byre to escape. My mum and brothers teased my dad mercilessly about this kissing and he did not like it at all.

Dad's Aunt Essie and Uncle George with their family

Bob and Sam McKinney both lost their lives in the Second World War

Aunt Essie was married to my grandfather's elder brother, George, and they lived in Upper Frank Street, Mountpottinger, Belfast. He was an expert stable man and had gone into Belfast as a young lad to work with the heavy horses in Craig's Coal firm. He talked about horses endlessly and it was a sad day for him when motor lorries replaced the large, gentle beasts. He was tall, was as bald as an egg and at home wore a little tasselled cap much like a tea cosy to ward off the draughts. When he managed to get a word in between aunt Essie's non-stop chatter he talked enthusiastically about his horses – the big carthorse variety he had spent all his life tending. He was in his element at wakes and in the company of older farmers like my grandfather Kennedy.

Great uncle George and great aunt Essie's two sons, Bob and Sam McKinney, were killed in the Second World War. They were in the RAF. Bob was shot down flying in a transport aircraft while Sam died in a motor cycle accident at an aerodrome not long after the end of the war.

A daughter was married to a chap whose Christian name was Valentine. In those days such unusual names were only for film stars and it was contracted by the family to Val. My uncle George could not bring himself to use even this form and, in his inimitable style, nicknamed him 'Valve Rubber' but never, of course, in Aunt Essie's presence. My uncle George's wit was priceless and enjoyed by his large circle of friends – especially in the farming community.

The afternoon when my dad suffered his first heart attack is etched in my memory. It was Sunday and I remember him moaning over the kitchen table and being violently sick. This was in 1952 and my grandmother was living in Pansy Cottage a few yards from our house at Ballyearl. His sister Annie's husband, John Kerr, unwisely gave him a sup of whiskey, a country cure for all ills and my father, who never took alcohol in any form, was lucky to survive the well-intentioned treatment.

Following a spell in the Royal Victoria Hospital in Belfast he made a partial recovery but was effectively disabled for the rest of his life.

The next few years were difficult for everyone. He eventually returned to work in the UTA workshop in Duncrue Street but with a blue card to restrict him to light tasks. He found the bench work frustrating and he hated being inside rather than out on the railway tracks and in the transport authority's hotels dealing with electrical plant. His role in the Electrical Trades Union did not diminish and it was only recently that my brother Eddie, who also worked on the railways for a spell, heard how dad had fought hard to improve the lot of apprentice tradesmen. Dad never talked much to us of this aspect of his life.

He found it hard to follow the medical advice and give up smoking Gallaher's Blues. During his vain attempts to cease the habit he became untypically irritable and my mother once or twice in despair sent one of us over to Forsythe's shop in Ashley Park to buy him a packet of cigarettes and thus cheer him up.

His attempts to lose weight always foundered on my mother's baking and our frequent fried meals. They had both been brought up on farms where consumption of milk, eggs and butter was held to be good, especially for children and almost every meal involved the frying pan.

I remember Procea bread, a low calorie loaf he had been advised to eat, and cream crackers and his scathing comments about their taste and consistency. For someone brought up on soda and potato bread and endless varieties of high calorie home baking, it needed great resolve to alter one's lifestyle to exist on these poor substitutes for real bread. He did eat them but he ate the other breads as well. He later found walking any distance difficult and was often beaten when faced with steep hills. I recall the frequent stops he had to make, ostensibly to look at cattle in the fields but really to give himself time to recover his breath.

The favourite walk up the steep Rea Hill, Carntall to his sister's Aggie's home was only possible given his determination and endurance of pain and then only in the early days of his illness. Later he hired Willie Forsythe, our greengrocer, to take him up there in his big car.

Around 1956 the bus route past our house on the Doagh Road was diverted along the Carntall Road to allow alterations to the main Belfast to Larne carriageway to be carried out and Ballyearl folk had to walk to and from the Fingerpost at Mossley to catch the buses. This gave my dad great difficulty but he persevered and enlisted me to take the bicycle down to meet the bus when he was coming home in the evenings. Riding the bike was easier than walking. I was glad to help him but I felt so sad that my dad could not keep up with the other men. I knew he, too, was devastated.

One night in the summer of 1958 my mother woke me in desperation. She thought my dad was dead. He had had another turn and when I went into their bedroom he was sitting beside the bed, pale and obviously very ill but at least still alive. I'm certain that this was a close call but he perked up as I later found to be typical of patients suffering from heart disease. The doctor who came summoned an ambulance and he left the house, as it turned out, for the last time.

This was in the first fortnight in September, 1958 and it proved a sad time in Ballyearl. A well known local farmer, George Crawford, died suddenly in his Land Rover in Allam's Market, Belfast and within a week our neighbour Edward Higgins took a heart attack and died while cycling to his son's home at Glengormley. I remember the commotion and noise as his coffin was brought into the house next door before the funeral.

Jackie and Ken McKinney, c.1957

My dad died at 8 o'clock on the evening of Friday, September 12 1958 in Ward 18 of The Royal Victoria Hospital Belfast. He was 43 years old. My mum and I were at the bedside most of this day but, towards evening, we were asked to wait outside the ward while a team of doctors and nurses attended to him. I vividly remember a doctor eventually walking down the ward to us and, before he reached us, I knew what he was about to say. My dad was dead and my mother just disintegrated with grief and exhaustion. It would be some time before she would be able to face the stark reality of what had occurred and the consequences for the five of us. The last thing I had done for my dad was about two hours previously he had asked me to light a cigarette and hold it in his mouth for a puff.

His body lay in our sitting room among a sea of flowers, mostly chrysanthemums, awaiting the funeral on the Sunday. I did not go into the room during this time but I can never forget the overpowering smell of these flowers. To this day they have an unpleasant connotation for me and I'll never like them.

During August and early September I had been working as a holiday relief postman in Carnmoney, cycling round the country roads and lanes – possibly the best job I have ever had in my life. On the Monday after my dad's funeral the postmaster, Israel Abernethy, could not find a replacement and he asked me if I would carry on. I did and it was the best thing that could have happened to me. I couldn't forget the events of the past week but the countryside was a solace and being busy and working with sympathetic colleagues helped me enormously.

My district was Ballyduff and here every farmer and householder seemed to know of my situation and their compassion was evident. Even the dogs seemed a bit friendlier that week.

I returned home that first Monday and my mum was doing the washing and weeping, it was a sombre time for all. My own most difficult time came each night when the five- past- six bus from Belfast stopped at the Ballyearl stop and the minutes passed and my dad did not burst through the back door with his usual joke and a big smile.

I knew then that our lives together as a family had changed.

Chapter 3: Friends and Neighbours

Ballyearl is situated about ten miles from the sea. The Three Mile Water at Mossley is the nearest river that appeared on a map nevertheless we children found plenty of opportunities to play near water. There was a little stream which ran just above and at right angles to Ashley Park. It came along the edge of a meadow and underneath the Springtown Loney to enter Girvan's Ten Acre field and run behind the hedge beside this lane. It branched sharply to the right at the intersection of the loney and the main Doagh Road and finally disappeared beneath the main road around one hundred yards from our house.

These right-angled turns had a major consequence in times of heavy rain. The swollen stream broke through and flooded the road right beside our big gate. This happened regularly and was no great inconvenience to children who relished the excitement. We had a grandstand view from our parlour of the lorries and motor cars splashing through about ten inches of muddy water. This water soon drained away into the field across the road but when a bungalow was built there without any great under building to bring it up above road level, the house was surrounded by water every time a flood occurred. It never reached up far enough to run straight into the bungalow but occasionally it was not far off doing so.

Old Mr and Mrs Knox who lived in the bungalow had less reason to celebrate as they erected a flood barrier of sandbags to keep the water from seeping into their home.

Every cloud has a silver lining and once the rain had stopped we left our grandstand seats in the parlour and rushed out to play in welly boots at our temporary riverside. We floated bottles stoppered with corks to keep them afloat, we sailed paper boats and crudely made wooden Queen Marys and Queen Elizabeths. The currents were ideal for races. I remember making such liners from a piece of planking for the hull, a bit sawn off a brush shaft for the funnels and small nails hammered in to form the railing. We often made these and sailed them in the small streams but collisions with the banks was a problem. The big floods afforded space for a virtual flotilla to be launched.

Another great position for playing in water was in the Ten Acre field at the point where the stream came through underneath the Springtown Loney. The level of the ground was about two feet higher than the water. The stream was around three feet wide and cattle drank here. Over the years their feet had trampled down the high bank in two distinct 'bays'. This made a perfect place for us to paddle in the muddy water and to sail our toy boats. Usually the water was just the right depth to suit our purpose. Sometimes, however, if there were many others there we started into dam building. Using a combination of clayey sods and large stones we created a grand barrage across the path of the stream.

We even carefully smuggled an old section of drainpipe into the field to build into the dam and so prevent it overflowing into the field. We always chose a day when Boss Girvan was busy at the other end of his farm otherwise the dam would not have lasted too long. His farm hand, Ben Ross, lived up in the Springtown lane houses and was often around this area in his tractor but we trusted Ben. He got on very well with children and was always giving us rides on his trailer or ruckshifter.

To this day I have retained an interest in fiddling about with water and on walks it takes very little to attract me. I will happily poke about in puddles with a stick creating diversions but I am wary that no other adults are about to see my childish fascination. The straight stretch of water running at the edge of the field from Ashley Park was the fishing section. There were sticklebacks, spricks as we called them, in abundance – swarms of small fry in Spring and the swiftly darting females and the larger red breasted males at all times of year. We caught them simply by leaving two-pound jam jars lying against the current in the bed of the stream. We seldom failed and took our prizes to be kept on the window ledges of our homes. The spricks never lived long and I remember the sadness when the morning after a catch I saw my sprick turned belly up in the jam pot or old bathtub I had employed in a futile attempt to curtail the mortality rate.

When I was over ten years old I was allowed to take the trip to the more exotic reaches of the Layde. The stream, just a bit bigger than the one in the Ten Acre, was so named as it was the lead supplying water for Mossley Mill dam. It flowed past Ballyclare Junction railway halt and eventually through Mossley alongside the railway track to become the Three Mile Water running into Belfast Lough. The gang from Ballyearl usually approached it from one of Girvan's fields on the other side of the main Doagh Road.

At this point there was a large culvert beneath the railway line and it was here that we waded through the deeper water to cross to the Ballyhenry bank. It was then possible to follow the widening stream to the point where a weir marked the channel taking water to Mossley dam. I'm not sure that we had our parents' permission to go so far and I remember one day bravely tiptoeing across the weir and back again in my blue Wellington boots.

Not far from the Layde there were a number of bridges over the main Belfast to Ballymena railway line but one sticks out in my memory. It was very narrow and had been constructed to give cattle access to and from fields on either side of the track but because it was so different from the other road bridges it appealed to me.

We always returned home from expeditions to the streams with our boots squelching and our socks wringing wet. Our parents were very tolerant and the water gave us endless, simple amusement. Occasionally we brought back trophies – a frog, tadpoles or the usual spricks in jam jars. The Layde was rumoured to have trout but I never saw any and would have had no idea of how to catch a trout if I had seen one.

One time I discovered a football corner post complete with its team flag washed up against the Layde culvert near Ballyclare Junction halt. It had come from Andy McKeen's field beside the railway junction where Lyle and Kinahan's football team played for many years. I loved football and treasured this relic but I'm sure it didn't long survive my dad's continual search for firewood.

When I was a bit older I was one of a gang who made a very daring raid one summer afternoon. In the late 1950s there was a rationalisation programme on the railway network. This led not only to a surfeit of wooden sleepers, as the young McKinneys found out at a cost to their leisure time, but to redundant coaches. A line of these were shunted into a siding at Ballyclare Junction where they lay idle for years. One whole coach was parked in a field beside Carnmoney Brae to serve as the changing rooms for a Belfast football team. The railway line at the bottom of Girvan's field intrigued young boys and we made our way across the Layde and onto the track to clamber up into a carriage for a reconnoitre. I have to confess that I was a bit of a scardey or 'couff' as my mother would have said, and I stayed on the safe banks of the Layde. I was aware that my dad worked for the UTA and if I had been caught he would have suffered no end of embarrassment. Mind you no damage was caused, just a bit of bravado on a quiet summer day in Ballyearl.

There was no mains water in Ballyearl until about 1965 when our hand pump and well became redundant. Before this most houses had their own wells or shared a supply with a group of neighbours. It was all a bit haphazard. I just do not know how the Ashley Park residents fared for a supply. I think water was piped in from a source in one of Mr Girvan's upper fields. I do remember one summer of great drought when a new spring had to be brought into use for Ashley Park. It was opened at the field end of Pumptown Loney, a short laneway connecting the road and our football field. The name suggests that this source had been used before.

I clearly remember workmen digging out a deep,wide trench and installing a hand pump. We boys took a keen interest in any form of construction and were able to inform curious parents of the nature and progress of any new works. The residents and, I believe, many other families in this dry summer, carried water in pails for all domestic needs. There was a great community spirit generated by the emergency and folk gathered at the pump to chat as the water was drawn. Remarkably William James Girvan was overcome by the mood and not only permitted non-tenants to take the water without charge but was seen chatting at the pump and, a rare occurrence, smiling at all and sundry. Mind you I do not remember an amnesty for footballers in his grazing fields as part of his improved disposition.

I think it was around 1958 that reorganisation of local councils in Northern Ireland brought Ballyearl into the district of Antrim Borough Council and bin lorries, a rarity in our area, began to collect our rubbish. Before then we only had an ash pit at the top of the garden in a bricked area. The more I think about it the more I realise we had little refuse to dispose of in our pits. We burned or reused most of the paper waste. Many magazines ended up in the toilet cubicle with the Deluge. The Radio Times was a favourite for this purpose, something to do with the texture of the paper, I believe.

There was no plastic in general use yet and, even in the immediate post war period, canned items were not common. Indeed the empty cans were prized as containers for small items of hardware, especially nails. Bread was unwrapped and anyway my mum baked most days and provided fresh sodas, wheatens, pancakes and scones. Fancy cakes were her proud speciality.

I can't recall whether we had a main sewer connection at the time when the mains water arrived in Ballyearl – around 1964.
The water connection was done by Hubert Hay who was a plumber from Whiteabbey. He loved talking. His mother had attended Skilganaban school around the same time as my mother's family so she was constantly talking to him about his relations. He wasn't hard to distract, mind you. He frequently sat yarning over his ten o'clock tea for an hour or more.

After the mains water was installed the trusty old Deluge cistern was scrapped but the septic tank remained for a year or two. Eventually around 1970 when a main sewer was put in along the Doagh Road Hubert returned and set about digging a trench up the side of the house and across the yard to connect our drains. A new toilet was installed in the upstairs bathroom and we became very modern indeed.

Brother Ken and I got to know the McKinney farm at Mossley very well because we stayed there for spells when my mother was in hospital. This would have been when we were both attending Mossley Public Elementary School. Granny McKinney was a truly kind and goodhearted soul. She was just a wee bit over concerned for our welfare and anxious that we did not fall ill. I have a photograph obviously taken at school during a spell at the farm because I am wearing two pullovers, it must have been in the summer because they are short sleeved.

We slept in an old-fashioned iron bed in a room which had access both from the main house and from the adjoining farm buildings. It had formerly been the room of the live-in 'servant man'. The bed typically was smothered in homemade patchwork quilts. The stay there was always a big adventure for us and the farm with the animals became a fantastic playground.

One evening we were helping my grandfather pulp turnips. We threw the turnips in to the hand pulper and then uncle George or one of the farm hands would turn the handle to grind them up for the cows. Ken flung one a bit too vigorously and it flew straight through one of the byre windows giving a bad fright to the cow which my grandfather was milking. We heard his shouts and the cow's excitement and, too terrified to await a certain telling off from our grandfather, we ran off up the back lane to skulk in the stack garden until his anger had passed.

Jackie McKinney, aged eight in two pullovers at Mossley School

Granny McKinney, c.1956

When our dad came home from work we were eventually tracked down to our hidey hole beneath the upturned milk cart outside the dairy. Fortunately grandfather, perhaps having cooled by then and having discussed the affair with dad, laughed off the whole affair.

Granny always dressed in sombre black including a wee black cap affair pinned to her head. She kept a black string bag full of silver sixpences hanging on the newel post of the stairs.

We each got a sixpence frequently. She was a generous lady to the end of her days. Later when she went to live with my aunt Aggie at Carntall I was a teenager and once a month I rode the bike down the Cullyburn Brae to Monkstown to fetch her pension. I remember the amount was six pounds ten shillings and she insisting on giving me, in spite of my protests, one whole pound for each trip. At the time I was paid the same for a full week's holiday work on different farms.

Granny McKinney had a simple formula for cooking – everything was fried. We ate fries maybe three times a day. I remember her big pan hanging on a crook and chain over the open fire and her breakfasts were special, with fried soda bread as crisp as toast. Attached to the side of the fire was a tank producing hot water for cooking and for mixing up food for fowl. There was no running water in the house, this was carried in from the well in the garden in pails and stored in large crocks. I remember my granda taking toast every night before bedtime. This was made using a large wire toasting fork over the open fire. He liked cloves in his tea at night.
At Christmas granny made ginger wine and it was the sweetest I have ever tasted anywhere. The McKinneys all had a sweet tooth. Granny kept a bag of white mint imperials to hand and these were given to us often. She spoiled us mercilessly.

The jam maker extraordinaire at Mossley was aunt Aggie. When we were there in the late 1940s she was unmarried and spent a lot of her time doing farm chores, mostly with the calves and fowl but she loved gardening and making jam. In the summer she stockpiled jars of rhubarb and gooseberry jam on the kitchen shelves and this had to last through to the following summer. When you realise how much jam the family munched through it was no wonder that she had to be so busy.

She had a regular routine on Sunday evenings when she took her embroidery up to the loft window just beside our bedroom and happily sewed or knitted away until bedtime. This was a favourite pastime even though two of her fingers had been badly disfigured by whittle she sustained from an infection. Perhaps she was dreaming of a handsome knight, or at least a youngish farmer, riding into the yard to carry her off to his farm in the hills. In a way her dream came true but, as with all dreams, the reality was less glamorous.

Aunt Aggie had never really had any opportunities for social intercourse, she was much too busy with house and farm work. The knowledge that she was courting came as a surprise to my mum and dad. They were down at the Mossley farm as usual for Christmas night with the family. Everyone met in the parlour, the only time in the year all the McKinneys came together. The house was thronged with adults and children and it was a special delight for my brothers and me to make friends with our older cousins. It was a sober affair with the emphasis on eating and chat, two things our family did very well.

Three sisters: aunt Aggie with May and Annie

At one point in the evening my dad noticed that aunt Aggie had gone missing and the mystery was not solved until a later night when my dad got the low down from those in the know. A farmer from the Rea Hill in Carntall had taken to having regular assignations with Aunt Aggie - in the byre of all places. This must have been where she had drifted off to on Christmas night. Willie Hall, her suitor, was definitely not in the first flush of youth, indeed he was wracked with asthma and wheezed following any physical exertion.

It was also later suspected by some family members that a factor in his ardour was that his invalid mother needed nursing care and a wife would provide the cheapest option. He had a reputation for being a wee bit near with his money which from exaggerated local gossip he had large quantities. I can't confirm the money bags theory but I know from what I was paid for working on his farm on Saturdays for a time as a teenager that he did not throw his money around with wild abandon. My standard payment was a sack of potatoes every now and again and the odd ten shilling note and as much rhubarb jam as I could eat.

It was hard to buy records and other essentials of a teenager without hard cash and uncle Willie Hall did not part with this too readily. Mind you the spuds were renowned as the tastiest in the neighbourhood. His farm was dry and south facing unlike the thick clayey loam at Mossley.

However I know that in spite of the inevitable nursing duties, aunt Aggie was very happy at Carntall. Her garden there was bigger and her jam making certainly did not decrease. My dad loved to visit here. From some of the fields there were spectacular views over the length of Belfast Lough. I remember watching for the Lairds Isle, the Ardrossan ferry, sailing up the lough daily in the summer time. There was a spring in a field beside the house with the coldest water I have ever tasted. In every way it was an idyllic place for the summer months. Uncle Willie suffered from asthma and had serious problems with his chest. He continuously coughed up phlegm into handkerchiefs. He had the habit of spitting from his sofa directly into the big, old fashioned hearth. His aim was the wonder of all who visited and watched the spittle fizzle into the open fire.

Aunt Aggie was a simple soul with very few aspirations in life other than a quiet corner, a bit of food and a garden to potter about in. She hurried everywhere sometimes breaking into a wee trot and with her arms swinging to and fro at her sides. As children we were very fond of her and were happy to paddle about the farm after her. Later at Carntall we ate her jam and home baking with relish.

With uncle Willie's reduced capacity for working the farm declined. They kept a couple of cows for domestic milk supplies and a few pigs. Just as she had done on the Mossley farm aunt Aggie looked after a coop of chickens. Eventually uncle Willie's two nephews, John and Hall Kennedy who lived at Irish Hill near Straid took over the management of the farm. I continued to go up to the Rea Hill on Saturdays to lend a hand and worked alongside the Kennedy brethren. They were a serious- minded, sombre pair and continuously promoted their religious beliefs vigorously and offered me gospel tracts, I presumed, to guide me along the narrow path.

Although he never had learned to drive uncle Willie kept an immaculate, grey Ford van in one of his empty sheds. Unlike my father's cousin, James Moore, Willie had never made it into a field to develop driving skills, he had just relied on a horse for his farm work. His brother, John, lived next door to the farm and chauffeured Willie around the district in the van. John, no doubt tired of this commitment, tried to persuade uncle Willie to let me have a go at the driving. It did not happen and I never found out why this arrangement failed to get off the ground.

I gave support to aunt Aggie when uncle Willie's health seriously deteriorated and he was admitted to the Belfast City Hospital. I stayed overnight with her the night before he died.

Following uncle Willie's death aunt Aggie soldiered on at the farm for several years. She had been granted the right to 'have her day in the place' a common arrangement for a farmer's widow in those years. Eventually she moved to live in Whitehead to be close to her sister, Annie, who lived in the resort.

In Whitehead her lifestyle changed dramatically. She bought a television set and developed a passion for sport, especially boxing and wrestling bouts and football that she delightfully pronounced 'saucer'. She also spent long hours on rug making, a fine achievement considering a deformity she had in at least one of her fingers. The good news for my brothers and myself was that the production line of rhubarb jam making was as busy as ever!

She probably never had much money and she spent little on clothes or luxuries. She made do with small fires and her large house in Whitehead was a cold place to visit on a winter Sunday afternoon. She had storage radiators fitted to provide some extra heat but these were not effective as she did not often switch them on. One relative, swore that on a visit he left his hat on a storage radiator and it stuck to it.

She was fond of serving Unox Luncheon meat at tea times and we often joked about this among ourselves. When my mum was ill my brothers Edwin and Wesley stayed with her at Lestannon Avenue in Whitehead for their summer holidays. They loved it and made many friends among the local children. One young playmate, Stewart McKinney, no relation of ours, turned up much later as a teaching colleague of mine in Abbots Cross Primary School.

Aunt Aggie soon had lots of friends in Whitehead and she even took up bowling which surprised us all. She proved more resilient than we had expected. John Kerr, her sister Annie's husband, had an electrical business in the town with a shop and an apartment above it. This was just round the corner from her home at Windsor Avenue and after he died the two sisters were in each other's company very often. I can picture them sitting in the glass conservatory behind the shop chatting and sewing, Annie talking and Aggie listening and busy with her needle.

My dad disliked Whitehead which we often visited on the train using up one of his free passes. He got three of them every year but it was a matter of pride that he never surrendered them and could therefore reuse them over and over again. He must have known every ticket collector, guard and porter on the railway network. He also kept a pass key and let us into a first class carriage on our jaunts. I kept this pass key for years as a souvenir.

Cousin Ina McKinney, daughter of Uncle George and Aunt Bessie

Uncle George McKinney

Uncle George with the rake in the hayfield at Burns' garden

We liked to paddle in the sea at Whitehead and I vividly remember cutting my foot on a piece of a milk bottle sticking in the sand on one visit. The highlight of the train journey was passing through the tunnel just before entering Whitehead station. Our Kerr cousins Agnes, Mary and Joan, although much older than us, were very pleasant and we all always got on exceptionally well. Although they were girls at this time we disregarded this species entirely. They all eventually became nurses. Mary married and emigrated to Canada but sadly died at a young age from cancer. Joan also went to live in the USA following her marriage to an American soldier. Agnes lived locally and at her wedding my aunt May struck up a relationship with Sammy Cranston, a pal of the groom. They were married shortly afterwards.

Uncle George was the character of the family. He grew up close to my father but they were very different in outlook and temperament. He had a milk run around Ballyduff, Mossley and Carntall. There was no better man for this job. He had a line of patter for all and his witty remarks about almost anything made him well liked. He was the darling of all the ladies, old and young.
He had a slight touch of what must have been epilepsy and suffered occasional 'turns'. I worked beside him on the farm during the school holidays and I never saw him have any such episodes. I think they diminished as he got older. He was great with the horses, both the heavy cart horse and the lighter hunter which drew the milk cart. It was a special treat for us to have a ride on the milk cart or occasionally on the back of the carthorse.

There was a small dairy on the farm and the milk, unpasteurised at this time, was bottled after being strained and cooled. Later bottled supplies in crates came from Dobson's Dairy to be distributed on the milk run.

Also the farm supplied milk in one-third pint bottles to Mossley School where my brothers and I drank it there, first pushing our fingers into the little hole on the cardboard top and inserting a mushy straw.

The dairy always had surplus bottles of school milk and when we stayed on the farm we often drank our fill after returning to Granny's from school.

There were sometimes crises with the milk horse. It tended to be more temperamental than the farm work – horses. I remember hearing stories of it either falling or lying down between the shafts. It was quite a job to unyoke it and get it operational again. And on at least one occasion the horse took off in panic with the crates and uncle Geordie was thrown to the ground.

My dad steered clear of these adventures only helping out at busy times such as the hay or corn harvests. I know my grandmother sheltered her younger son; he was relieved of heavy duties because of his weak chest. I heard that uncle Geordie suffered some fairly severe cuts to his head from a milk bottle disintegrating and flying out at him from the bottler.

While uncle George learned to drive he remained very nervous at the wheel and tended to give a commentary on the boldness of other motorists and pedestrians daring to come anywhere near his van. He often drove a van because it was possible with a flimsy wire barrier behind the seats to transport pigs, often large sows, in the back. The only difficulty was that he needed someone to help him give a sow a leg up into the van through the back doors. His heart condition in later years did not stop him assisting in this operation. Going into Allam's Saleyard in Belfast he was terrified of zebra crossings always afraid that someone would step on to the crossing at the last moment causing him to carry out an emergency stop. This was especially hazardous with a sow on board.

Inevitably, one day this happened on the way home and the sudden braking caused the sow to slide up the slippery floor of the van, crash through the wire and end up, Heels McGarry, in the front seat. He had to wait until he arrived home to extricate the sow from its position jammed hind end up between the seat and dashboard.

Wedding of George McKinney and Bessie Stewart

After my dad's death in 1958 I had to assume much responsibility for helping my mum manage the family home. She leant on me in much the same way that she had depended on my dad to run the finances and other household affairs. I got to know her very well then. Mum, like almost all her brothers and sisters, had an innate emotional instability. She found it particularly hard to cope with big events like my dad's illness and death. As she often said she had been told after his first heart attack in 1952 that he could die suddenly at any time. This put an intolerable strain on her. She watched, and when it was necessary, nursed him over six years with the constant realisation that his life would eventually be curtailed in its prime. There were few strategies available then to treat coronary heart disease and the doctors simply used medication to contain its advancement.

The year following my dad's death in 1958 was without question the most difficult in my life. My mum just went to pieces and nothing seemed to lift her from the depths of despair.

At one point her brother, Jimmy, who was close to her in age and temperament, arranged for mum to see a doctor on the Lisburn Road in Belfast. I went with her and afterwards we were passing through the city centre to get the bus home when I had the bright idea of taking her to see a film then showing at the Hippodrome. She agreed reluctantly but at that time did anything I suggested. The film was Kenneth More in A Night to Remember - not the most cheerful choice. I have seen it again many times since and each time it brings back memories of the black cloud that hung over Ballyearl at that time.

Mum had spells in hospital in this period and I stayed with Edwin and Wesley running the home and going to Stranmillis College each day on the bus. Ken was serving his time as an apprentice electrician in the UTA and stayed with my aunt Sylvia and uncle Alfie in Belfast during the week returning to Ballyearl at weekends. Edwin sat his Qualifying Exam that year and no provision was then given to candidates for his special circumstances. He certainly warranted such consideration.

Wesley suffered regular bouts of chronic asthma. When he was eight years old I remember once having to summon the doctor in the middle of a really bad bout at around two o'clock in the morning. The young doctor who treated him wondered how we were able to cope.

At this time with my mum in hospital I remember the four of us being taken for Sunday lunch at aunt Grace Patterson's home at Sizehill, Lisnalinchy, Ballyclare. These were great meals. The Patterson's ate well and aunt Grace was so very kind and good to us. Our uncle John Patterson transported us in his Triumph Mayflower, a car which seems to have been passed round the Kennedy family over the years.

Uncle John Patterson was a bit of a character who was fond of a refreshment or two when he could manage it. One twelfth of July he took my mum, in one of her good spells at this time, and aunt Grace and family to see the Orangemen at Antrim. Sometime that day he had sneaked off to the beer tent. On the way home my mum was terrified out of her wits as John, driving the Mayflower raced Harry Park, a UTA driver, in his double-decker bus back to Ballyclare. My mum used to claim that John was a much better driver after he had had a few so it was no surprise to find the Mayflower passing the finishing post, probably John Baird's pub in Main Street, a short bonnet in the lead.

I remember one incident at our house at Ballyearl very clearly. We had an old armchair in our kitchen that was often pulled up close to the fire. One of us had been sitting here and then went off to do something else. A burning coal fell out of the fire and rolled under the chair. It was some time before it was noticed and by then it was already well alight. Mum quickly went into action and dragged the burning chair out into the garden. I helped her, thinking at first that it was a hopeless case, but she was fearless and, although she received a few burns on her arms, her courage saved the day and our house.

When I think back now I wonder that we didn't have more incidents like this. It was mother's regular custom to light the sitting room fire by carrying a shovelful of red hot coals from the kitchen fire. We had a bit of smoke about the place for a while but fortunately no disasters. There were fireplaces in both bedrooms but these were seldom lit especially after we got electricity when electric fires were used.

One time she had arranged to have the kitchen chimney swept because the crows had built there and blocked it. In the course of the work the sweep went to investigate the small bedroom flue and eventually took out two large bags of straw and twigs which had accumulated from attempts at nest building over the years. This was obviously a highly dangerous state of affairs. It was fortunate that a stray spark from the common chimney flue had not set the house on fire.

One evening my brothers, Edwin and Wesley, were sitting watching television when a young jackdaw fell down the chimney and flew about the room shedding soot everywhere it landed. The lads were utterly startled and it took some time before they recovered sufficiently to usher their unusual visitor out through the back door!

The clean-up afterwards was indeed a difficult and time-consuming operation.

The fire was especially dangerous when mother used the damper to increase the draught to heat water for the Saturday night baths. I remember often feeling with my hand the heat from the fire penetrating through to the outside gable wall in the yard. At such times we surely lived dangerously in Iona.

When Ken and I bought a car, an Austin A35, I took mum to Ballyclare every Tuesday to get her widows' pension and to shop. Samuel Tweedie probably felt the draught when mum's horizons were extended. This was a happy time for our family. We boys were all at home and she relished looking after us. She was in her element doing just this.

Ken McKinney with Mum in the back garden at Ballyearl

My first pay cheque arrived in time to clear off a number of bills we had accumulated and, with Ken also moving up the pay scale in his apprenticeship, we were in clover. There was tremendous fun at home then and mum's health was good. She was always happy when she had plenty of people around her and responsibilities were shared.

Mum never really liked being a housewife; I think she found the never ending housework tedious and she liked the challenge of something different. She enjoyed gardening, only possible in a small way in our little plot, and she adored cutting firewood. She would have played cricket in the garden with us but, as ever, was afraid of what the neighbours might think.

She tackled sawing the railway sleepers with the rest of us, except my dad, and this was hard going with the primitive saws we had then.

Indeed just after Ken was married in 1965 she broke her leg stumbling from a pile of sleepers where she was wielding an axe. We had to bring her bed down to the parlour until the break healed.

She was very good with her grandchildren, first Ken's son Paul and then Wesley's daughters, Jennifer and Gillian. Unknown to their parents, when she was babysitting she allowed them outrageous privileges and never cared what mess they made so long as they were amused and happy. She often got them baking and the arrangements for this concentrated more on fun and enjoyment than the end product. She never was one to mind a bit of mess so long as it was all in a good cause.

Often in these days the whole family congregated at Ballyearl on a Sunday afternoon. This was all she really ever needed to make her happy. Family news was recounted and there would be the sound of laughter as old family jokes and stories were endlessly repeated. As for outings, she wanted nothing more than a visit to Woodburn Presbyterian Church, better known as Aldoo, and the Quarterlands of Carrickfergus, either to visit relations or simply to drive around her childhood haunts. Time and time again we saw the stile and fields she had crossed to get to Straidnahanna School and Sunday after Sunday, as we passed the farms of all her relations, she would identify each and extol their seed, breed and generation.

Our mother's underlying problem had been that she found it impossible to live on her own while at the same time accepting that she could never bring herself to stay with any of us. I suppose that, like old Granny Higgins our neighbour, she just couldn't live without her 'weans.'

The months following my dad's death were difficult for all but throughout the period we did try to remember the good times at Ballyearl and the way, with humour and hard work, mum had striven to give her four boys the best possible foundation for their future. In doing so she created memories we would never forget.

Chapter 4: The Boss, The Chase, and Albert's Trousers

We were very fortunate with the friends and neighbours we had in Ballyearl. In all, I suppose there were just about thirty households but there was a fair selection of characters living in our little village. Ballyearl, though, was not really a village, merely a collection of houses along and just off the Doagh Road but village is the only term that I can think of that is suitable.Our house was one of four semi-detached villas on this main road. Next door to us lived the Higgins family. They had been there for as long as anyone could remember. Beside them was an invalid, Mr Robert Hunter, and his wife, Hansina. They had come from Straid and I think they had been in Ballyearl from the time the houses were built. Eventually Robert became more frail and Mrs Eileen Gerrard arrived to stay there and nurse him. I think perhaps Hansina died before Robert. Mrs Gerrard had two children, David and Lesley and they went to Mossley school with us on the nine o'clock bus. Following Robert's death and the sale of the house, Mrs Gerrard and her family went to live in one of the houses at Springtown.

Eventually the Martin family moved in here from the Glen Road near Bruslee, Ballyclare. It was great news for us to discover that, not only were there two boys in the Martin family, Stewart and Herbert, but that they were in our age group. A few years later Trevor was born. I remember this event very well. Ken and I were not forced to take a long walk up Springtown Lane as we were when Edwin and Wesley were born but I was aware of the usual excitement and secrecy which such home births tended to create. We played and fought with 'Stewarty' and 'Herbie' Martin for many years. Stewart loved cricket but Herbie played any game and he was very placid and easy to get on with. Stewart and I were more of a kind, a bit hot-headed and many a good squabble we had. On some days in the heat of a game skin and hair flew but next day we had forgotten it all and played together as usual.

Mr Martin was an incredible jack-of-all-trades and when he wasn't engaged in renovating his own house he did odd jobs for many Ballyearl folk. Indeed, his expertise was such that my dad came under increasing pressure from my mother to match Tom Martin's expertise and work rate around the house. Mr Martin always seemed to be hammering or busy up a ladder. He was particularly good at improvising in his use of materials and nothing was ever wasted.

He installed a special coke-burning stove and went regularly to Belfast Gas Works to buy fuel. This was unheard of in Ballyearl. We tended to use expensive coal in our range or paraffin oil in the cooking stove.

Mrs Martin was a skilled dressmaker and made clothes for, among others, my aunt Bessie. They were mobile too. In the early days Mr Martin had a motor bike with a sidecar which he rode to work and to take the family on outings.

Later he had a range of small cars and vans. The one I remember best was an old green, almost khaki coloured, Ford which was sound enough to make the trip to Monaghan where the family had come from originally and where their relations still lived. Mrs Martin rode a bicycle to all parts of the district. Cycling was a common mode of transport then. Not, I hasten to add, for my mother because we just knew somehow that she would never have kept her balance for very long on a bicycle. She wouldn't have survived a week even on the quiet roads then in our district.

My mother and Mrs Martin quickly became friends and their friendship lasted until my mother's death. Oddly they began and continued to call each other by their formal names – Mrs Martin and Mrs McKinney. To this day I do not know Mrs Martin's Christian name.

The Martins' neighbours were Tommy and May Scott and their nephew, John Strange who lived with them. I remember Tommy coming to see May Strange, as she then was, from his work as a railway man at Ballyclare junction nearby and I remember their marriage. He often arrived early in the morning, having spent the night shunting wagons in the sidings there. The noise of shunting steam engines was the familiar night time sound in Ballyearl. He was a friendly soul and one time acquired some fame with my dad by fixing our wireless set – simply by giving it a hefty thump or two with his fist. Ever afterwards when we had a problem with faulty equipment we gave it what became known as the 'Tommy Scott Treatment.' It was amazing how often it worked.

May Strange had a wooden shed in her back yard where she did dressmaking and I recall it being heated like a sauna bath. Before you got to the door you had to negotiate your way across the yard and past their dog, Rover. I wasn't always successful. Rover was old and cross so I only went there on errands under protest.

May Strange was a kind hearted lady and a teacher in the Mossley Sunday School where my grandfather McKinney was superintendent. On the morning of our qualifying examination in Ballyclare PE School, her nephew John and I were waiting for the bus in her house and May offered up a prayer for our success. It did the trick and for some years we both travelled to Ballyclare High School on the bus with other Ballyearl scholars.

May was an accomplished singer and often performed with her sister, Belle, at local concerts. I well remember May and Belle singing sacred songs and choruses at Mossley Sunday school. Another sister, Sadie, also taught in the Sunday school. They were all part of my grandfather's team of teachers and I remember how upset May was when she heard of my grandfather's death following his fatal accident.

May, Tommy Scott and John Strange moved to Carrickfergus and then William John Horner, a native of Mossley and a bachelor, lived here for several years. Though small in stature, he had been a blacksmith in the Belfast Shipyard and rode a large "sit-up-and-beg" bicycle. He had a most peculiar way of getting into the saddle. He would push the bike along for a bit, hopping beside it with one foot on the pedal then, at the right moment, he would swing his leg up over the seat and spring into the saddle. He was good at this manoeuvre but I watched avidly just hoping that some day he would come a cropper. As he rode along his posterior swayed from side to side with his toes only just touching the pedals.

For many years he courted a lady from the Kings Moss, Mary Ann McCrum, and she often accompanied him on bicycle trips. She, though, was an accomplished cyclist and rode her cycle much more sedately than her boyfriend. They were both a little deaf and I have it on good authority that communications shouted to each other were clearly heard next door. I know that their relationship proved unfruitful, at least in terms of an eventual exchange of marriage vows.

Next along the road was Pansy Cottage. The first people I remember living there were the Kerr family. I believe that Norman, the husband, was a cousin of my uncle John Kerr, my aunt Annie's husband. The cottage had formerly belonged to his father. Norman Kerr worked in the engine room of Mossley Mill. His tragic death following an accident at the mill was one of those dark days that I remember so vividly from childhood.

One morning part of Norman's clothing caught in the whirling machinery and he was dragged into the engine and killed. His daughter Anne went to Mossley school with us and was our regular playmate at Ballyearl.

I remember Mr Hamilton taking Anne out of class that day and eventually hearing the gory details of the tragedy circulating in the playground. The mill workers always sat up on the boundary wall overlooking the school yard during their lunch break and it was inevitable that we would hear about the accident from their conversations that day. My uncle Davy Darragh was an engine fitter in the mill at this time and I believe he had attempted to extricate Norman from the machinery.

We were always escorted to the works canteen for our school lunch and passed the engine room so we knew its position well. Indeed, this machinery and the two mill fire engines housed nearby were the focus for all the boys' curiosity. Our imaginations ran wild over the details of the accident. Soon after the funeral Mrs Kerr and her children moved to live in Larne.

My grandparents came to live in Pansy Cottage about 1950 when my grandfather McKinney retired and uncle George took over the farm at Mossley. Before improvements could be carried out to the cottage my grandfather was killed in an accident on his bicycle near Monkstown.

Although my grandmother was devastated by his death this became a good period for us all because my father liked having his mother and sister May living close by and we adored having our granny McKinney just a matter of yards from our house. Our nearness was a comfort to her. We went to see her very often and Ken and I were old enough then to be of some help to her with the household chores – especially pumping water from the hand pump just beside the back door. We were, of course, experts at this job from our experience at Iona!

The cottage was enclosed at the back with sheds made from railway sleepers. The Kerrs had also worked on the railways. I remember the chickens she kept in outhouses around a yard behind this back door. At one time Willie Forsythe who lived in Ashley Park and delivered fruit and vegetables in Ballyearl kept his van in the large shed at the side of the house. He was not too careful when brushing out the van and the floor was covered with discarded nuts and bruised fruit. I remember that rats were a constant problem and my granny's favourite cat, Fluff, struggled to keep them under control. I'm pretty sure Fluff succumbed, either to a bite from a rat or from the poison spread to control the rodents. I remember granny being very upset.

Rats were always a problem in the Pansy Cottage sheds. Later when my uncle George moved to live here, he bought a large henhouse and erected it in the side garden. There were soon nests of rats beneath the hen house and I don't think I ever saw so many rat holes in one place. Typical of many farmers, uncle George was not unduly upset by this, he used to say that the rats ran around winking at him. Pansy Cottage became the centre for the McKinney Christmas celebrations and almost every Sunday friends from the family circle came to visit granny.

I remember two regulars, Willie and Maggie McBride who were connected in some way to our family. When they came they were treated like royalty. We always knew to stay clear of the house when their car was seen beside the gate. My grandmother had relations called Moore and they were also regular visitors. Of all these relatives the one I liked best was James Moore, cousin of my father and a bachelor farmer from Carntall.

He was a colourful character. He had a very strong country accent and a hearty laugh. He loved sweeties and his coat pockets were usually filled with them. Living with his sister, Tilly, in a remote hillside farm on the Rea Hill, he never mastered any form of motor transport and went everywhere on the bike or the bus. He continued to use horses on the farm even when all other farmers had moved to tractors. He did try to learn to drive in one of his fields in a small car which he bought. Sadly, or perhaps fortunately for other motorists, he never made it on to the road. He was a regular visitor to my aunt Aggie and uncle Willie Hall's farm quite close to his own in Carntall.

The visitors to my granny's house often arrived on Sunday nights and we got to know them well but I always struggled to remember how they fitted in to the family connection.

Eventually my dad's young sister, May was married and my grandmother moved to the Rea Hill to live with aunt Aggie and uncle Willie Hall.

The next residents of Pansy Cottage were Matthew Crawford, usually shortened to Mattha, and his wife. She was just known as 'old Mrs Crawford' to distinguish her from the two other Crawford families in Ballyearl. They had moved from a farm near Raloo outside Larne and were used to a more isolated country existence. They considered Ballyearl almost urban. Mrs Crawford at first presented a strange picture to us all. She was quite small and always wore a woolly cardigan, black bonnet pulled down close to her ears and a dark skirt and black stockings. Her face was very wrinkled. She told us that her grandchild had said that her face was like a map. A flowered pinny apron gave her a dash of colour but this was worn only on weekdays. She could have come straight out of a William Conor painting. She visited our house very often and my dad got on particularly well with her. They argued constantly, but happily, about theological affairs and endlessly discussed church affairs and details of local clergymen.

She seemed to know all the ministers in East Antrim. Mattha was a lot less sociable. Indeed he was gruff and short tempered. His complaints about various matters and people were relayed daily to us by his good wife. He did tend to mention that he felt that my grandmother had overcharged him for the furniture and effects she had sold him with the cottage. My dad disagreed and was rather proud that a feeble old woman had managed to put one over on such a hard-fisted farmer. Mattha struggled to fit in with the sophistication, or what passed as sophistication, in Ballyearl. In this context two incidents stand out in my memory.

Mattha went to bed early and he never seemed to realise that he needed to pull the bedroom blind before undressing. Unfortunately, his bedroom window overlooked the bus stop and folk could not help seeing him prepare for bed. The bus stop in summer was the gathering spot for some of the local men who met there for a yarn. At one stage darts were played as an evening pastime. My dad was a member of the club and I remember him telling my mum how they had watched this spectacle and tittered at Mattha's exploits. The highlight of the performance, apparently, was Mattha's unfailing custom of giving his behind a good scratch before getting into bed. These men were really very mischievous but I can understand how they were so intrigued. I'm sure Mattha never realised what was going on, at least the blind was never pulled down.

The other incident concerned Mattha's attempts at wall papering. In this instance we had all the details supplied by Mrs Crawford. We got a daily report on his progress and there was no doubt that this was Mattha's first attempt at such work. He had trouble with the corners and became frustrated at his failure to get the edges of the wallpaper rolls to meet. When he had finished Mrs Crawford told us that she was disappointed to find that she could slip the poker in at the top of the wallpaper and down behind where the two corners joined.

The Crawfords were taken to church in Carnmoney every Sunday by their son, Tommy, in his small covered van. There were only two seats and poor old Mattha had to struggle in and out of the back of the van on his hands and knees. not unlike a calf being taken to market.

Beside Pansy Cottage there was a narrow passageway laneway known as Pumptown Loney because it led up to the site of a former spring. I remember a well being opened during a very dry summer and the supply used by the residents of Ashley Park. Normally, though, it provided us with a playground. The boxwood hedge on one side was very thick but in places had been eroded leaving large gaps. There were also overhanging beech trees. These hedges were perfect dens, especially one area which was virtually enclosed and where it was impossible to be seen from the laneway. This became a gang hideout and the scene of little girls' tea parties.

The other side of the laneway had a thick hedge sheltering the back of a large tin shed in Jimmy Forsythe's yard. Willie Forsythe kept his van and motor car in these sheds. At the corner beside the road was a pool of horrible smelling glar, the result of a blocked drain somewhere in the vicinity. On one never to be forgotten occasion my brother Ken fell into this mess. I can picture him coming up the road towards home and we could smell him before we saw him. He had to be scrubbed many times before my mum was satisfied that he was anywhere near clean. As she scrubbed she scolded him while calling down imprecations on the head of poor Jimmy Forsythe. He lived with his brother Johnny and at one time I think a sister in the first of two semi-detached villas just on the corner of the road up to the terrace called Ashley Park. These were grandly called Ashley Villas. I remember the brothers having a shop in the house. I think the shop that Willie Forsythe had at 6, Ashley Park and which we all knew and used for sweets and lemonade must have been the successor to an earlier one in Ashley Villas.

Jimmy was a tall man and a bit awkward. I remember a neighbour lady stating once that Jimmy always made her feel a little nervous when she saw him coming round the corner of her house. Johnny, his brother, had a very florid complexion and was rather stout in build. He always wore a white shirt and it stuck out of the top of his trousers. The brothers worked in the Whitewell Laundry whose yellow vans were seen all round the district at this time. They went to their work and travelled everywhere on bicycles.

Jimmy brought the Belfast Telegraph, the weekly magazines and comics round each night and on Saturdays the sports edition of the newspaper – Ireland's Saturday Night. Ken and I were fervent football followers and waited for its arrival impatiently every Saturday night. It arrived on the 8.30 bus from Belfast and not long after it had passed we knew that Jimmy would push the paper in through our door. I think it was the sight of big Jimmy coming round the corner of the houses in the dark that frightened the women. If our radio wasn't working, perhaps because the wet cell battery was uncharged, this was the only way we could hear that day's football results.

Johnny Forsythe died suddenly and, eventually to the great surprise of everyone in Ballyearl, Jimmy married Sadie Sherrard who lived with her sister, Mary, in one of the Springtown houses. The two ladies moved in with Jimmy and this led someone to reflect that Jimmy had found it hard to find a woman then suddenly he had two. Sadie was renowned for being house proud and it was said in Ballyearl that she even polished the coal shovel.

Frank and Gretta Rea lived next door to the Forsythe brothers and were good friends of my parents. Gretta's family had come from Straid and Frank's from Millvale, Ballyclare so the conversation covered the people they all knew from these districts. Gretta was very jolly and liked nothing better than a good laugh. She gathered up information on the doings and folk of Ballyearl and related this to all and sundry.

On one occasion the shop assistants in Samuel Tweedie's shop made up a piece of outrageous gossip, told Gretta and then watched as she did the rounds of the houses passing on the news. She was the 1950s Ballyearl version of Facebook!

The Reas often played board games with my parents – usually Ludo and Snakes and Ladders – and I remember the teasing and laughter which were always a feature of these evenings.

Frank was one of my dad's best friends and helped him with jobs around the house after his heart attack. They were both members of the seven o'clock bus 'club', the group of men who caught the first bus into Belfast each morning. My dad and Frank sat together not needing to speak too much at this early hour. I know that was one reason why my dad was so comfortable in his company. Frank had spent a lot of time on the farm of John McKinstry at Skilganaban just opposite my granda Kennedy's farm and he was a strong and careful worker. Every summer he cut the boxwood hedge of Pansy Cottage for my grandmother and everyone marvelled how he could leave the top so level. He also dismantled our kitchen range when we changed to a Devon grate. I clearly remember him throwing the large pieces out through the open window into the back yard.

Springtown lane ran up the side of our house and garden so we were very familiar with the people who lived here. Over the years these included many strange and wonderful characters, though often they only stayed for a short spell. The cottages were small and not always in good repair.

Providing continuity through this line of tenants was Ben Ross, his wife and their large and diverse family. Ben was the manservant of the Girvans of Ashley House and seemed to spend his entire life on a tractor. He was very patient with children and we got many rides on the back of trailers and ruckshifters.

In summer we bounced along the lanes and fields jumping on and off as we liked. Ben just sat there and drove seemingly oblivious to what was going on behind him. Another lady called Maggie Harrison, the sister of Mrs Ross lived with or beside the Ross family. Sam Gordon, a big, bluff Belfast docks worker, visited some week nights and every Sunday afternoon. We saw him getting on and off the bus. Sam was a friendly man and spoke to us all, though in his rather gruff, Belfast accent.

Maggie Harrison died and with little ado her children were incorporated into the Ross household. We were never quite sure exactly how they were accommodated, indeed I wonder if Mrs Ross knew, but they were happy, pleasant children and went to school and played with all the others in the Ballyearl gangs. Big Sam continued to visit the children and the Rosses long after Maggie's death and he obviously cared deeply about their welfare.

I remember some of the people who lived up in Springtown for peculiar reasons. We spoke to almost everybody who went up or down the lane. It was an important Ballyearl thoroughfare. George Watson and his wife were there in the 1950s. He drove a large lorry for a Belfast feeds merchant and one day he told me that pepper burned a hole in your stomach. I have no memory of the context of the conversation but I never forgot his words. Mind you I still used pepper. I later thought it odd that he found pepper harmful but had no problem smoking cigarettes in the close confines of his lorry cab. It is strange the impressions which remain from childhood.

Old Willie Grace lived in Springtown for a time with his niece, Rosetta, and he became a favourite of my uncle George who knew him from the time he lived in Mossley. He had a white moustache, smoked a pipe and reminded me of Santa Claus in civies. He was fond of making grand statements of simple philosophy. Uncle George greeted him one day by remarking 'Willie, I think it's going to rain' 'Oh well, George,' he replied, 'it won't be the first time!'

In a bungalow almost directly opposite our house lived an old man, Johnny McCurdy, and his unmarried daughter, Helen. He had had a leg amputated and walked with the aid of shoulder crutches. He came here on retirement from a farm near Glenavy. He was probably the first of the many older men in my life that I have befriended and whose company I have enjoyed. He was well off because, apart from anything else, this bungalow had been built with the best of materials for Jamsie Girvan, the son of William James Girvan of Ashley farm. My dad liked visiting old Mr McCurdy because they were both familiar with the business of farming and conversation was easy and relaxed. I remember him coming home after one evening session and telling my mother that in the previous two hours he had bought and sold cattle worth hundreds of pounds while in his pocket he hadn't the price of a packet of 'fegs.'

Jackie McKinney in one of WJB Wilson's caravans, c.1950

The McCurdys had a wonderfully trim front lawn and, to keep it in order, Johnny had a push lawnmower that was the Rolls Royce of such machines. It purred over the grass with almost no effort needed to push it. The old man could operate it with some difficulty but as his health declined he relied on me to do this job. It was a real pleasure. Together we kept it like Mossley Bowling Green.

He managed to use the scythe and other implements in spite of his handicap. In many ways he treated the gardens like his former farm. He had apple trees, strawberries, gooseberries, and blackcurrants and he planted potatoes, beans and many other vegetables. His daughter, Helen, helped him look after two coops of chickens in the large back garden. His shed of tools and implements was amazing to behold and he let me borrow them to use in our garden. I loved the summers there making hay, though on a small scale, going through all the usual procedures – cutting with his scythe, raking, coaling then building the hay into ricks. It was just a disappointment when we ended up burning it. The old man, and the young fellow were just playing at being farmers.

He often incurred the wrath of his neighbours because of these fires. The smoke drifted over the washing hanging out on lines and I remember my mother berating him to me when the wind direction brought the smoke our way.

One time I accompanied him on a visit to his daughter's farm near the Langford Lodge wartime aerodrome in Glenavy. We went on the bus and I was his guide. We had to change at Smithfield bus Station and for me, and I think for him too, it was a big adventure. I remember eating crab apples in the orchard. There was a huge aircraft hangar close to the farmyard.

When his health collapsed he moved to Killead to stay with his other daughter but I continued to go over to help Helen with work in the garden. Helen was distinctly odd in appearance and in her habits. She was painfully thin, her hair was sparse and she giggled like a schoolgirl when she talked. I went one time to Glengormley on her large bicycle to get her a prescription from the pharmacist and, once I lost my fear of falling off, I enjoyed building up to top speed. The big cycle had good brakes unlike most of our bikes. Helen went to church by bicycle to the Kings Moss Gospel hall. The Fenning family, father and mother in front and the two children,

Alan and Beryl at the rear, went past our house twice every Sunday walking to the church from their home at Mossley. They were so regular you could have set your watch by them.

After her father had left Ballyearl, Helen McCurdy carried on in the bungalow on her own at least for some time. She was very brave and attempted most jobs, managing very well even with the scythe and the lawnmowers. One job she had less success with was wringing the necks of fowl when she needed any for the table. It was known that following her feeble attempts to stretch the birds' necks she hung them up on the clothes line where the poor creatures flapped about until they eventually died.

Next door to the McCurdys in a similar type of bungalow lived the Houston family. This comprised Sammy and Ruby Houston and their only child, Wesley. Sam Houston was our 'Man from the Prudential' and he travelled the district in his little Austin car collecting his weekly insurance payments.

I remember falling foul of him on more than one occasion because I became implicated in teasing or bullying his son Wesley. Wesley never became involved in our games of football or cricket and didn't like any form of vigorous play so he was often the butt of unkind taunts from other boys. I'm afraid I joined in too often and I'm not proud of my behaviour. This even occurred on the bus on the way home from Ballyclare High School where he was a fellow pupil. Mrs Houston was very active in the Mossley Women's Institute and on several occasions tried to enrol my mother into the membership.

Next door to the Houston family lived Mr WJB Wilson. These initials distinguished Willie Wilson from his more famous brother RJB Wilson, a farmer and agricultural contractor from Carntall, not far from my uncle Willie Hall's farm. Bob, as RJB was known to his friends, was held in high regard in our district because, among other things he was a JP and it was known that he worked closely with the police. If you could get to Bob in time it was rumoured that he could get you off minor charges without penalty or summons to appear in court. I cannot verify this but my aunt Aggie, Bob's neighbour at Carntall, certainly believed it, not that she was ever likely to need his assistance in such matters.

The district seemed very law abiding at this time and the kind of offences which we heard of were minor – usually to do with cycling. In around 1954 I was summoned to appear at Whiteabbey Court where I was fined for riding my bicycle without lights. Other common misdemeanours involved carrying others, usually in my case, my brother, perched on the bicycle frame. Offences such as these weren't serious enough to petition Bob Wilson.

Willie Wilson attracted children, almost always boys, around him and to his house like wasps round a jam jar. For boys the attractions were television and caravans.

The first television set I ever saw was in the home of George Crawford, a wealthy farmer who lived between Ballyearl and Mossley. Once he invited some children over to see a football match on television in his parlour. I have no memory of which match it was, perhaps a cup final of the early 1950s. I think, too, that George and Mrs May Crawford invited some of their Ballyearl neighbours to watch the broadcast of the 1953 coronation. This occasion was a special opportunity to see the new wonder of television but not long after this we had a standing arrangement to visit Willie Wilson's house every Saturday night to view the evening's television entertainment.

His sitting room was typically crammed then with up to ten boys eager to catch every flicker of the programmes – from In Town Tonight at 7pm through Jim Hardy in Wells Fargo to the Saturday night variety show – Billy Cotton's Band Show or The Norman Evans Show. This comedian was a special favourite of Willie Wilson's and I remember him laughing so much one night that he rolled off the sofa where he always stretched out to watch the programmes. We had great fun. Very occasionally he had visitors and we were denied our night's fun or he had to tend to his grandfather who was in his nineties and usually went to bed early before the television was switched on. We didn't often see old Granda Wilson, as he was called, but the few times I did I was frightened of his gruff voice and abrupt manner. The family were known to be well off but the old man always wore a jacket that was literally green with age around the collar.

There was an understanding that when Granda went to his room Willie would put the light on in his sitting room. When we saw this signal we knew that the coast was clear and we headed over and knocked on his door. I never remember being turned away.

There always seemed to be at least one or two caravans in his driveway. He kept some at Sligo and sometimes went there in the summer to service them or indeed stay in one on site. He took boys with him for a few days but my dad never allowed me to go along for the free holiday. I was disappointed that we couldn't go there with the others.

We went off for day trips in Willie's Standard Vanguard motor car and I think I accompanied him once or twice to tow a van to a site in Portrush or Port Ballintrae. Most of the boys we played with congregated over at Willie's house and Willie never seemed to have any objections. It seemed to be a case of the more the merrier. There was no doubt that a playmate, Reggie Magee, was the dominant force in this group. He seemed to spend all his time after school at Willie's house. As he grew up he rapidly became Willie's right hand man. Reggie could turn his hand to almost any job and Willie gave him responsibility until he was virtually indispensable to his various caravan enterprises.

We also did have a regular arrangement to go with Willie on a Friday night to Sullatober near Carrickfergus. A lady called Sally, a distant relative or friend of Willie's family, stayed in Ballyearl as Willie's housekeeper from Sunday to Friday night. He took Sally back to her home on Fridays and went to collect her on the Sunday evenings. There was a long lane up to her farm and we got to know her family from our frequent visits. The Vanguard had a long bench seat in the front and a steering column gear shift and occasionally he got one of us to sit in front of him and steer the car. There was less traffic around in the 1950s but this was a hazardous liberty.

Quite often we all gathered in the caravans in Willie's driveway, talked and made plans for the summer trips to Sligo or other resorts in the west of Ireland. Nowadays, when I hear names like Sligo, Ballisodare and Killarney I think automatically of Willie in his waistcoat and shirt sleeves with his wee terrier, Spot, or Spat as he pronounced his name, yapping at his heels.

I remember using Willie's .22 air rifle to take pot shots at rats in the river running down past his garage. This is the only time I have ever handled a gun in my life. Our parents probably only heard the half of what we got up to in Willie Wilson's garden.

Because he was so obliging Willie Wilson acted as a kind of unofficial taxi driver to many folk. He was certainly very kind to our family and when my dad died it was his telephone we used to make the funeral arrangements and his car that took me to fetch my mum from hospital following one of her illnesses. I never heard of him refusing anyone. Willie Wilson's house, garden and caravans were a kind of young boys' paradise.

In my early teens I found the summer holidays a bit of a drag. I was too young yet to help on uncle George's farm and too old for the antics of the gangs that the younger boys formed in Ballyearl. Consequently I'll never forget the summer when Mr Bob Webb arrived with his car and trailer to begin construction of a new bungalow just opposite our house. He was the 'Bob the Builder' of my childhood. The bungalow was being built for his mother and father-in-law Mr and Mrs Knox. He was good fun and always referred jovially to Mrs Knox as 'the old battle axe.' I was really an extra hand on the site, if an unpaid one, and I really enjoyed the experience. He had one other regular worker, Tommy Conn, and it says much about how well I liked him that I still remember his name. He came from Hollywood and seemed to be a jack-of-all trades engaged in brick laying, joinery and labouring. There was another rather shifty individual called Paddy who appeared when plastering was required but I never found him as friendly as Tommy. I used to sit in on the ten o'clock tea sessions when the wee black cans were used to boil the tea and I joined in, or more often just listened to their conversation. They got hot water from our house. Tommy Conn told me all about his current girlfriend and he was pleasant and terribly good natured.

I remember a lorry arriving regularly with lime mortar and I think we added cement to this to make the mix for the building. I often wheeled this mortar to Tommy when he was laying bricks. I was sorry when that summer holiday was over. I knew that the bungalow would be finished before I had any other time off school but I did go over to the site when I returned home in the afternoons.
The Knoxes became good friends of my parents. They kept chickens in their garden and Mr Knox was a keen gardener. I remember he used to leave parcels of vegetables for us on our garden wall, very often on Sunday mornings. My dad's attempts at growing vegetables were never very successful so mum appreciated these gifts. Although Mrs Knox sometimes displayed a sharp tongue she never approached Bob Webb's condemnation as a battleaxe. I'm sure he was just joking.

Sometime later Bob Webb the builder returned to Ballyearl to construct another bungalow a bit further up the road towards Houston's Corner for a daughter of the Knoxes. I can't think why, but I was never so highly involved on this building site. I think Tommy Conn had left Bob's employment by this time.

Eventually Mrs Edna Bennett and husband Albert with their children, Bertie and Alice moved in to swell the population of Ballyearl.

Albert Bennett became the centre of one of the most peculiar incidents that I can remember happening in our neighbourhood.
One summer's day the Girvans were rucking hay in the meadow just past the Bennett's bungalow. To this day I clearly remember the scene in the hayfield on this beautiful, sunny afternoon. It seemed that it would end as such days normally did with a set of very tired adults and children making their way back to their homes well satisfied with the sweat and labour of their valuable contribution to the Girvan's hay harvest. Everyone always enjoyed the jokes, gossip and repartee of a useful community enterprise.

No one had the least suspicion that this day would turn out to be such a momentous occasion in the history of Ballyearl.

The men were forking the hay up to the ruck builders and we children cavorted about in the loose hay and generally had a great time enjoying the rush and excitement of this pleasant task on a fine day. Albert Bennett was on top of a ruck tramping down the hay when he suddenly shouted out 'Hey, those are my trousers, there's a chap just gone up the road and he's wearing my good suit!' A hasty discussion took place after which the boss, William James Girvan Senior, always one to favour the direct approach, shouted out 'After Him' and with the boss well to the fore brandishing his pitchfork a hue and cry commenced. We children brought up the rear.
The culprit indicated his guilt by immediately breaking into a run. I have to say, though, that few people having seen boss Girvan, pitchfork in hand and yelling his special brand of abuse, would have done otherwise. Somewhere along the road the boss acquired a

bicycle and by the time we had reached Ballyclare Junction railway halt he had abandoned it and was making his way along the banks of the Layde stream in full pursuit of his quarry. I was in the rearguard but eventually joined the men at a small wooden crossing over the river. This was simply a series of railway sleepers that had been positioned to allow farm carts and cattle to cross the stream. There, shouts and threats were being addressed to what I took to be the thief skulking underneath, knée deep in the water. The boss stood guard brandishing his pitch fork and making regular splashes in the stream just to let the miscreant know that he was still there. I saw enough to realise that the man was terrified and near exhaustion.

After what must have been the longest hour in this fellow's life a policeman arrived from Whiteabbey station to arrest him. Willie Wilson had been commissioned to go to the police station and fetch a constable to make an arrest. The burglar, for it was soon established by the sight of Albert's trousers that such was the case, was clearly relieved to see the arrival of the law. The haymaking was forgotten as everybody triumphantly accompanied the officer and the thief up through the fields to the main road. I don't remember whether Albert Bennett ever recovered his new suit trousers but this curious incident had certainly produced a red letter day in Ballyearl.

Chapter 5: The Families from the Street

Right at the extremity of what we understood to be Ballyearl's boundaries lived two Crawford families. To the east towards Mossley there was George Crawford's farm and at the other end almost opposite what is known today as Ashley Road and we knew then as Girvan's Wee Road, lived another Mr and Mrs Crawford. I never discovered the latter's Christian names and that probably indicated their superior status. Their bungalow was relatively small but had a very long garden and at the bottom, a large green house. Their son Norman had no other employment but tending the garden and greenhouse. I think he suffered from what was then called 'nerves'. He drove a lovely, little convertible Hillman Californian car and it was the envy of all the young boys. His father owned, or was reputed to own, one or two cinemas in Belfast. What was certain was that every weekday he travelled into Belfast in the early afternoon and returned on the eight- thirty bus every night. He had a rather florid complexion and favoured light tan overcoats with a natty cap, certainly not of the shipyard 'duncher' type, and shiny brown shoes.

Although he was always immaculately dressed, when he got off the late bus he had some difficulty in negotiating the short walk up the footpath to his bungalow without one or two stumbles. He was usually a little bit the worse for wear but was very pleasant and chatty, always in a clipped, rather posh accent and as he got older his walks became more and more unsteady.

Our acquaintance with him was generally restricted to a few polite, casual remarks as he passed our house on his way to or from the bus stop so we were really surprised when, at the time of my father's death, he called into our house on his way home and sat and wept with my mother, commiserating with her on my father's death.

Mrs Crawford was a leading figure in the Mossley Women's Institute, a group of ladies that my mother could never bring herself to join despite many invitations to become a member. She much preferred to spend the evenings sitting at home darning socks or even playing Ludo or Snakes and Ladders with us.

A notable achievement of the Mossley Women's Institute was to petition successfully for a street light to be provided at the Ballyearl bus stop.

George Crawford's farm, now the Ballyearl Leisure Complex and Courtyard Theatre, could be seen as the eastern boundary of Ballyearl.

It was a prosperous enterprise aided by George's main occupation as a cattle dealer. In the 1950s few farmers had suitable vehicles to transport their stock to the markets in Ballyclare or Belfast. George Crawford, with his landrover and cattle trailer, travelled around the small farmers in the district offering them prices for their cattle. He had a keen sense of their potential value in the big markets and was able to trade them there at a substantial profit. In those days without sophisticated communications farmers were not so aware of the prices prevailing at the town markets as they would be today. Many would not have had a wireless set or telephone.

George left much of the day-to-day running of the farm to Henry Johnson who had been a 'servant man' on the farm for many years. May Crawford suffered from a chronic illness. She was a kind, gracious, lady who lived a life free of the household chores which were the daily lot of most other women in Ballyearl.

The Crawfords had suffered their share of misfortune. I remember one night being wakened out of my sleep and immediately sensed that something was amiss. I could hear my dad talking to someone. It seemed he was shouting down from his bedroom window. There was a peculiar red glow in the night sky which penetrated our window. I then heard him explaining to my mum that he had heard footsteps on the road outside and, on looking out, had seen young Helen Crawford running past. She had stopped for a moment and hurriedly explained that their hay shed had caught fire and was now well alight. She was expecting the fire brigade and endeavouring to recruit helpers to assist in extinguishing the fire. As my dad spoke to her the clanging of the fire brigade's bells was heard in the distance.

We all got out of bed and, in the company of most of the people of Ballyearl, trooped over to see what we could do to help. It was an amazing sight. I can still visualise the huge flames and the silhouettes of the fire fighters from Mossley, Glengormley and Ballyclare against the orange sky. The fire hoses were eventually linked in to Mossley Mill dam and the night of the Crawford's hay shed fire was the talk of the countryside for years. I remember we were even allowed to take the next day off school to recover our missed sleep and this really did emphasise the significance of the episode in the neighbourhood.

Oddly enough a few years after the hayshed had been rebuilt, it was again destroyed by fire. This was another cruel blow to the Crawford family.

When Ballyearl folk wanted to go over to the Carntall Road, perhaps to Bob McKinstry's grocer's shop, they used a path that ran up the side of one of George Crawford's fields then led over a stile past a cluster of small cottages. In the end one of these lived a remarkable old lady called Beanie. We never knew her surname. The cottage always seemed to be sooty and her appearance was black, from her shabby clothes to her dark skin. She often sat on a chair outside the cottage. It might be a dreadful thing to admit but I thought her the personification of a witch. It would not have surprised me had she produced a broomstick from behind her door. I suppose it was inevitable that, though she was totally harmless, she became a figure of fear to youngsters. The ultimate dare was to sneak past Beanie's front door on a pitch-black night.

Jimmy Aiken, a character from Ashley Park who liked to amuse and astound children, claimed that he went over there every Saturday night to pare Beanie's toenails. And, of course, this tall tale was readily accepted by his young audience.

At right angles to the main Doagh Road and not more than 50 yards from it was Ashley Park, a terrace of twelve houses owned by the Girvan family. Miss Lillian Girvan was a regular sight going from door to door each week collecting the rent money. She was a bit of a recluse and this seemed to have been her only appearance in public. I always thought that it was a rather demanding role for someone of such a retiring disposition.

For some reason this terrace was usually called the 'Street' by Ballyearl folk and in the days of my boyhood those of us who lived on the Doagh Road had young friends from Ashley Park. Many of the adults who lived there were slightly eccentric and brought fun, drama and a bit of colour to our lives.

In the late 1940s and early 1950s there must have been up to twenty children of my age living in Ballyearl and many more who, though a little older than me, always joined in our exploits especially in the summer evenings and at weekends. Many dads often took part in our football matches with great gusto. My dad was, I'm afraid, never one for football or energetic games.

Strangely, there was always a dearth of girls around Ballyearl and I suppose, before I became a teenager this mattered little. In those days, girls certainly did not readily join in the boys' vigorous games. I remember the girls congregating in their 'wee houses' created by the gaps in the hedges of Pumptown Loney. Here they played happily with dolls and tea sets or made mud pies. The boys preferred to ride bicycles, catch spricks, play football or go on manoeuvres with Reginald Magee's sham army.

Ashley Park, Ballyearl

Ashley Park overlooked a stretch of waste ground which comprised our football pitch. This was thought to belong, as all the surrounding land, to Wm. James Girvan but strangely he did not bother much with this field and did not crop or graze it. More significantly he never chased off trespassers in his inimitable style but gave youngsters free rein to use it openly. We enjoyed this privilege until a catastrophe struck. Samuel Tweedie began to renovate his shop and he used this area to dump the builder's waste material and rubble. We carried on playing games over the mounds of spoil but it was never again the same popular pitch. We were very disappointed that Mr Tweedie had been so heartless. This was surprising as his son, Leslie, often played here with us all.

It was just a bit inconvenient to move our custom to Bob McKinstry's shop on the Carntall Road but in our eyes Mr Tweedie's action merited a trade boycott.

The tenants in Ashley Park did not change very often and I still remember the names of most who lived there in the 1950s
In number one at the end closest to Tweedie's grocery shop lived the Montgomery family. Isabel Montgomery had been a McNeill from Sunnyside in Mossley and was a member of Carnmoney Presbyterian Church choir. I played football later with her brothers, Dessie and Noel, or Johnny as he was nicknamed. Her husband Robert, or more commonly, Rab, was a big sturdy fellow who drove a lorry for a Belfast firm which he parked at the end of the terrace. He played football with the local boys and eventually Ken and I took part with him in matches for the Churches League team at Mossley.

I clearly remember being taken with other team members on the back of his large flatbed lorry to play a local derby at Monkstown. When our team played there it was a good idea to have a hasty means of escape after the match so the lorry was a convenient means of transport.

Sadly, Rab was later killed in an accident with his lorry in Donegal. They had two girls but I only remember the name of one – Reda. She was a bit of a tomboy and had inherited her father's boldness. She would give a slap in the face to anyone who annoyed her. Next door lived the Downs family. I can recall Mrs Downs, a large lady always dressed in black, standing with one hand on the doorpost and cheerfully engaging in conversation with passers-by, adults or children. I remember four sons, Cecil who collected scrap iron round the district in an old lorry and who lived in Springtown after he got married, Austin, Stanley and Victor.

Austin, or Unky as he was nicknamed, was a few years older than most of my pals but he got on very well with younger boys. He had a deal of bravado, was certainly more daring than his younger pals and sometimes involved them in his dubious exploits. The McKinneys tended to stay on the fringe of these in case our parents found out but we were attracted to him nevertheless.

Austin was a great fellow for 'sodding' cyclists who came up the Doagh Road but another of his stunts was a bit more unpleasant. He prepared cardboard boxes as parcels beautifully tied up with string. He left these on the main road and then lay behind the hedge, well concealed hoping for interesting developments. Eventually a motorist would stop and often, curious to find out more about the package, opened it up on the spot. Inside was a mass of cow manure scraped off a cow pat in a field. I never was brave or fortunate enough to actually witness 'an unveiling' but going from Austin's reports, the expression on the motorist's face and his language was well worth the uncomfortable stint behind the hedge.

Austin was also an accomplished fighter. He gave me a boxing lesson on one occasion. I remember he stressed the importance of a good stance – a bit like that of Freddie Mills, at that time a British champion middleweight. Austin then added his own creation – a move which was meant to surprise an opponent. This involved suddenly and, with lightning speed, throwing both arms up in the air, a bit like a victory salute and letting loose a murderous scream. I didn't point it out to Austin but my fear was that, if this procedure failed to surprise an opponent, I would receive a most damaging punch on the nose just when my raised arms left me defenceless. But then I did not often engage in the noble art unless my temper had gone entirely and in such circumstances all traces of tactics were quickly forgotten in flailing fists.

Stanley Downs, the eldest of the Downs' sons, was the epitome of friendliness and in later years when I met him he greeted me warmly and spoke fondly of Ballyearl.

Victor Downs was an enigma. He had a few odd habits. A neighbour who visited us regularly told us of seeing him take his cat for a walk on a leash made from a ball of wool. Like Austin and Stanley he worked in Mossley Mill but later took a night shift job on the cleaning squad there, perhaps because he wouldn't be exposed to as much teasing then as he apparently endured on the regular day shifts.

In Number 3 lived the Cooper family. The father, Joe Senior, was a regular traveller on the 7am bus to Belfast with my dad and, at that early hour, his other silent companions. He smoked a pipe and he was the first person I knew who had a little metal lid on the top of it. I remember him as the quiet one of a very lively, interesting family. His wife, who was always Mrs Cooper to us children, was very musical and played the banjo expertly. There were bonfires every 11th of July on the ground in front of Ashley Park and she led the music and the singing and generally was the life and soul of the party. The Coopers were involved in the Mossley Scout troop and the hockey club. I am sure that when I was briefly in the Cub Scouts, we went on a bus outing to Castlewellan and Joe Cooper and Raymond Wilson from Mossley were the star entertainers in the sing song we had on the way home.

David Cooper , the youngest son, was a fine hockey player and either he or his older brother, Walter, for a time drove Bob McKinstry's lorry to deliver groceries. Later he emigrated to Australia.

Next door to the Cooper's lived Jack and Nessie Lusk. She was a sister of our neighbour, May Strange and he was a farm worker who specialised in working with horses. Their dashing daughter, Isobel, became, for me at least, the pin-up girl of Ballyearl.

In number five lived Jimmy Aiken with his aged mother. I remember her death and being told of how Jimmy and Mrs Cooper produced some fine music on the accordion and banjo at her wake. Jimmy Aiken had many accomplishments. He was an amateur conjuror and would amuse youngsters by producing three-penny pieces from behind their ears or by pretending to swallow sixpences. He often played the accordion for us and was roped in to provide the music at occasional Ballyearl social gatherings. He was very patient and good natured. I believe he had a Scots background. He had a club foot and walked with a distinct rolling gait. He used to call the footballers over to him and tell us about matches he had watched at Hampden Park, Glasgow. He recited the rhyme:

Ten thousand eyes watched Casey as he rubbed his hands in dirt
Ten thousand eyes watched Casey as he wiped them on his shirt.

He travelled with us every morning on the nine o'clock bus. We were on our way to school. He appeared at the bus stop with a large black bag slung over his shoulder. He told us, and of course we believed him implicitly, that he had a monkey in the bag. I must have been about thirteen before I realised that this was not true. I was a bit disappointed. Much later we heard that he was a second hand clothes dealer in Belfast and the bag contained some of his stock.

Next to Jimmy Aiken lived the Forsythe family. This was the house we visited most often because it served as a confectioner's and tobacconist's shop. There was barely enough room inside for the counter and a few shelves to carry the sweetie jars. A curtain separated the business end from the living quarters and the Forsythes never had much privacy. In spite of this a tall chap known as Norman, or fondly Spud, Conway managed to find enough spare space to court daughter, Martha, for a number of years. This was ultimately unsuccessful because the relationship foundered after years of regular Saturday and Sunday night visits.

We knew about this because we went to Forsythe's shop every Saturday night to stock up on sweeties for the next day's church service and to see us through a night watching television with WJB Wilson. I remember that a labourer from a farm up on the Rea Hill came down to Willie Forsythe's on his bike every Saturday night. He bought a bottle of appleade and a Bounty chocolate bar and stood at the counter talking to Willie and happily munching his weekly treat.

The Kennedy family lived at number six. The father, John, was a great friend of my dad, indeed he could have been a distant relative of my mum's Kennedy family. With his wife, Maggie, they had a large family of boys and girls and the oldest, John, junior, and Sinclair were among our closest playmates. John was a good footballer and went on to play with the Irish League side, Linfield. He was a true Ballyearl celebrity.

In number eight lived Jack Gillespie and his parents. I think he may have had a younger sister but I now have no memory of her name. Jack had a complete obsession with mechanical vehicles. Everywhere he went he convinced himself he was driving a car or sometimes a big lorry. He carried a saucepan lid as a steering wheel and he was able to produce expertly the various sounds of his vehicle accelerating, braking or stopping. Coming to a halt he'd change down through the gears then reverse the vehicle into a parking space. It was an exhilarating performance to watch as he made his way down Ashley Park and along the main road towards our house. His family emigrated to Canada in about 1952 so we never discovered whether he was able to find a career in motor transport.

The Smith family lived in number nine. The father, George, had an important job as a foreman with the well known building firm, McLaughlin & Harvey. He was tall and burly and I remember just after I went to Ballyclare High School he came over to our house and presented me with a book on calculus. This kind action was typical of Geordie's nature. I think his wife had died some years before and his daughter, Lillian, ran the household. She was a favourite of my mother and I believe that Lillian would often help mum by taking Ken or me for a ride in our pram. Stanley Smith was tall and eventually joined the army. I remember seeing him on leave wearing his khaki dress uniform and peaked cap. He had the bearing and smart appearance of a natural soldier. Tommy Smyth, his brother, became a plumber and was a regular hockey player in Mossley.

Number Ten, Ashley Park was the home of the McCormick family. Ivan McCormick, a playmate of mine was the only child of David and Anna McCormick. Ivan was mollycoddled by his mother and always struggled to fit in with any group of rowdy boys. He seemed to have a problem with coordination and football seemed to be beyond him. We'd stick him in goal but we knew that he would be a certain disadvantage to any team. He was in the Carnmoney Company of the Boys' Brigade and walked with Ken and me most Thursdays to the parade night. Ivan had the greatest difficulty in keeping in step when marching. He didn't seem to realise it but when the company went on the march there would be the regular sound of feet perfectly in step then in between these Ivan's step could be heard. In this procedure he was a forerunner of Corporal Jones in the television series Dads Army!

Despite this he often won the award for the Best Boy of the Year at the annual Boys Brigade display. He deserved it, too, because his mum, probably realising his problems with the marching, made sure he was turned out immaculately every parade night with no part of his uniform missing. I often went over to fetch him on Thursday nights and usually had to wait in the house for a time while his uniform preparations were completed by his mum. His dad was the quietest man I ever met. In all the years I called for Ivan I never heard him speak a word to Ivan, his wife or to me. He just sat and read the newspaper.

Reclusive was a word which did not spring immediately to mind when thinking of Mrs McCormick. For some unknown reason over many years she and Mrs Glenn, the old lady who lived next door in number eleven, carried on a noisy and bitter feud. Regularly, sometimes twice a week, the two ladies would appear at their front doors and loudly berate each other in the most intemperate language. This was a public performance and we in our back garden, perhaps two hundred yards off, could hear every word uttered without difficulty. In those days before television this was Ballyearl's own soap opera and very entertaining it was, too. Why they didn't shout at each other from their back doors where fewer people would have overheard their quarrels remained a mystery.

Mrs Glenn lived with her daughter, Winnie, and two young boys, Reggie Magee and Richard McMillan, they seem to have been taken into their household sometime during the war years. Mrs Glenn was small and stout, wore dark framed spectacles and usually had mutton dummies (plimsolls) on her feet. She always reminded me of Old Ma Murphy from the Dandy comic. She was very fond of cats and the house appeared to seethe with them. She was good natured, except of course, when Mrs McCormick appeared on the scene and in the days when supplies of lemonade were scarce she kept a crate of bottles in a corner of her front room. She kindly handed them out to the pals of Richard and Reggie.

Richard McMillan was renowned as one of the brightest pupils at Mossley School. His work books were a treat to behold and his homeworks were often used as models for the other pupils. He loved music and could whistle in tune like no one I had ever known. He took up the harmonica and became an expert in no time. He was an early version of Van Morrison. But, Dick, as we called him, was tough and no one picked fights with him readily.

Reggie Magee was definitely a one-off, a distinct, eccentric individual. In his younger years, before he began to spend most of his time over at WJB Wilson's house helping with his caravans, he loved to play at armies. This suited him because he could affect a posh English accent and military bearing and allowed him to carry out his role as Colonel-in-Chief of the Ballyearl Battalion with aplomb. Like the Grand Old Duke of York, swizzle stick in hand, Reggie marched his young soldiers from one end of Ballyearl to the other, not tolerating a word of dissent from anyone. My youngest brothers were eventually recruited into the Ballyearl Brigade.

There was a curious incident concerning Reggie that I remember well. One morning a death notice appeared in the Belfast Newsletter of a certain Reginald Orr Magee of 11, Ashley Park, Ballyearl. Mrs Glenn dealt with Hagan's the grocer from Monkstown and their traveller, Billy Bill, saw the death notice and sped up to the house to offer commiserations and of course, collect an order for extra supplies for the sad event. He knocked the door and got the shock of his life when it was opened by Reggie in apparent, sound health. This incident, in common with other affairs involving Reggie, attracted little attention after the initial surprise and there were not to my knowledge any consequences. Reggie later obtained a job as an assistant in a shoe shop in Belfast and those who saw him on the way to work on the bus and didn't know otherwise would have taken him for a manager or chief executive. This was exactly as Reggie wanted it.

The last house in the row was the home of the Montgomery Family. Mrs Montgomery worked in the canteen at Mossley Mill. She had three daughters, Grace, Ruth and Peggy the eldest, living with her. They were older than us but good looking, pleasant girls and well thought of in the district. I remember Grace going to the Kings Hall in Belfast to do ice skating. This was an unusual pastime for those days. For some time her boyfriend was Billy Millar from Glengormley. He became an actor at the Group Theatre, Belfast and later went on to become the famous Hollywood star, Stephen Boyd, actor in many popular films including Ben Hur.
Now that's an appropriate way to round up the list of celebrities from Ballyearl's Ashley Park!

These people from Ashley Park were without exception friendly and entertaining and provided a rich dimension to my young life. I recall my association with them, young and old, with pleasure.

Chapter 6: Rations and Roundsmen

Often when I am helping to carry in the weekly shopping from Tesco I wonder how we ever managed in Ballyearl without a supermarket. My mother made do with a delivery of groceries once a week from the lorry of our grocer, Samuel Tweedie. Billy Montgomery, his van man, would carry in to our house one cardboard box containing my mother's 'goods'. This is how she referred to these supplies. Sometimes she called them her rations, a relic from the restrictions of the recent wartime shortages. As well as the box of groceries he refilled our paraffin container from a tank on the lorry.

We needed the paraffin for the oil stove my mum had for cooking and for the oil lamps we used before mains electricity reached Ballyearl. In the early 1950s this stove was a large two-burner affair. It was ungainly, often leaked and anything that was cooked on it often had the distinctive and unpleasant smell of paraffin oil. We also had a small Primus stove, another paraffin device which specialised in flaring up in flames reaching the ceiling if it was not properly prepared before lighting. It tended to be hard on the eyebrows if you dared stand too close before it snored into life.

One began the complicated operation of starting it up by putting some methylated spirit into a little tray beside the burner. This was lit and you waited until it had burned out. Next, a small pump was used to build up the pressure and force the paraffin through the heated pipe to the burner. Applying a lighted match at the right time was a crucial judgement. Poking it with a special pricker was essential if the jet sooted up. I remember one occasion my mum became so frustrated with her repeated failure to light the stove that she flung it out into the back garden.

The oil lamps we used around the house were also smoky and they had glass globes that had to be cleaned regularly with newspaper. The globes were easily broken. The best light of all came from a Tilley lamp. These used paraffin and also operated on the pressure system but with a gauze mantel which glowed and produced a strong, bright light. We never had one at Ballyearl but they were used on my grandparents' farms.

The delivery of groceries followed the visit to our house of Tom Vint, Samuel Tweedie's assistant who travelled round the district collecting orders for the shop. I remember Tom Vint generally came on Saturday mornings just as we were getting up. He would immediately sit down by the fire and grab our copy of The Weekly News and wait patiently and comfortably until my mum was ready to give him the order. When my dad was there he found Tom's chatter a bit annoying and usually tried to make himself scarce until he had gone.

Tom had all the commodities in his head and shot out the names for my mother to reply with a yes or no. I can hear his litany still in my head. ' Tea, butter, margarine, lard, soapflakes, Briskies, Brasso and so on. There was a fairly limited range of the items available then and it didn't take long to complete the task once Tom set his mind to the job in hand.

In addition to the weekly order, mum visited Tweedie's shop daily, or more likely sent one of us down to do the messages as this was called. 'A small Tide – a brand of detergent – half a pound of butter, a packet of Briskies and a pot of jam' would be a typical list for a Monday. Samuel Tweedie marked these purchases down in a book and every so often we received an invoice for payment. This was compiled by Ella, his clerk, in her most beautiful copperplate handwriting. She had an office at the rear of the shop with a large glass window where she could watch the customers' arrival and departure.

When I was a boy, we seldom, if ever, went outside Ballyearl to do shopping. Indeed we had no way to reach other centres other than by bus. It was only when my mum began to receive her widow's pension from 1958 that she went to Ballyclare to fetch the allowance and was then able to shop around for a few items. Following my employment as a teacher in 1961 we acquired a little car and thereafter I took her to Ballyclare every Tuesday after I returned from school to do the shopping and get her allowance. These were halcyon days because, with my salary and Ken's wages as an apprentice electrician, we were suddenly quite affluent.

The one thing that we couldn't get done without going to Ballyclare was having the wet cell radio battery charged. It was carried on the bus, left in Samuel Girvan's electrical shop for a few days and then collected ready to allow our wireless set to get underway again. I couldn't be deprived of Radio Luxembourg for too many days.

In the 1950s there seemed to be an endless stream of travelling tradesmen who came to our doorstep. There were at least three bakery vans visiting Ballyearl – Inglis with Jimmy Wilson from Mossley as server, City Bakery with roundsman, Matt Millar, and a quaint little electric van from McWatters Bakery. They all had their separate days so mother got fresh bread daily. She also baked soda bread and all kinds of fancy cakes and buns herself, usually for weekends. I remember the McWatters' salesman coming to our back door with a wooden tray slung around his neck containing a selection of his bread and the items he knew my mum favoured. He marked up the purchases in his book and on a card my mum kept. She usually paid him on Friday or Saturday.

Mum's bill from Samuel Tweedie's grocer's shop

In those days all door-to-door salesmen had fine leather pouches for their money and they had the knack of upending them expertly to get change without spilling any coins.

Over the years we had a succession of milkmen though uncle George McKinney who was the Mosley milkman never seemed to cover our area. His round covered Upper and Lower Mossley. The milkman I remember best was called Robert and was very friendly. I was his unofficial helper for a time during the school holidays. I used to go down to the Mossley Finger Post crossroads to meet him at about eight o'clock in the morning. I then sat, dangling my legs over the back door of the van and ran into the houses delivering the bottles while Robert drove. I'm sure I speeded up his deliveries. I accompanied him round the Carntall and Straidnahanna districts and would finish up in Ballyearl after about an hour's work. I really loved this adventure. He gave me a shilling or two at the end of each week but this was a bonus – never the prime purpose of my offers to help. It got me round parts of the district that I did not usually cover on my bike.

Our greengrocer was Willie Forsythe from Ashley Park and he came around twice a week. Willie was a quiet, easy going character and his problem was that he never managed to get up early enough to get good quality supplies of fruit and vegetables in the Belfast market. By the time he arrived the best fruit and vegetables were gone. As a result his produce often was, as we'd say today, well past its 'sell by' date, and certainly not very fresh. But Willie was personable and obliging so most of the Ballyearl folk gave him their custom. There was no alternative. He owned a succession of ancient vans the most extraordinary of which was one that had previously served as a hearse. In many ways this vehicle matched Willie's temperament.

Willie was the Drum Major of the Mossley Pipe Band and he was scarcely recognisable in his busby, tartan cape, kilt and white putties. My dad took great amusement from a report he had heard of advice Willie gave to his band members prior to a Twelfth Day parade. 'Now, don't look at the people – let the people look at you.'

He and his wife Martha had a confectionery shop in Ashley Park where we were frequent customers and where dad got his cigarettes. Martha was painfully thin and frail yet walked up and down to Mossley every day to work as an operative in the Mill. Their daughter, Martha was the senior member of the Ballyearl girls' gang. Her hair was kept very long and it fell half way down her back in tresses. We always thought that she was lucky to live in a sweetie shop.

We had no refrigeration in those days and, even after an electricity supply became available sometime in the 1950s, we couldn't afford many appliances. It was well into the 1960s before mum obtained a vacuum cleaner and a refrigerator. Indeed we had no need of the former simply because we had no carpets. Every floor was covered with oilcloth – linoleum as it was called – or red tiles.

It was essential that we had a butcher to call. I think ours came three times a week. We ate a lot of beef then. The butcher who visited was Mr E. V. (Victor) Murray who had a shop in Whitewell, Glengormley and had an extensive country run selling meat. My mum always stressed how clean his van was and he himself was always well turned out in a spotless, white apron.

I remember he often wore leather gaiters and I knew that he was interested in horse racing. He was friendly with the Girvan family and I believe he often travelled to race courses throughout Ireland with William James Girvan. At one time the Girvans had owned a horse called Lord Glenfield that achieved considerable fame by winning one or two notable races. Victor often told me about its exploits.

Jamsie Girvan, the son, sometimes created a makeshift course for the horses by opening and closing gates in the big Ten Acre field beside our house. He put straw down where the course crossed Springtown Loney. We'd watch Jamsie putting the horse through its paces over these fields. He was an accomplished jockey if rather heavy for a racehorse. It was very exciting to hear the thump of the hoofs on the turf and see the clods of earth fly up into the air. Victor Murray kept a close eye on all these activities as well as selling his beef and sausages.

Another regular visitor, on a Friday night I remember, was the Boot and Shoe Repair man. He had a sack into which he'd pop any footwear for repair. He would then bring back the resoled boots and shoes the next week. I don't remember his name but he liked to exchange gossip with mum and dad. I remember the smell of the new leather and the pleasure of putting on boots, we always seemed to wear boots not shoes, that were watertight again. In those days of post war austerity and shortages children and adults were often forced to face the cold of winter in footwear with thin soles or with holes in them that let in the rain.

We had the services of a barber who came to the homes in Ballyearl to cut our hair. Neil Patton from Carntall did the rounds in the evenings to earn a bit of extra cash from his position training in Herbie Boyd's barber shop in Ballyclare. He was enterprising and occasionally would meet pupils coming out of school on a Thursday, his half day from work. He set us up on the ditch and went to work using hand clippers. They tended to pull out rather than cut the hair. All he had to do then was to call round at our homes for payment. There were many handyman hairdressers in these times and dads often took on this job to save money. The standard method was to place a pudding bowl on the head and simply snip off any hair below the bowl. Unfortunately it was always easy to detect such a utility cut from the distinct line on the head created by the bowl.

Neil Patton later opened his own hairdresser's shop in Ballyclare. I tried to avoid having my hair cut here because it would have brought back memories of those after school haircuts on the ditch outside Mossley school. I remember how in the Ballyclare shop he did finish off by rubbing into the hair a greasy smearing of brilliantine – he called this concoction 'Come Back Soon'.

Insurance salesmen were common in our district. They called every week to collect the small contribution towards the premium. Our neighbour, Mr Samuel Houston, was the Ballyearl 'Man from the Prudential' and called to collect our weekly premium.

There were beggars regularly going round the houses collecting pennies. There was one called Jimmy Glass who came regularly to Ballyearl. He was very proud and feisty and considered that he had a right to financial support. He could become very awkward if a donation was refused. His visits usually came around the time of the Ballyclare May Fair. I was always a bit wary of him, especially if I was in the house on my own. If I saw him approaching our door, I hid behind the sofa until he had disappeared, usually muttering insults but only to himself.

The most unnerving experience I ever had with a traveller occurred one day when I was on my own in the house. The front doorbell rang and I nonchalantly opened it expecting to see one of our regular tradesmen. Standing there was an Indian gentleman wearing a red turban and positively jingling with bangles and showy jewellery. His suitcase was open but I did not stay around long enough to inspect his wares. Leaving the door wide open I turned tail, fled down the hall, shot through the kitchen, out the back door and cleared the garden fence in one bound to cower in Girvan's field until I reckoned that the strange foreigner had moved on. When I told my mum and my brothers of the incident they found it totally hilarious and for many years I was not allowed to forget about the day the Indian knocked at our door and frightened me out of my wits. In mitigation for my behaviour it must be stated that in the 1950s foreigners were not a common sight in Northern Ireland. To me the Indian was straight out of The Arabian Nights or other exotic tales we had heard in school.

The best time for youngsters in Ballyearl was the summer. I don't remember anyone going off for a holiday except perhaps on occasional day trips on the bus or train to a seaside resort like Bangor or Portrush. Our family was fortunate that my dad had a quota of free passes for the train. I remember going to Newcastle on the old County Down railway route through Comber and we also went often to Portrush, boarding the steam train at the Ballyclare Junction or Mossley halts to visit our favourite destination.

Other than this we were happy to play with our friends in Ballyearl. We made great use of bicycles and whizzed about the lanes and byways. Often the bikes we owned were not too sound mechanically. Brakes did not always work well and sometimes a foot had to be applied against the front tyre to slow down before stopping.

I remember when I was about fifteen cycling through Mossley on my way to work on Billy Blair's farm and using this method to slow the bike. I was thrown over the handlebars and was fortunate to fall on my hands so softening the impact. It was a close shave and the memory of this incident still has the capacity to make me tremble. A good feature about cycling was that one learnt how to carry out running repairs. I quickly became an expert at fixing punctures and changing inner tubes using a few of my mum's kitchen forks, rubber solution and patches cut out of discarded tubes. This experience was good practice for mending punctures in the bladders of the case balls we used for football. Some older lads organised cycle races on Sunday afternoons on a course around Ashley Park, Pumptown Loney and part of the main Doagh road. This ended tragically when one Sunday a young man from Kings Moss crashed into a motor car and was killed.

When we had no bikes we trundled hoops. These were the rims of old bicycle wheels without the spokes. They were pushed and steered with bits of bent bull wire called cleeks. They were incredibly good fun and every child seemed to have one then. Jack Gillespie from Ashley Park was the hoop champion.

The main games, however, remained football and cricket. A proper leather football, known as a casey, was a regular Christmas present and a good one was a luxury. Following continuous use they soon deteriorated. They lost their shape to become swollen and bloated, or the stitching joining the panels parted and caused the inside tube to stick out like a large hernia.

There were no plastic balls and the rubber ones which were available did not last long before they were punctured by thorns from the many hedges around Ballyearl – especially next to our house. The only thing to do then was to pierce the ball with the tip of a hot poker to allow it to inflate and deflate as it was kicked. Those days of post war shortages taught one to be inventive.

We improvised a cricket pitch along the gable of our house stretching into the back garden. The rules were elaborate, the most important being that anyone hitting the ball into Granny Higgins' garden was considered out. This sanction was essential because a ball's retrieval from the old lady's property was tricky. She usually took up her watching station at her parlour window as soon as a football or cricket ball appeared. My mum played occasionally and helped us shape cricket bats from scraps of wood.

Climbing trees was another popular pastime. I remember the first morning of our summer holidays one year when Ken and I were out of the house like a shot to enjoy our new found freedom. We headed up Springtown Loney where Ken climbed a beech tree and made his way, hand over hand, along a branch yodelling like Tarzan. He went just too far and, in trying to drop down from the branch, fell on the ground in a heap. Together we skulked back to Iona where mum soon realised that he had broken his arm. So much for a trouble-free break from school!

The biggest hazard for the McKinney boys was their front gate. It was just the right height to clamber up on. No one could stop us doing this and, inevitably, we each fell over it at some stage of our boyhood. At least two of us still have traces of the scars on our foreheads.

Winter had a special attraction for youngsters. There seemed to have been more snow in those years. I clearly remember my dad and other men from Ballyearl shovelling the snow from Springtown Loney in the heavy snowfall of 1947. The drifts reached the height of the hedges and it took a considerable time to clear the snow sufficiently to allow the residents to make their way up and down the lane.

Building snowmen and having snowball fights was great fun but I thought the slides we created on the smooth surface of the main road were better. I remember a line of adults and children, wrapped up well with scarves and gloves, waiting their turn to skim down the long, icy track. Inevitably some spoilsport sneaked out when darkness fell and sabotaged the runway with salt or cinders – Mr Sam Tweedie, our grocer, was usually the number one suspect. The best slides were always not far from his shop.

The normal pastime was football. We played in fields, back gardens and often just on the road. The only opportunity we had to watch a proper game was in one of Andy McKeen's fields at Houston's Corners where a Belfast Amateur League team – Lyle & Kinahan – played their home games. At 2.30 pm on a Saturday afternoon, a small band of boys from Ballyearl, happed up in mufflers and Welly boots, would meet up with a number from the Kings Moss district and patiently watch the road from the Corr's Corner bus stop down to Ballyclare Junction for the players to appear. Strung out along the road and laden with hampers and bags of kit and equipment the two teams, and with a bit of luck a referee, were easily recognised ambling down from the bus to their changing rooms in one of Andy's sheds or, for a time, the waiting room at Ballyclare Junction railway halt.

The home team contained our football heroes, among them Gus and Bap, two rotund and red-faced half-backs, no longer in the first flush of youth and a slim young goalkeeper called Dickie. The pitch was the only grassy area in a sea of rushes and was often waterlogged. One afternoon there was so much water in the goalmouth that Dickie had to be given a sheet of corrugated iron to stand on to keep him from sinking into the mire. The teams had proper corner flags, real football shirts and a round leather ball, beautifully dubbined to keep it waterproof. Sometimes they even had two balls and we were able to borrow the spare one to have a match – Ballyearl v Kings Moss – along the sidelines.

The touchline had one unusual hazard. Old Andy McKeen was such an enthusiastic supporter of Lyle and Kinahan that he was totally unable to contain his excitement. Darting up and down the touchline, and unknown to himself but very evident to anyone who came within range, Andy would kick out, first with one foot then the other, bellowing all the while imprecations on the referee and opposition.

I still remember the names of some of the teams in this league – Bethel Young Men, Craigavad, Combe Barbour – even today they evoke some of the magic of those afternoons in the field of mud and rushes behind Andy McKeen's farm.

After the match we trudged back home as satisfied with the entertainment as those who had been at Windsor Park in Belfast. Mother always had the damper out in the fire preparing for our bath night. The perfect day was finally completed with a bag of sweeties from Willie Forsythe's shop and a couple of hours of television in our neighbour Willie Wilson's parlour.

Chapter 7: Upper and Lower Mossley

While our small cluster of houses took its name from the townland of Ballyearl, one mile away, Mossley, had grown up around the Henry Campbell & Company's Linen Spinning Mill. The name Mossley, came from the mill's establishment in the 19th century by entrepreneurs from near Mossley in Lancashire.

Next to Ballyearl, where we lived and Carnmoney where we went to church, Mossley was the place my family and I knew best when I was growing up.

Mossley was then, and to some extent still is, composed of two distinct parts – upper Mossley beside the mill dam and lower Mossley stretched along either side of the main Doagh Road. In those days both parts were dominated by terraces and villas built to accommodate the mill workers. In my school days in the late1940s nearly every family in Mossley had at least one person working in the mill.

Lower Mossley was older and indeed one of the two rows of terraces straddling the main Doagh Road was called Old Row. These houses had small yards and backed on to the main Belfast to Ballymena railway line. They accommodated families who had a long family connection with the mill and their tenancy was tied to employment in the mill. Directly opposite was Sunnyside where the houses were roomier with long gardens at the rear. Some eventually acquired garages, facilities which were uncommon then.

About the middle of the Sunnyside terrace was McCullough's shop. Mrs McCullough was a large lady and, in typical pose, filled the doorway of the shop, using one hand to prop herself on the doorpost while closely monitoring the mill, road and school opposite. She had a jolly laugh and her husband, who had been in the navy, worked in the mill but was also a part-time barber for boys and girls - an early example of a unisex salon. As a young girl my aunt May McKinney had her hair cut there occasionally but hinted that she always felt uncomfortable with the process.

The McCulloughs prided themselves on being able to supply all customers' needs from their stock. My uncle George McKinney, who went there regularly for his Park Drive cigarettes and Wrigley's chewing gum, swore that there was nothing that Willie McCullough could not bring down the stairs from his store room. Uncle George was the milkman in Upper and Lower Mossley for many years and his knowledge of the people and their backgrounds was comprehensive. His genial nature endeared him to all the housewives and nothing made him happier than exchanging banter with them on his morning round.

Upper Mossley consisted of three terraces for workers and some detached villas for managers in the mill. The Red Row and the White Row curved around the Mill Dam, pleasantly fringed by trees and with swans and various species of water fowl.

The houses in the White Row were finished in grey cement and were much sought after as their spacious rooms were suitable for big families. The Red Row, as its name implies, was built from brick, and any special status it had arose from its position beside The Villas. These had everything one could then aspire to in accommodation – large rooms in traditional upper class style and surrounded by box hedges and lawns. These were intended for managers in the mill.

Between the Red and White Rows, set well back from the main road and dam and approached by a potholed track, was Uppertown, a terrace generally regarded as the least favourable housing in Mossley. The roofs were utilitarian, corrugated iron and the row was known locally as Tin Top. I often visited a friend there and can vouch for the cold and damp of his home.

The track up to Uppertown continued past the end gable of the terrace towards the hockey and cricket pitch which the works club used before they moved to new facilities at the nearby recreation grounds. Also, behind Uppertown there were two brick and concrete air raid shelters constructed for the residents of Upper Mossley during the 1939–1945 war. My brothers and I knew them as the scene of irregular activities usually involving adolescents on dark evenings. We were never to be found there and if our parents had heard reports of us joining in such goings-on we would have been punished and restricted to Ballyearl.

Mossley Mill in its pleasant rural setting with the hill of Carntall in the background

We were allowed to go to hockey matches here and approached the pitch from the fields, crossing the railway line by a narrow bridge provided for cattle. This seemed a big adventure for young boys. The mill owned a lot of the land in this area and held water rights on the streams which originally had powered the works. The sluices were still in place and were familiar to my brother Ken and myself from those of a similar nature in our grandfather's fields at Skilganaban. There was a weir on the stream close to the hockey pitch and it was a grand dare to take off our boots and socks and walk across the narrow cement ledge with the shallow water trickling over our bare feet. Had our parents known this we would have been banned from the hockey matches.

Also, not far from the pitch and close to the river, was a large stretch of dumping ground for the mill called the Brick Hill. I think it had been the source of the clay used to bake bricks when the mill houses were under construction. The mill lorry, I believe the firm only had one then, brought loads of linen waste from the spinning process to be burned here. The fire smouldered continually and a pungent, acrid smell arose. It always seemed present everywhere around Mossley and I can sense it in my head to this very day. More than anything it connects me to my boyhood. The strength and direction of the smell varied with the weather conditions. In Ballyearl we knew that rain was expected when the smoke from the Brick Hill could be smelt on the east wind from Mossley.

When I look back now I realise how important Mossley dam was in our lives. My brothers and I had to pass it on our way to Sunday School and The Boys Brigade company in Carnmoney. There was always something of interest to us there. At the water's edge, where a pool formed at the inlet from the stream, there were huge shoals of sticklebacks – known as 'spricks'. Swans and ducklings abounded and their seasonal behaviour was a delight to observe. There must have been bigger fish in the deep water because Bob Mackey, who lived in the Red Row, was often to be found fishing there in his waders.

It was great fun, too, in winter when the surface was frozen, to skim stones or lumps of wood over the icy surface and try to see whose missile could reach the furthest. But the dam was most impressive for me in the moonlight. I remember one time at Ballyclare High

School when required to write an essay on a lyrical theme I really went over the top on a description of the dam by moonlight. Mr Thompson, my English teacher, even though he was a bit of a sentimentalist himself, had to tone down the piece to keep it within the bounds of credibility.

Beside the dam and reaching as far as the roadside railings was the area where coal for the mill furnace was stored. It was piled in vast mounds and these were replenished daily by a stream of blue lorries from the Brown Ash Coal Company. Smoke poured from the mill chimney every day of the year except for holidays and the furnace had a voracious appetite for coal. These vehicles along with the red James Boyd & Sons quarry lorries and the green and cream UTA buses made up a large part of the traffic on the Doagh Road in the 1950s. When I was at Mossley school there was a fatal accident just outside the school gate involving a young boy from Old Row and one of Boyd's lorries.

I remember Mossley folk as uncommonly house proud but one resident did go a little bit overboard with the splendour of her household furnishings. She was fond of loud colours, especially red, and she loved bright lights. This, of course, was not long after electricity first became available and the new fangled light fittings attracted others too. The house was said to resemble Buckingham Palace – not that many Mossley folk in those days had seen the Queen's residence. She tended to keep her window blinds open all the time. Most people knew that she liked to show off her furnishings.

Beyond the villas and the mill dam was what we called The Park. This comprised the official recreation grounds belonging to the mill and supposedly for the exclusive use of the workers. Like other linen mills, Mossley was very active in promoting a wide range of sporting activities for its workers – hockey, cricket, bowling and tennis among others. Teams competed in local leagues and included some players with no direct connection with the works. There is no doubt of the contribution the Mill made to local sport in terms of the recreation facilities provided and the opportunities for relaxation and pleasure offered to men and women, young and old, in the Mossley district.

There was a splendid bowling green and pavilion surrounded by neat box hedges. When he retired from leader of the Mossley Scout troop Mr Hamilton, our school headmaster, became a fervent bowler and in the summer term would take some senior boys up to the green for a trial game though most of us preferred hockey or football to what was generally reckoned an old man's game. There were no lady bowlers then. They had to stick to hockey and tennis.

There were both asphalt and red clay tennis courts and these were constantly in use during the summer, especially in the evenings. I remember one time seeing some of our teachers – Mr Hamilton, Mrs Frame and her husband, Sam – playing tennis there. Mrs Frame was a good hockey player and I think she did play at least sometimes for the Mossley team. Beside the tennis courts was a small hockey pitch used in our time by ladies while the men's pitch was still situated beside Brick Hill. It was a perfect surface for football, level with short grass, expertly maintained and, best of all, had proper netting in the goals. Football, though, was banned and Mr Tom Dubois, the groundsman, was ever vigilant and kept an eye out for trespassers – especially footballers.

For a period Mossley sported a good cricket team and the club used the newly laid hockey pitch in summer. Hockey was a thrilling game to watch and we came to admire skilful players from the four Mossley elevens, especially those like Harold Burns and Brian Gilroy who played for Ulster and, I believe, Ireland. The sound of the hockey ball rattling against the backboard of the net following one of Brian Gilroy's short corners and the loud cheers which followed, can be recalled to this day. One player, Geordie Preston, acquired the nickname 'Push-push Preston' from his constant call from the wing to give him a pass!

Spectators were thrilled and opponents surprised to witness the extraordinary feat of Harold Burns's brother Jimmy, who had lost an arm in an accident in the mill, keeping goal expertly. His only problem seemed to be that when he overbalanced he required the assistance of a colleague to help him get back on to his feet. I noticed that he was as eager to engage in robust play as other members of the team. Indeed, Mossley hockey elevens had a reputation for such tactics especially when local rivals Parkview from Doagh provided the opposition.

The hockey teams were dominated by certain families – Burns, Gilroy, Patton, Dubois. One lady enthusiast, Teeny McKeown, (née Patton) a member of the Mossley Women's team, brought her baby in the pram and parked it beside the pitch while she played her Saturday match. It was little wonder that the child, Cecelia, grew up to be a keen hockey player.

Eventually the old Brick Hill pitch was replaced by a new expensively drained one at The Park. A modern pavilion was built beside it to accommodate the growing membership and to cope with outdoor and – a new sport here – indoor bowling. Sadly the former bowling pavilion, in its 1930s splendour, was destroyed in a fire around 1960.

 Our first acquaintance with the Park was as small children when we were taken there by our mum to use the swings and roundabouts. I cannot think of any other site for miles around which then had such a facility for youngsters. My brothers and I became familiar with the swings, both the ordinary and boxed – in type for very young children, the long, shiny metal slide and the mechanical rocking horse but we had to wait until we were much older before we were allowed to have a go on the Plank. This was a long, wooden seat attached to a stout iron frame by rigid bars that swayed from side to side when propelled by two persons standing at either end. It was exciting when it was pushed hard but was prone to make those using it, and not just for the first time, dizzy even a little sick.

The park and green keeper was Tom Dubois and he was revered and feared by adults and children alike. He lived in a cottage opposite the Park and he and his sons, Dick and Stanley, were keen sportsmen.

He kept his tools and machinery in a green shed at the edge of the hockey pitch and on a Saturday afternoon in summer, bowlers could be seen making their way rather shiftily towards the little tin hut. The clubs were not licensed for alcohol consumption and I believe bottles of stout could be obtained from this unofficial bar. If we were aware of this it was never a closely guarded secret.

Between Tom Dubois's cottage and the Manse Road was the most surprising recreational facility of all. Few people are now aware that in the 1930s Mossley had a fully functioning swimming pond. The site was beside a small stream that provided the water to feed the basin. The pool itself was quite large and, although it was filled in some time in the 1960s after it fell into disuse, the flat grassy space where it had been situated could be picked out until quite recently.

In about 1960 there was an overgrown path leading down to the pond from the Carnmoney Road, just opposite the Mossley Ladies hockey pitch. There was also a green wooden fence and one afternoon I daringly explored the changing facilities. Inside I saw a diving board and the pool with green, slimy water.

The pond was totally out of bounds to those who were not club members but a story circulated that one of my class mates, Logan McKinstry, a daredevil if ever there was one, had been swimming here. It is more likely, though, that this arose from a bit of exaggeration on Logan's part.

Mossley Swimming Pond, c.1930

Tree planting at Mossley Recreation Park, c.1930

Thinking of Mossley as it is now, it is hard to visualise just how much it was dominated in the 1950s by the mill and its workers. Each weekday began with the mill horns wakening and summoning the village people to their jobs. I think the first horn went off at 7 o'clock, another sounded at 7.50am with the final call coming at 8am. There were lunchtime horns and at 5.40pm to conclude the working day. They could be heard in Ballyearl and provided a useful time check.

Those who worked in the mill had very mixed backgrounds. I dare say they reflected society in those times. At the top there was Colonel Henshall and the members of the Campbell family. They were connected by birth or marriage to the original Henry Campbell of the firm's name. The Campbells and Henshalls were directors and managers and were revered in Mossley as if they were royalty. My uncle George saw it as a matter of pride that he, a farmer, did not owe the same allegiance to the Campbells as the mill workers. He would certainly not have doffed his cap when, on his morning milk round, he met the Colonel driving to the works in his large car. This vehicle was well known on the roads beside the farm. However, he would have been forced to admit that it suited him to rent fields from the mill estate.

A few of the very top managers lived in residences on The Avenue, a tree lined route to the mill only used by directors, visitors and important office staff. There was a variety of tradesmen involved in the maintenance of plant and equipment. Some of them visited Mossley school to carry out general repairs and inspect the heating boiler. Andy Hunter, who lived in Old Row, did something important in a maintenance capacity and was a regular visitor to our classroom which led through to the boiler house.

I knew many of those who were employed in the mill and I found them to be decent, hardworking, respectable people. When I was a student I worked as a postman and Mossley was on my round. Like my uncle George McKinney I found it pleasant to go from door to door and make friends with so many of these folk both young and old. I was regularly offered tea in many homes and at Christmas I appreciated their generous tips.

When I joined the local football team, I played with many lads from lower and upper Mossley who had been at school with me. Young people tended to choose either football or hockey although there were many who were good at both and moved from one game to the other with ease. My brothers and I idolised the older boys and tagged along when they gathered in groups to discuss sporting performances - quite often after Mossley Sunday School on a walk to Teeny McKeown's sweetie shop on the Carntall Road.

David Hunter, a family friend, who worked after school on the McKinney farm

Reeling yarn in Mossley Mill, c.1930

In addition to sport, a number of these young men were also members of Ballyduff Silver Band. A dance band, the RAJA, so named because it was formed by Ross Aiken and Jack Anderson and included other musicians from Old Row and Sunnyside. This popular band played all over the district. Looking back to those days the comrades I remember include Ross Aiken, David and Alex Hunter, Noel and Dessie McNeill, Tom and Bert McBroom, Jack and Jim Anderson, Jim Beck, Billy Dunn, Tommy Kernohan, Joe and Billy Scott and many others whose friendship I was fortunate to enjoy.

In the 1950s and early 1960s men and women, teenage girls and boys travelled to work in Mossley mill from all parts of the district - Doagh, Ballyclare, Monkstown, Whiteabbey, Carnmoney among others. Up to ten single and double decker buses lined up on the Doagh Road and along the mill boundary wall every morning and evening to load or unload the lively crew. Then, at least during the working day, Mossley became a hive of industry.

At lunch time the workers gathered in groups at the Finger Post crossroads of the Doagh and Carntall roads or lounged by the roadside. Many visited McCullough's shop in Sunnyside or sat on the railway bridge parapet and gossiped. From here they had a perfect view of our school yard but we were warned against communicating with them. Sometimes rude remarks drifted down to us in the yard but we pupils were usually too engrossed in our playground games to pay attention to them.

From the time I started in Mossley school at 4 years old until I left seven years later to attend Ballyclare High School I enjoyed meeting and making friends with Mossley people. They were interesting, decent, hard working folk and I will always remember and appreciate the contribution various characters made by their humour and fellowship to my development as a youth and young man.

Chapter 8: Henry Campbell College

Mossley Public Elementary School 1922.
Back row (from left): George Darragh, J Hughes, Sam McConnell, William Archbold, David Lough, Mollie Vint, unknown, A Parke.
Middle row (from left): Cissie Blain, M Blain, Sarah Darragh, M McNeilly, E Forde, Winnie Glenn, M Ritchie, Charles Beattie, Edward McKinney.
Front row (from left): B Gillanders, N Seaton, B Gregg, T Armstrong, Willie Andrews, A Blair, J Martin, B Walker, Sammy Hunter.

The McKinney family have enjoyed a long connection with Mossley School.

My brothers and I went to Mossley School as had my Dad, uncle George and aunt May McKinney before us. For my brother Ken and me it was Mossley Public Elementary School but the name had changed to Mossley Primary School by the time my other two brothers enrolled.

My grandfather's small farm business, Ashfield Dairy, used to supply school milk for the pupils. When I was young and visiting the farm after school I liked to scoff the third of a pint bottle surplus to that day's requirement. Later uncle George brought the crates to the school. They had been delivered to the farm early in the morning from Dobson's Dairy in Belfast.

Some former pupils used to boast that they had attended Campbell College, using the name of the famous Belfast boarding school. They then clarified their boast by stating that they had meant Henry Campbell College. Mossley school was managed for many years originally as a National school, then a Public Elementary school and finally as a primary school by the directors of the mill so the Campbell College title was not entirely inaccurate.

Aunt May McKinney (centre) at Mossley PE School with good friends Meta Patrick on her right and Annie Montgomery in centre of front row

The school premises were situated right at the end of the Old Row terrace and not ten yards from the main Belfast to Ballymena railway line. It had been established for the children of mill workers and in my day was still under the mill's control. The maintenance was carried out by men from the mill and Mr Hamilton's deference to the members of the Campbell family left no doubt about who was his real employer.

Whatever its name, when my brothers and I attended, we sat, or perhaps suffered at the feet of Mr Sidney McC Hamilton, its illustrious headmaster. Mr Hamilton came to school each morning on a lady's bicycle with a carrier basket at the front. I remember him taking off his bicycle clips before entering the front door. He lived in The Castle, a large house but nothing like as grand as the name suggests. It was situated between The Villas and the recreation grounds in Upper Mossley. It was enclosed by a high wall but this was not enough to prevent adventurous boys from gaining access to the apple orchard in the enclosed grounds. In the autumn there were frequent sermons from Mr Hamilton about the ethics of breaking into other people's property and we pupils felt that he had mainly orchards in mind.

Every school day, with my brother and some pals, I waited at the Ballyearl bus stop for the nine o'clock bus to take me to Mossley School. For some reason it was mostly boys there in the mornings, perhaps the girls walked the mile or so to the school. Typically then, school boys wore baggy, short trousers made from flannel or hard wearing corduroy and grey, knee length socks and leather or wellington boots. The trousers were held up by braces, called galluses by my dad, or sometimes green and yellow or red and yellow elastic belts with a snake- shaped metal buckle. Our socks usually sagged around our ankles, sometimes by choice or indifference, but also because of the poor quality of the elastic of our garters. Socks and pullovers were invariably darned again and again to hide holes caused by excessive wear.

Dad and Uncle George McKinney at Mossley School in 1922

The footwear was mended frequently, too, but not always before the soles became thin enough for holes to appear. Some poor souls continued to wear black, canvas plimsolls, popularly known as Mutton Dummies, throughout the winter. It is no wonder that wet feet were common.

In summer the boots would have changed to black shoes or Moses sandals and ankle socks. Woollen or corduroy jerkins were popular and the pullover worn inside might have been a thick home-knitted garment. I occasionally stayed at my grandparents' farm in Mossley when my mother was ill. I was then often sent to school wearing at least two pullovers. My grandmother was afraid of me catching a cold while in her care.

Later brightly coloured Fair Isle, short-sleeved pullovers became available for those who could afford them.
Burberry overcoats were expensive and I think I had to wait until I attended Ballyclare High School before I acquired one. As the eldest in the family, I was lucky not to have to wear hand-me-downs from others in the family but in those days adults' clothing was often adjusted by a dressmaker to suit children.

Miss Nan Campbell from the mill family owners often came into the school to talk to Mr Hamilton and it seemed like a royal visit. She always had a little white, terrier dog which was given freedom to scamper below desks and nose into every corner of the room.

Normally Mr Hamilton was a stickler for cleanliness and would usually not have tolerated an animal anywhere near the premises. However Miss Campbell commanded deference and normal rules did not apply!

In my time at the school the accommodation consisted of four rooms with tall, wide windows and high ceilings which appeared to have been created from one original, teaching space. There was at least one partition which could be moved back but I think this seldom happened. Some wooden barbells were attached to the brown painted wainscotting on the walls but I only ever saw them being used as props in a school play about a circus. Ken, my brother, in a leopard skin leotard, hoisted them once in his part as the circus strong man. Plays were rare and I suspect that this one took place under the direction of a student teacher or perhaps the American exchange teacher who came to us for part of a year in about 1950. Mr Hamilton was happy to limit acting and dramatic scenes to his daily teaching.

Strangely, my most vivid memory of the school building concerns the boys' toilets. They had an odour all their own and this arose from the brown ceramic urinal troughs. I'm sure they were clean but were certainly smelly. As usual, boys tended to gather here at break time and I recall unspeakable acts of a competitive nature which involved the wall of the urinal and did not improve the hygiene of the arrangements.

I think that while I was a pupil some improvements were made to the infant classrooms because I have a faint memory of their becoming brighter, possibly by the addition of skylights in the roof of the building. After I had left Mossley School, more extensive renovations were carried out to the premises and, while the work was being done, the pupils were moved to an unused flax store on the main mill site. One of my brothers remembers the disruption caused to the smooth running of the school. I am certain of the effect this must have had on the fastidious Mr Hamilton. He liked every detail of the school arrangements to be in good order and always under his control.

Our headmaster was completely obsessive about preventing litter and would tell us how to dispose of sweet wrappers on the way home. We were instructed to roll them up into a small ball in our palms and then drop this into the bottom of a hedge. There were then no litter bins, of course, in the countryside. He liked everything to be neat and tidy both in our personal appearance and in how we packed schoolbags and stowed our books beneath the lids of the heavy, double desks.

I heard recently from a former teacher in Mossley School of an incident that perfectly illustrates Mr Hamilton's obsession with tidiness and order. This occurred soon after the staff and pupils moved into a new school on the Manse Road, Mossley. The splendid new building obviously offered a challenge to the headmaster to ensure that no untidiness would be allowed to spoil the pristine condition of the premises.

It appears that as part of the Christmas treats for the children a travelling entertainer visited the school to introduce some seasonal fun. Fernie was well known in schools as he made his way round the area on his motor cycle and a sidecar for his props. He was a distinctive character and the children especially enjoyed his ventriloquist act. In the course of his first visit to the new school, he lifted a chair that was on the stage and prepared to set his foot, and boot, on it. Suddenly, Mr Hamilton arose briskly from his seat in the front row of the audience, dashed up the steps on to the stage and, glancing at Fernie, very pointedly took a sheet of newspaper and spread it on to the chair before Fernie could desecrate it with his boot.

The interesting sequel to this disruption to Fernie's act occurred the following year when Fernie set out to repeat the charade of the boot and the chair. This time, however, before he dared set foot on to the chair, he directed a meaningful glare towards Mr Hamilton in his usual front seat then ostentatiously drew out a white handkerchief from the recesses of his costume and placed it very deliberately on to the chair. Those behind the headmaster, sadly, missed the look of quiet satisfaction that momentarily passed across the headmaster's face.

When I heard this story it showed me that the passing years had not diminished my former headmaster's passion for tidiness and order in all things.

In the 1940s and 1950s there was a regular service of steam trains on the railway line beside the school and they played quite a part in school life. We could distinctly hear the puffing and rumbling of engines labouring up the steep incline from Belfast and the swoosh of those on the downhill run from Ballymena.

It wasn't just the noise that intruded. There was a bridge close to our playground and the smoke, billowing from the engines passing through the bridge, sometimes drifted into our room through the tall, classroom windows. Mr Hamilton would jump up at the approach of a train and slam the windows shut but he did not always manage this in time and then wisps of smoke hung about out classroom for some time afterwards. It was rumoured that a parent had removed her child from the school because she found it hard to keep up a supply of clean shirts to replace those soiled by smoke from the trains. Mind you, I think she was known to be a little bit fussy!

Another implication of the proximity of the railway was that there was a strict rule against going onto the line or embankment for any reason. This was a cardinal offence in Mr Hamilton's book and likely to make him tremble with anger. There was trespassing there occasionally, though I was neither brave nor foolhardy enough to try it on myself.

The most memorable incident involved a senior pupil, Stanley Dubois, who, desperate to retrieve the ball from the grass embankment, climbed the tall spiked railings but, perhaps because he had been warned that Mr Hamilton was on his way out to the yard, rushed his jump back to safety. He was fortunate to land without injury but was upset to see the headmaster approaching at speed and inquiring sarcastically why he had left the turn-up of his trousers on a spike of the railings.

Like many teachers, Mr Hamilton enjoyed playing the part of a show man and I believe he enjoyed acting up for all he was worth to his submissive audience. I feel he gained considerable amusement from the effect he created.

He did not tolerate pupils who used poor equipment, especially the old nibbed pens we had then. These got abuse simply because they were perfect for dropping on the soft wooden floors as darts. This tended to ruin them as writing implements. I remember Sidney, as pupils dared to call him among themselves, angrily snatching one pen after another from the hands of terrified pupils and exclaiming "What's this feeble object, Sir? This is only good for gardening, Sir." (The 'Sir' was his usual form of address to all male pupils). With a bellow of rage he would then fling the pen out of the window on to the railway embankment. I used to wonder how many discarded pens, pencils and rubbers would eventually be unearthed on the railway bank beside this stretch of line.

Mossley PE School c.1948. Back row (from left): Billy Scott, Wesley Houston, unknown, Billy Douglas, unknown, Tom McBroom, David Moore, Tommy Kernohan, Sammy Millar, Jim Berry, John Herron, Jim Smyth, Desmond McNeill, Alex Hunter, Alan Fenning, John Strange, Tommy Higgins, Bert McBroom, Logan McKinstry, Robert Hilditch, George White.
Fourth row (from left): Rose Grace, unknown, Merlie Wilson, Martha Forsythe, Beryl Fenning, Susan Boyd, unknown, Joan McCready, Nellie Stevenson, Joan Gault, Beryl Aiken, unknown, Sadie McAuley, Meta Downes, Marion Blair, Jean Downes.
Third row (from left): Hazel Montgomery, Betty White, unknown, unknown, unknown, unknown, Bea Montgomery, unknown, Jackie McCready, Dorothy McCready, Anne McAuley, Joan Ogilby, Dorrie Ritchie, Betty Anderson, unknown, June Downes, Dorrie Larcombe, Ena Larcombe, Marie Montgomery.
Second row (from left): Ias Montgomery, unknown, unknown, unknown, Pearl McNeilly, Sally Hunter, unknown, ? Ritchie, unknown, Leila Blair, unknown.
Front row: Kenneth Carson, unknown, John McNeilly, Sammy Scott, William McAuley, John Bell, Sinclair Kennedy, unknown, David McWhirter, Drew Stewart, unknown, unknown, Roy Kidd, Reggie Magee, unknown, John Kennedy.

I now realise that most of Mr Hamilton's rages were simulated – just a show put on for the pupils. I suspect he enjoyed this act and he was good at it. He was so good in fact that I, who giggled very easily, had great difficulty in suppressing my sniggers when he was dealing with some poor miscreant.

He was a firm believer in spanking as a punishment, usually for moderate misdemeanours. Other measures were employed for more serious offences. It had all the features of a ritual. Typically, he would charge out from behind his desk, trembling with bogus rage, rush down between the rows of double desks, grab the offender by the shoulders and haul him – girls were not spanked – out into the aisle then push him to the front of the classroom. Here, with the class now fearfully silent, he adopted the same procedure. First, hitching up his trouser leg, he'd place his left foot on the seat of a front desk then hoist the victim by the shoulders, usually still but occasionally struggling, up and over his knee. Using the flat of his hand he would administer several whacks to the seat of the boy's pants.

I suffered this often and I remember most of all the smell of clothing, possibly mothballs from his suit and the close-up view I got of the knots in the floorboards. At this delicate moment the sound of a suppressed snigger from the audience did not improve Sidney's mood, indeed it usually meant that the perpetrator would be added to the queue for a spanking. I remember one day giggling out loud when, in the course of the spanking, Mr Hamilton's smacks produced clouds of dust from the offender's trousers. On another occasion, a boy wearing hobnailed boots was shoved along by the headmaster. He shot to the front of the room and, unable to stop in time, skidded into the piano.

I know that I received more spankings in our headmaster's class for giggling aloud than for any other reason.

The cane, too, was much in evidence. During certain lessons, if he was in a poor temper, he would stride up and down the columns of desks swishing the cane and whipping it against the loose folds of his trousers. Occasionally he used the cane at the front of the room but for serious offences he sent the boy out to the cloakroom to await punishment. I am sure he was aware of the psychological impact of the waiting on the offender's nerves. I was sometimes in this position and I remember dreading the sound of his footsteps approaching from the classroom. The awful sense of isolation was always the worst bit of the punishment. He had a habit of prefacing the caning with a personal appeal to the offender to improve his behaviour or performance. I remember him mentioning the shame my family would feel if they were aware of the punishment I was to receive. This worked because I knew that, had he found out, my dad would probably have given me another dose of punishment.

If he was working at his desk and was interrupted by a bit of extraneous noise from a section of the classroom he would grab any object close at hand, maybe a bunch of keys or a blackboard duster, and fling it towards the centre of the disturbance. This was extremely effective and normally produced instant silence.

I have to say that I preferred a spanking or the cane to Mr Hamilton's all too frequent, none too subtle remarks. Some comments were much worse than others but they all left an imprint on my emotions. I will never forget one day, just before I went to Ballyclare High School, when my homework did not please him. He dismissed me from the line-up at his desk with the remark, "Ah well, Sir, very soon you will be someone else's problem." A good spanking would have been sooner forgotten.

I always felt that he considered my passing the Qualifying Examination a bit of a minor miracle.

Mr Hamilton hated disorder and grubbiness. Workbooks with greasy food stains or marks from rubbing out answers with a moistened forefinger would be flung into the air with disdain to the back of the room. On one occasion a girl, known for shabby work, produced a jotter badly messed from an encounter with her cat. With great ceremony he picked the book up by the tips of his fingers and, sneering all the while, carried it through the door and supposedly down to the boilerhouse.

But I must admit that he was also amusing even though it was often at someone's expense. Any foolish remarks or silly behaviour by a pupil would be met by the comment to a bystander, 'Excuse me, Sir, would you go out to the door and see if the wee black van and the men in white coats have arrived yet?' Someone new to the class and not yet familiar with his ways might actually head out of the room. This, of course, only added to our amusement.

A really silly attempt at a simple arithmetic problem would be met by Mr Hamilton taking the pupil aside, almost always a boy, and asking him first to make a circle with the forefinger and thumb of his left hand and then to push the forefinger of the right hand through this circle. The pupil was then told to withdraw that finger quickly enough to catch the right forefinger in his right hand. The pupil was then sent to his desk to attempt the impossible task. Every so often Sidney would ask 'Sir have you caught that yet?'

Spectators, safe from his sarcasm, found this highly amusing.

He would dismiss a piece of poor work with the remark 'You're improving, Sir, definitely improving.' He'd wait a moment then add, 'But it's round the waist, Sir.'

He was very fond of quoting poetry especially that of Rudyard Kipling. I developed a liking for these verses when I was a pupil in his class. The poem 'If' was a special favourite of his and much quoted in class. He also often read to us from Kipling's 'Just So Stories' and the 'Mowgli Jungle Tales'. This fitted in with his interest in Scouting but there was also the feeling in Mossley that he resorted to aggression and not just inside school. Often when he saw two boys arguing he would offer to 'hold their coats' and we all had a pretty good idea what he was condoning. It was rumoured, and indeed later confirmed by reports from elsewhere, that it wasn't unknown for Sidney, when he was upset by an opponent on the hockey field, to invite his opponent to an assignation behind the pavilion after the game to settle the argument. I would dearly have loved to have been there and offer to hold the coats, or perhaps more appropriately, the hockey sticks.

In those days spellings and tables were learnt by repeating them aloud endlessly. We were often asked to rhyme them off to our teachers: 'Two ones are two, Two twos are four,' and so on. As this was being done the teacher might be engaged in some other menial task. One day a younger pupil from another class was reciting her tables for Mr Hamilton beside his desk. She did so in a distinct sing-song lilt and after a short time Sidney stood up and went over to the piano in the corner and began to play an accompaniment, stopping to say mock seriously, 'Is that the right key for you, Miss? Oh well, carry on anyway.' At such times it was hard not to break into laughter. Sometimes this was acceptable but at others it was dangerous, you were never very sure how he would react. He could be very unpredictable in his responses.

In my early years at the school it was quite common for pupils who were weak at their work to be held back a Standard, the name used to denote class level, for more than one year. It was bad enough for them when this involved working with younger pupils in the same classroom but it became particularly distressing when their contemporaries moved out of the classroom to another Standard with a different teacher. By their size and physical maturity these youngsters were obviously out of place. The work that they did also drew attention to a lack of progress commensurate with their age.

On the other hand I do not recall any taunting of these children by other pupils because of their handicap. Neither have I any memory of bullying at the school. Certainly, there were the usual disputes, even involving fisticuffs in the yard and almost always connected to the football games, but nasty name calling was rare.

There were indeed some pupils whose behaviour occasionally gave the teachers cause for concern. One of these was Reggie, a playmate of ours from Ballyearl.

He was a bit volatile at times in school and could flare up in short, impulsive outbursts of violence. One day in Miss Auld's room something unsettled him and he stood up and flung his pencil case in the teacher's direction.

Fortunately it merely struck the piano. In some schools, nowadays, this would not be unusual but in Mossley it was unspeakable. Eventually when the dust had settled the matter was cleared up quite amicably. I think the fact that Reggie lived in the same house as Miss Winnie Glenn made it easier to have the matter resolved with the minimum of fuss.

Miss Glenn worked in the mill office and seemed to act as an unofficial school secretary to Mr Hamilton. She was meticulous in such tasks. She took a lot to do with the school Savings Scheme, a movement which in those days seemed to command as much priority as the curriculum. And in fairness to Reggie this was his first and last venture at armed revolt – future fitful episodes only took place in Ballyearl.

To my knowledge only one boy was ever moved from the school for being harassed by other children. This was a friend of ours from Ballyearl.

He was just a little different from the normal boy and, as an only child, was mollycoddled far too much by his mother for his own good. Her decision to transfer him to Glengormley School meant that he had to travel four miles every day to get to school. Incredibly, he went by tricycle which must have done nothing to help him integrate and make friends in his new school.

Some new pupils coming to Mossley School took a while to fit into our surroundings. They found it especially difficult if they came from Belfast and the totally different culture of schools in the city. Most adapted well and I remember one who came into our class, Ronald Berry, who in no time at all acquired the nickname, Soapy, the genuine mark of acceptance. The origin of the name, as with all nicknames, was a mystery. His prowess at football probably helped his integration.

Reginal Magee, Colonel-in-Chief of the Ballyearl Volunteer Brigade (Under 12 Division) in his command caravan with Jack McKinney and Tommy Higgins lurking in the rear

One or two rather pleasant girls joined the school in my final years and it was probably a sign of my growing maturity that they made more of an impression on me than the boys.

A family of new residents made an impact on the entire village when they arrived in the Old Row from Belfast. They were quite a large family and two boys at least joined the school. The older boy, Billy, liked to think of himself as a 'hard man.' I believe he had spent some time in a Borstal institution and his reputation for toughness and unruly behaviour quickly spread through the playground. Plenty of scuffles, of course, took place here on a regular basis but Mr Hamilton's brooding presence kept them from developing into anything of a serious nature. For a week or two Billy was cock-of-the-walk, all of us avoiding contact with this boastful fighter. Then one day news circled round the yard that an unofficial contest had been arranged after school between the bully boy and Samuel Fleming, a senior boy of a deceptively placid temperament.

I remember the occasion well to this day. By a quarter past three quite a crowd of boys had gathered at a field gateway, far enough away from the school to prevent the noise of battle and the shouts of spectators from reaching Sidney's ears. This situation was, I believe, a kind of 'High Noon' at Mossley, a reference to the climax in the popular John Wayne film of the period. Spam, as Samuel Fleming was affectionately known, carefully and deliberately drew on a fine pair of brown leather gloves – the kind my dad wore on formal occasions – and, with no preliminaries whatsoever, proceeded to pound Billy's nose with a series of straight lefts. It was no contest and in next to no time, the bully slunk home with his tail between his legs, his face a mass of blood. The spectators, though delighted with this unexpected home victory, were a little disappointed with the brevity and the lack of spectacle the fight had promised. We soon dispersed and headed home, certain what the talking point would be in the playground over the next few weeks. Mossley had triumphed over Belfast and fear had been banished from the playground where football and its minor rumpuses could resume unhindered.

Mossley Scout Troop Reunion c.1960.
Back row (from left): Wesley Houston, Neville Whitley, Norman Blair, Brian Gilroy, Harold Burns, Joe Robinson, Jim Anderson, Stanley Dubois, Ross Aiken.
Fourth row from front (from left): Unknown flag carrier, Tommy Kernohan, Willie Graham, unknown, Billy McCoy, Derek Dubois, David Cooper, Mervyn Gilroy, Bobby Sloan, Peter Street, Jack Anderson, Jim McCrudden, Bert McBroom (flag carrier).
Third row from front (from left): Billy Scott, Alan Fenning, Joe Scott, Jack Adams, Sidney Hamilton, Logan McKinstry, Samuel Fleming, Billy Douglas, unknown.
Second row from front, sitting (from left): Alex Hunter, Reggie Magee, Billy McWhirter, Victor Fleming, Richard McMillan, Desmond McNeill.
Front row (front left): Unknown, Sinclair Kennedy, Bobby Lough, Neil Higgins, unknown, Robert McAuley, Drew Stewart.

Billy's family received a lot of sympathy when it became known that the mother had severe psychiatric problems and theirs was not a happy home. Her husband did odd days of work on my uncle George's farm and, like too many others he employed casually, was lazy and unreliable.

I remember one day at lunch time when we saw, amidst a noisy scene, Billy's mother being led into an ambulance and taken off towards Antrim. I think on that afternoon we were spared any remarks from Mr Hamilton about the arrival of the wee black van. I was one of a small number of senior pupils who were kept behind after school, no doubt with our parents' permission, for extra coaching for the Qualifying Examination, the test used to allocate places at grammar schools. This was a bit less formal than regular school lessons and, as we ground or way through arithmetic problems and questions from a yellow book of Intelligence Tests, Mr Hamilton coached us and the surprising thing for me at these lessons was that Mr Hamilton appeared to be just like a normal human being. The fire breathing dragon was obviously reserved for ordinary school lessons.

Mr Hamilton was Scout Master of the Mossley Scout Troop and for a short time I was in the Cubs. I liked the yarns we heard from Akela, Mr Jack Adams, the rough British Bulldogs contests and the handball games, though the wood in the schoolroom floor was not smooth and splinters in the fingers were a frequent hazard of this game.

I left the cub scouts under a cloud. I think it was the first time my quick temper got me into one fight too many for those in authority. It says a lot for the respect we had for Mr Hamilton that his appearance in front of his troop of scouts at the annual St George's Day parade dressed in corduroy shorts, garter tabs, red and green scarf and woggle did not produce a single giggle. There was one day in the year, Thinking Day it was called, when he and the other scouts came to school in full uniform. Many of the pupils were enthusiastic members of the troop.

The scouts had a two-wheeled 'Trek' cart drawn by senior boys. It appeared in the school yard just before the annual camp or when collections of waste paper were made around Mossley.

Before I left Mossley School I had transferred to the Lifeboys, the junior section of the Boys' Brigade company at Carnmoney Presbyterian Church. This treachery did not go down well with Mr Hamilton. Every time he got a chance he had a jibe at the activities of the B.B. organisation. He would compare real camping, as he called it, done by the scouts in proper tents with fires under the stars with the practice of sleeping on the floor of church halls, more usual at B.B. camps.

One time the Mossley Cubs played a football match against the Lifeboys in Carnmoney and afterwards we all walked home together down Carnmoney Brae and past The Castle, Mr Hamilton's home. The cubs decided to go up to his door and tell him the result – a clear victory for the Lifeboys. I rather sheepishly followed at the rear of the cub group. Before we left the somewhat subdued troop leader I tactlessly announced that I had scored two of the six goals. His silence and the glum expression on his face told me that this news had not exactly gladdened his heart.

In addition to Mr Hamilton, another teacher who taught there when I was a pupil at Mossley School was Kathleen Frame – Katie as we called her but certainly not in her or Mr Hamilton's presence. She lived in Larne and passed our house every morning on the way to school in her car. She was popular with parents and pupils alike and taught children in the middle classes – second and third standards.

Strangely I do not remember who taught me in the junior forms –Junior and Senior Infants and First Class. It may well have been Mrs Frame who then moved up to the older children when Miss Marty Auld joined the staff. I do know that she taught my brothers in their first year at the school.

Mossley Primary School moved to a new building off the Manse Road in the 1960s. I had then been in teaching for some time, visited the school and talked to some of the staff including Mrs Frame. I was pleased to find her still fit and as lively and bubbly as ever. She was glad to see me and indeed, to my surprise, remembered me well. We talked about old times in the former school building and some of its features. Then she said with a smile, 'You know, Jackie, you were always a terrible giggler.' I had to admit that she was right and I assured her that, while the giggling had subsided, I still enjoyed the funny side of life.

I think there would have been no more than eighty pupils at the school by the time I left and when I was enrolled in 1944 there might have been fewer and therefore more composite classes with a single teacher. This makes it difficult to remember when I moved from one Standard to the next. It is complicated because we were sometimes taken in the afternoons for practical lessons, such as handwork and needlework, by a teacher from a different standard and moved around from room to room.

Before I left Mossley PE School another male teacher, Samuel Walters, joined the staff. He was from Millvale near my grandfather's farm outside Ballyclare and had recently been in the army. He took us for gardening. In the Spring we went over each week to the school plots beside Sunnyside terrace. My uncle George always brought a cart load of manure to the plots from his farmyard. Mr Walters was friendly and cheerful, a pleasant change from Mr Hamilton's stern formality. He never was my class teacher but I did Handwork with him, mostly weaving cardboard looms with strands of raffia for table mats or winding scraps of wool on to cotton reels to make doilies. At Mossley School I also learned to knit. I think this was with Mrs Frame who took the boys along with the girls. I was never very good at needlework but I can still do plain knitting – we never progressed to the more difficult purl stitches. We were meant to be knitting scarves but I accidentally cast on and off so many stitches, sometimes in great bursts, that my edges were seldom straight. I remember Mrs Frame saying that my scarf was more like the shape of a motor car. She was very pleasant and we laughed a lot about my frequent mistakes. Later when I taught in primary school I was very proud to be able to show off my knitting skill to some very surprised young girls.

The most unusual teacher in my time at Mossley was Miss O'Connell from the United States of America. She was certainly different and innovative. I remember her speaking in a pleasant drawl. She helped us make hobby horses using brush shafts for bodies and card to cut out and paint as heads. We even found string for the hair. This cannot have been easy in the days of post war shortages. I remember us prancing around the classroom astride our brush shaft horsies. I suspect that Mr Hamilton might have been a little peeved at such outrageous freedom. It probably offended his obsession with keeping pupils in their seats and well under the teacher's thumb at all times. No matter, we certainly enjoyed ourselves and I have not forgotten the pleasure we had from this activity.

Miss Marty Auld, teacher, on right with my rather glum brother Edwin, second left in back row, in 1953. Back row (from left): David McKinstry, Edwin McKinney, Brian Hamill, unknown, Ronnie White, Drew Vance, John Bell, unknown, Jackie McCready, Robert Rankin. Middle row standing (from left): Unknown, Sandra Anderson, Dorrie McNeill, ? McNeill, Lesley Gerrard, Thelma Auld, unknown, unknown, unknown, unknown. Front row, seated (from left): Betty Scott, Doris Auld, Roberta Adair, unknown, Jim Kernohan, unknown, unknown, June Downes, unknown, unknown, Doreen Anderson

I must have really taken to Miss O'Connell because her last day at the school is clearly etched on my memory. We had an assembly, an unusual event in itself, and we sang the hymn:

'Blest be the tie that binds / Our hearts in human love.'

Eventually she left on the three o'clock bus to Belfast and we cheered and cheered as she waved to us from the bus window. Every year after this at Christmas, a large parcel arrived at the school containing 'candies' for the pupils from our former American teacher. I'm sure Mr Hamilton didn't approve of the bubble gum which was included. It was much too messy, but nevertheless we all enjoyed this seasonal gift.

I attended Mossley School from 1944 until 1952 the years of tough post war austerity and very different from the affluent society of today. Basic materials such as pencils and paper were scarce and schools did their best with what was available. As ever, teachers were ingenious at using scraps and waste containers from home, or in our school, Mossley Mill. Nevertheless I was happy there with the limited resources in the company of many friends from the district.

To obtain a new pencil or a new jotter from Mr Hamilton you had to surrender the stub of the old pencil and demonstrate that there was not a single unused line in the jotter. He was very strict on this matter although his stock of pen handles and nibs must have been extensive to allow so many to end up on the railway embankment.

We took turns at mixing up powder to make a thin watery ink and this was poured into the desk ink wells from a crock jar with a stroup. I remember what a luxury it was later to be able to afford a small bottle of Stephen's Radiant Blue ink for our homeworks – 'ekkers' as these were known – and perhaps have some red or green ink to rule the headings and margins. Ball point pens were rare and expensive. The teachers sometimes used them as markers. I'm sure even if they had been more widely available, Mr Hamilton would have banned them, simply because of the messy work they would have encouraged.

In the junior classes I remember the pleasure of handling plasticene with its sweet, oily smell as we rolled it on to wooden boards. We used counters stored, as so many things were then, in tobacco tins. There was no plastic and the colours of equipment and books were limited and muted. It was a special treat to be given oblong drawing books of sugar and tissue paper on which to draw with coloured pastel chalks.

Mossley P.E. School Class 1953. Back row (from left): Bert McBroom, unknown, Bertie Blake, Robert Brown, Sammy Fleming, Joe Brown, Billy Douglas, unknown, Robert Hilditch. Middle row (from left): Vivian Kidd, unknown, unknown, Rose Grace, Lena Beck, Jean Downes, Margaret Ross, unknown, Martha McBride, Dorothy McCready. Front row (from left): Jim McAuley, Billy Scott, Pearl McNeilly, Hector Cherry, Molly Adams, unknown, unknown, unknown, June Downes, Billy McWhirter, Ias Montgomery.

In the senior classes we wrote carefully in pen and ink on precious Vere Foster red and blue lined exercise books of good quality paper, no doubt made in Ballyclare. To make a blot on our exercise books was a serious matter but it was much worse if we tried to erase the mistakes messily with a rubber or, horror of horrors, experimented with bleach. The small jotters were made from poor quality newsprint and only suitable for use with a blunt pencil. Unless one had a proper rubber, and these were in short supply in the 1950s, correcting mistakes was difficult without creating a dreadful smudge, or perhaps even rubbing a hole in the page. If you did this, you risked a spanking or, at least some strong words from our headmaster. My mum was expert at removing pencil mistakes using a piece of bread. Although it required more skill, she had even developed a way of dealing with ink blots in which diluted bleach was the main ingredient. Some nights she was busy in our house tidying up spoiled homeworks, a slice of plain loaf and her small bottle of 'magic fluid' at the ready.

Every child either had or wanted a pencil case. These were popular Christmas presents and were usually made from plain wood in two tiers with the top tier sliding aside to allow access to the pens, pencils and rubbers inside. We all had proper, if small by modern standards, leather school bags. I held on to mine until quite recently.

In the senior class we were given an Arithmetic test every Friday morning and blue cards of sums, grubby with long use, were issued. These were copied into a square lined exercise book and completed in ink. I think we were positioned in the desks according to our weekly performance. There was a nasty little book of laborious sums – straight work they were termed – and problems in a book called Fountain Arithmetic. I encountered copies of this and other dull books we used in Mossley School, later in my teaching career.

Eventually the school moved into the age of technology and acquired a radio receiver. It was kept in a locked cupboard recess in the wall in Mr Hamilton's room with speakers in other classrooms. It had a gleaming walnut case and the sound quality was first class - how I would have loved to tune it to Radio Luxembourg!

Mr Walters was very fond of the wireless lessons. I remember exotic countries being described in Travel Talks every Friday at 2.00 and we were so fascinated by this novelty that total silence reigned. We also had the BBC Singing Together programme on Mondays and Rhythm and Melody on Thursdays. We joined with William Appleby in songs like 'Paul's little Hen' and 'The Minstrel Boy to the War has Gone.' Mr Hamilton remained a little wary of the radio singing lessons and he continued to teach us hymns with his trusty tuning fork and piano. When we sang as a choir he patrolled the ranks, ear cocked for anyone who was off key. Detecting the usual tuneless monotone from someone in the back row of seniors, he would snap "Stop growling, Sir!" at the bravely struggling singer. Sometimes on Fridays we had a special treat and the Story Books were distributed. These often featured stirring yarns about cowboys and Indians from the American wild west. Our standard reader was a dull text – The New First Aid in English Reader complied in a graded series A-E by Angus McVicar. It specialised in tales of heroic British adventurers like Captain Scott of the Antarctic. There were sections listing 'Interesting Facts' such as The Seven Wonders of the World. In addition to the usual Hanging Gardens of Babylon and The Pyramids of Egypt included on the list it was more surprising to see A Modern British Ocean Liner included. Mr Hamilton used to add one of his own - one of the notorious laggards in our class getting all his spellings correct.

The story books were much livelier and had no comprehension exercises to do at the end, a favourite trick of Angus McVicar. We read them together taking turns to read aloud and it was bad luck on anyone who dared to read ahead and lose the place. Often, when an exciting bit of the story was reached, the books were collected and we had to wait until the following week to find out what had happened next – just like the serials in the Saturday morning cinemas our city contemporaries enjoyed.

There was always a break in the morning for school milk. The small bottles had cardboard tops with a tiny hole perforated in the centre of the cap to allow the drinking straw to be inserted. They were usually opened by using a pencil but also, as often as not, simply by stabbing the top in with a finger. This resulted in a spurt of milk shooting up and over the desk and dousing whatever books happened to be there. Most days cloths had to be found to wipe up the mess.

The quality of the straws was poor and they became soggy and useless long before the milk was drunk. The milk was invariably tepid, no doubt because the crates had been stored beside a radiator before break time.

Unusually for this period the pupils at Mossley School were able to have school dinners in the mill canteen. A register was completed in the morning by Mr Hamilton then, once the money had been collected, it was taken over to the canteen by a senior pupil. This job was prized because, once you got out of school, you could easily make the assignment stretch for at least a quarter of an hour. It felt good to be given such responsibility. With a bit of luck you might even meet someone on the way and have a bit of a yarn to make the exercise last even longer.

Those pupils taking school meals would line up at 12 o'clock to await Mr Hamilton, our courier. He always escorted the line and made us walk smartly by stepping out and snapping his fingers repeatedly. This snapping of the fingers was a characteristic habit of his – he did it as we sang, as we repeated our lessons and at every opportunity.

On the way we passed the main power plant of the mill with its shiny brass pistons, rods and wheels of all sizes humming away smoothly amid the hissing steam and flying transmission belts. Everything was beautifully painted and polished to perfection. It probably did Mr Hamilton's heart good to see an operation like this working with such smooth precision. His aim, no doubt, was to have the school operate like these well-oiled machines.

We also passed row after row of the workers' bicycle sheds and a glass fronted building where the mill's two fire engines were garaged. They, too, gleamed and shone, ready for action which they seldom experienced. I never saw them in operation except when they were turned out to help extinguish George Crawford's hayshed fires or when crews used them to practise drills. I remember them operating with the firemen and engines from the Glengormley Fire Station. They were to be seen on Thursday nights using their pumps and ladders on sections of the mill premises. There was a small First Aid post beside the fire engines. It was all a marvellous sight for a young boy to examine every day on his way to lunch.

The works canteen was approached by a long flight of steps about fifty yards past the main gatehouse to the mill. At the head of these steps were two rooms, one of which was where my mum had obtained our free supplies of orange juice and cod liver oil just after the war. I remember going down here with mum and a young brother in the pram.

We had our meal in a little side room well away from the throng of workers in the main canteen.

The larger canteen space was also used on special evenings of entertainment. The Scouts put on an exhibition of their activities here once and some of my family attended. I have a hazy memory of other events held there too, perhaps to mark the end of the war or in connection with a royal celebration. The Campbell family and the mill management were very keen supporters of all celebrations of royal occasions.

The dinners consisted of the usual fare, heavy on sausages, mashed potatoes and lots of cake and custard. We had fish cooked in batter and this was very different for me because at home, fish consisted of herring or smoked cod fried in the pan. I loved the canteen way of cooking fish. With the nearest chip shop at Glengormley and well out of our reach this was a foretaste of the fish and chips I would buy in Ballyclare on late games days at Ballyclare High School.

Once when I was a senior boy, two pals and I were daring enough to boycott the school meal and head off instead into the main workers' canteen. The mill staff did not arrive here until 12.30, making their way noisily through a wide glass – ceilinged tunnel from the factory. I remember we were served big baps spread with margarine and mugs of very sweet tea. Kathleen Higgins, our neighbour at Ballyearl, seemed to be in charge of the issue of sugar and was especially generous to us with a commodity which was scarce at this time. Inevitably it wasn't long before Mr Hamilton heard of our mutiny and that was the end of our attempt to act as grown-ups.

On the way back to school from the canteen we were sometimes late enough to coincide with the workers getting out of the mill for their lunch break. They would gather at the gate in a seething melee and then, once the horn had sounded, charge out through the green iron gates chattering noisily, in a great hurry to be away from work. It resembled the stampede for the exits at a football stadium.

Beside this entrance were the mill offices and visitors' reception area. My aunt May worked here as a secretary for many years and used to tell us about the managers she worked for and especially about the awesome figure of Colonel Henshall. Always referred to simply as The Colonel he was the chief executive and had transferred the attitude to discipline he had employed in the army into relationships with all his subordinates at the mill. Most people I knew were terrified of him and certainly nobody dared contradict the Colonel.

The gatekeeper, I suppose today he would be the security man, was Jimmy Geddis, a likeable but strict figure who took his duties very seriously and made sure no unauthorised persons entered the works. In the mornings and evenings he would pay suitable abeyance to the Colonel when he appeared at the offices.

Once back at the school we had about half an hour for playtime.

The school yard was an awkward shape for football games but boys are ingenious at finding adequate space for a match, however unsuitable the terrain. We played diagonally across the yard, one set of goals chalked out at the corner of the black stone boundary wall and the railway bridge parapet. The other was on the brick wall at the back of the Old Row terrace and beside a narrow entry leading to the rear of the school building. As in most school playgrounds, the games proceeded directly through the girls who were peacefully engaged in skipping or hopscotch. Squabbles with the girls were normal but real rows were rare. A bigger problem was retrieving the ball when it went on to the railway embankment or into the backyard of the family who lived in the house adjoined to the school building. At one time this must have been a residence for the principal but never in my time. A dog patrolled in their yard and deterred even the most daring from scaling the wall.

In my last year at the school I went a bit wild and one day at lunch break, in the company of Logan McKinstry and a few pals, set off on bicycles, commandeered from senior girls, on an expedition to Monkstown and Nellie's Dam. Heads down close to the handlebars and pedalling madly, we did not stop until we were back in the playground., The thrill, I'm sure, came from just riding as fast as we could and being daredevils. We were imitating the famous motor cyclist of that time, Geoff Duke.

Another time, behind Sunnyside, where unauthorised activities usually took place, a curious stunt was enacted. This procedure was for an individual to turn around and around a number of times – quickly enough to make himself dizzy then to shove head between knees and keep still for as long as possible, all to be completed without passing out. If this were done in the right order and quickly enough a sensation of feeling 'high' would occur. I cannot vouch for this because, as usual, I was afraid of the consequences from Mr Hamilton if he were to find out and I just watched meekly. I cannot recall any peculiar reactions from those who participated. I dare say it was the 1950s equivalent of a 'hit' from an illicit hallucinatory drug. Inevitably Mr Hamilton found out. It was suspected that, as usual, Mrs McCullough was his informant, and a concerted campaign was begun to nip such dangerous behaviour in the bud.

Strangely in all the time I was at the school I never visited the mill on an educational visit. In those days this just wasn't done. I couldn't have told what went on there and depended on my aunt May and uncle Davy Darragh, who was a machine fitter here for a time, for any details of the processes and routines. Our knowledge was limited to what we could see through the mill windows as we passed along to the canteen – only workers in shirt sleeves and aprons tending the spinning frames. We could hear the droning sound of the machinery and the constant hiss of escaping steam through the many pipes which protruded from the building. That was the extent of our experience of the mill in operation.

Later when I grew up I was quite stunned to hear from friends who had worked there of the authoritarian regime imposed by the managers and the harshness of the working conditions in the absence of organised trade unions.

I suppose the nearest we came to an out-of-school expedition was a visit to the dentist in Carnmoney. Every so often, I think it was usually a Friday, Mr Hamilton would ask those in his senior classes if they needed dental treatment. Those who put their hands up had made a difficult decision – whether the hour's freedom from the classroom and a leisurely stroll up and down Carnmoney brae in the company of their pals compensated for certain torture in Carnmoney Dispensary House. It was here that Mr Baird, a bald headed, itinerant dentist from Ballyclare, administered basic but painful, dental care. I'm sure that we had no teacher to escort us on the road: perhaps a senior pupil was put in charge of the party. I just don't recall anything but a casual arrangement. Neither do I remember our parents being involved in giving permission for the visit nor approving of what Mr Baird decided to do. My mother told us of her painful experience at the hands of what seemed to have been the same dentist in Ballyclare. A good compromise, if you could manage it, was to go along and have your teeth cleaned. This, while not totally pain free, was certainly not as awful as other procedures we endured or heard described.

I remember the antiseptic smell of the surgery and the forceful grappling which Mr Baird employed to keep his young patients in the chair while he poked and prodded in mouths with his shiny instruments. He really was quite rough. I also have not forgotten the hideousness of his spittoon following an extraction – whether mine or that of one of my friends. I think we were taken into his surgery in twos or threes although how anyone remained there for treatment after seeing him at work on someone else is puzzling. Perhaps in those days young people did not question the demands of someone in authority, however threatening they appeared.

I also remember visits to the school by Dr Erskine, a somewhat elderly lady with lank grey hair who spoke in what we would have called a posh accent. She used a long glass rod to prise open my mouth and peer inside. She held my tongue down with a wooden spatula dipped in an antiseptic fluid and asked me to say 'Ah' repeatedly. The examination was quite civilised compared with the rigours we endured at Carnmoney Dispensary.

I clearly remember on my last day at Mossley School we stopped at three o'clock and I know that when I met the 3.05 bus at the Finger Post I was running strongly for Ballyearl. I'm sure I had said my farewells before going out of the school door but I was never one to linger around and wallow in sentimentality. The school had done a good job in giving me the opportunity to go to grammar school and for this I was grateful. My dad was ill at the time and I know that my emotions were unstable. I was happy at the school, not all of the time but then that is what one expects of a seven-year spell in an institution.

I have to admit though that, even in later life, Mr Hamilton remained an awesome figure and I never was entirely comfortable when I met him in different contexts. This was probably my fault more than his because he always greeted me warmly. Eventually he became the chairman of the church committee when I was a young member. On the few occasions when I dared express an opinion on an issue I had to resist the instinct to put up my hand before I addressed the chair. I did manage to overcome this inhibition to some extent but certainly, unlike fellow committee members, could never bring myself to call him Sidney.

The Finger Post at the junction of the Carntall and Doagh Roads, now gone, might be regarded as the western boundary of Mossley. Not far from the end of the Old Row stands the Orange Hall which could be the eastern boundary. My next association with Mossley would be in this building. There on a Saturday afternoon in a few years time, I would strip off for games with Mossley Young Men, the local football team.

By this time I was concentrating on my future career and my days at Mossley School seemed to be a part of a past which had gone; even the memories had already begun to fade.

Chapter 9: High Time at Ropeworks and North End Hut

Itransferred to Ballyclare High School in 1952 from Mossley Primary School and, with an enrolment of around 450, it seemed a really large school. Every term-time morning for the six years I joined others from Cloughfern, Whiteabbey and Mossley on the Ballyclare via Mossley bus at Ballyearl. What a motley collection of buildings met us on arrival at the school. Other grammar schools had buildings named after distinguished former pupils. At Ballyclare the names were less pretentious. Among ours were the Rope Works, The Cleansing Station, The Orange Hall and The North End Hut. There was also a small Nissen hut beside the tennis courts, the command centre of the prefects, and outrageous stories circled round the lower forms about what took place in there. I didn't ever find out because I never joined the ranks of the prefects.

Ballyclare High School, main building, c.1950

The staff, unlike some of the buildings, were far from old wrecks, and in my memory most were young, lively and colourful. I remember them in their room bases – gentle Mr Chesney and stern-faced Mr Grainger in the Physics laboratory, Mr Bell amid Bunsen burners and the smells of the Chemistry laboratory and music teacher, Miss Lusk among her 'nymphs and shepherds coming away' in the last room of the old building opposite the male staff room.

This tiny room deserves description. When all the male members were present there was hardly room for a cat. I can vouch for this because I sometimes had to struggle in to fetch the cricket bag, which for some reason was kept in their toilet cubicle. It was probably my imagination but the cricket gear seemed to emit a distinct musky whiff absorbed from its unusual base.

The fairly new prefabricated building had Mr Williams in Room 10 giving out his daily history prep and counting the school savings money, often at the same time. Mr Mudd in Room 11 read English poetry in grave tones with his black gown swathed about him. Mr Sam Thompson taught English in Room 12 and, though volatile at times, was a popular if rather eccentric master. He often told us stories of the cycling trips he made to cathedrals and public buildings in the summer holidays, a kind of Ulster Betjeman. In later years his thirsty visits to other buildings of a public nature outnumbered those to churches. It was always a treat to be asked to remain after school and help him unpack the new books that arrived from the county library. This was the only library I remember in the school then. We were rewarded with sweeties and an added bonus was the chips we bought on the way down to the late bus. Mr Thompson was an enthusiastic scout leader and looked rather smart on parade in his corduroy shorts and garter tabs.

This was not an unusual sight as all boys wore short trousers until around fourteen. He was by his own admission an indifferent umpire at school cricket matches. His attention tended to drift from the game to the hedgerow and the birds – the feathered variety, as he would say with a loud guffaw. The cry of 'How's that?' would startle him from his reverie and often his finger would shoot up nervously, irrespective of the validity of the claim. We bowlers knew how to exploit home advantage.

Next to Mr Thompson in this building were the French teachers, Messieurs Jim and Sammy Wilson in rooms 13 and 14. I had the taller Mr Jim and I remember his frustration, indeed anger, at a class colleague who, after three years instruction, still pronounced the French definite article 'le' as 'lee'. A case, perhaps, of the Cloughan Lane being just too far from the Champs Elysees!

The last room in this corridor was occupied by the lower forms of the Preparatory Department. The older prep children were taught in the Orange Hall on the Rashee Road and their teacher, Miss Ferguson, also took lower grammar school forms for Nature Study in this building.

Ballyclare High School in 1938. By 1950 aluminium classrooms had been erected beyond the spot where this photograph was taken. In my time as a pupil the 'Cleansing Station,' where we changed for games and P.E., not shown here, was to the right.

Her summer nature walks up Ross's Avenue allowed the young lads to saunter idly beside the young lasses and provided welcome relief from bold King Billy looking down from the Orange Lodge banner stowed on the stage.

Then there was the frail figure of Mrs Houston our Art teacher. Her voice quivered as she taught us elaborate lettering decorated with serifs. She looked ninety but was probably not a day over seventy. It was rumoured that in winter she kept herself warm on the bus journey from Belfast to school by sitting on a hot water bottle. Every pupil knew where she kept her handkerchief. It is sufficient to say that it wasn't in her pocket.

When I joined the school Mr Cunningham taught Physical Education for about a year in the assembly hall which doubled up as a gymnasium. We changed for P.E. lessons as we did for rugby and the girls for hockey, in separate rooms of the Cleansing Station, the name acquired from its wartime function in the town It was rudimentary and dark and certainly resembled a military establishment.

Although Mr T Davidson taught me Latin my most vivid memory of him is of his supervisory duties in the canteen. Usually a silent threat, like a dormant volcano, he commanded immediate attention when he gave tongue. No sergeant major was better at keeping order. One day following a particularly strident bellow I watched fascinated as his facial muscles strained to stop his teeth ejecting.

He took tutorials with senior pupils in the smaller Rope Works rooms. This accommodation took its name from a spell as a post war offshoot of the Belfast Rope Works. It had its origins as an emergency mortuary for Ballyclare during the Second World War. Fortunately it was never needed for this purpose. I don't remember any windows in the main building but the classrooms certainly exuded a heavy, gloomy atmosphere.

One day with three other boys I was having a Latin tutorial in one of the smaller rooms not far from the main entrance when our Latin lesson was interrupted. Mr Davidson had to stop teaching to make several trips to the main door in response to loud hammering and shouting. This door stuck regularly but on this occasion the noise came not from some one trying to enter the building, but from Mr Sam Thompson in an adjacent room giving his usual, enthusiastic dramatisation of Walter de La Mare's poem The Listeners. It begins 'Is there anybody there, said the traveller knocking on the moonlit door?' We gathered from the tone of his muttering that Mr Davidson was not amused by the confusion. We had the Two Tommys as caretakers. Tommy Rock was very small in stature and genial – not unlike Ronnie Corbett – while Tommy Ferguson seemed to be permanently stationed outside the canteen, a cigarette often glowing surreptitiously from his cupped hand.

While in the lower forms, instead of walking up to the school every Friday morning, I went over to Ballyclare Technical School to 'Stalag Luft Brownlee' for woodwork. This was an old ex-army hut heated like a sauna by a central, pot-bellied, stove, ideal for heating pots of strong smelling glue. Here Mr Willie John Brownlee commanded a fine range of mallets and edge tools. With these we produced elaborately jointed teapot stands and toothbrush holders. Well mine were just about recognisable as such!

Form Upper 4 1956. Back row (from left): Winston Cochrane, Gaston Gamble, Bryan Johnston, David Ralston, Jack McKinney, Stanley Steele, Jack Wilson, Marshall Irwin, Billy Gamble. Middle row (from left): Merrie Shannon, Dennis Boal, Stewart Rennison, John Craig, Robert Dunlop, Ian Hagan, Matt Millar, Gerald Bell, Diana Craig. Front row (from left): June Gregg, Doreen Agnew, Jill Murray, Rosemary McConnell, Form Teacher, Gloria Stewart, Pauline McCleary, Mary Cunningham.

At lunchtime the choice was either to stray with friends up the back lane alongside the rugby pitch or play football. Here there took place what my mother delicately called 'irregular gatherings' and, like her I will leave their details to your memory or imagination. To Mr Montgomery's displeasure football was played in the King GeorgeV1 Coronation Field, just outside the school fence opposite Ballyclare Foundry. Despite its grand title this was essentially derelict land with unpainted goalposts. It had been donated to Ballyclare Council around 1936 for public recreation, but never seemed to be in official use. Later a deal was completed between the council and the education authority whereby the Coronation field was exchanged with the school pitches on Foundry Lane and provided convenient space for the expansion of the school site.

I have memories of many occasions and incidents when I attended the school. Often the annual Grange-McCluney Cross-Country race brought an exciting finish to the spectators gathered at the final straight beside the Rope Works. In 1953 there were special school sports to celebrate the Coronation in June and we received souvenir books and cups and saucers. The weather was beautiful and the May Fair carnival remained in the Town Square until the coronation celebrations were over.

A most vivid memory of my time as a pupil concerns a day when the school came close to evacuation. This was long before the days of bomb scares. The cause was more mundane. The land on the northern boundary was still farmland then and the farmer chose a hot, still day to spread manure in this field. It was strong stuff and soon the smell went off the scale. Complaints from the staff and pupils were loud and long and some pupils and teachers came close to being sick. Eventually, fortitude in the face of adversity took us all through to half-past three and the performance was never repeated.

The highlight of my years in the lower forms was the Christmas parties. These were arranged in the evenings, a different night for each form. Young teachers, such as Mr Hooks and Mr Francey, joined in the fun and led the games. It was a rare chance to develop friendships begun in class time. Ten o'clock and the bus home came all too soon and forced many reluctant partings. Later the Old Ballyclarians' Saturday Night Hops were popular as respectable alternatives to the wilder dances in the local halls. I cannot remember ever attending any.

I can say that I really enjoyed my time at what must have been the friendliest grammar school in Northern Ireland.

Chapter 10: The Carnmoney Connection

The first minister I remember in Carnmoney Presbyterian Church was Rev. S.H.Nicholson. I must have beeen around nine or ten when I was pulpit assistant on Children's Day. Dressed in Moses sandals, white ankle socks, short grey trousers, shirt and tie, I recall the sea of faces which met us as we entered the pulpit but I loved it and, after this experience, it was either the stage or teaching for me.

Mr Nicholson was a tall gaunt figure and drove a large, black car, an Austin I think. It had taken on the purplish tinge peculiar to older cars at that time. I remember he died while baptising a child in Ballyhone above Monkstown, one of the outposts of the congregation. The family shared his own surname. The pulpit was draped with black and an air of gloom hung over the congregation the following Sunday.

Our family pew was in the gallery, four rows behind the clock, directly facing the minister. Not all gallery pews were so fortunate. From some upstairs pews it was only possible to see part of the minister's head. These were often occupied by rowdy, young people. As a small boy, my view of the choir, well of the bass singers anyway, increased as I grew taller. One gentleman's head only appeared when he threw it back to reach the high notes. Happily, my view of the young girls in the choir increased as I reached adolescence.

Boys Brigade, 53rd Belfast Company, c.1953
Back row (from left): Ivan McCormick, John Beggs, Jim Smyth, Stanley Carson, Tommy Gillespie, Arthur McClean, Samuel Fettis, Sammy Brown, Willie Smyth, Jackie Carson. Middle row (from left): Bertie Campbell, Chris Campbell, Tommy Campbell, Hubert Bell, Billy Drummond, Derek Abernethy, Jack McKinney, Martin Cowden, Jim Graham, Willie Pusey, Sandy Finney. Front row (from left): Lieutenant Robert Alexander, Rev H S Nicholson, Inspecting Officer, Samuel Kirk (captain), Lieutenant Bertie Jameson, Lieutenant Bertie Allen.

In the 1950s pew rents were still collected by the sexton, Jock McIlwaine, cycling to the congregation's scattered districts. The rents appeared to assign territorial rights that were guarded jealously. My dad discovered this one harvest Sunday when he was unceremoniously evicted from a pew by an overbearing lady who was keeping a seat for her husband, on elder's duty in the porch. The incident provided a lively dinner table discussion.

There was always sure to be a dinner table discussion after Mr Nicholson preached a 'Home' sermon. He did this periodically and we youngsters did not fully understand the inferences made but we gathered from the fixed attention of the congregation and the guarded comments afterwards from my dad that the tone was of strong advice on keeping the seventh commandment. 'He was letting them have it today,' dad would comment and I'm sure that, when we boys went off to play with our Mecano sets, he and my mum held a fuller examination.

Usually in the Spring and Summer months Mr Nicholson would announce which district of the congregation he would be visiting in the coming week. People remained at home – well there were not so many places to go to in these times – ready to receive him formally in the parlour.

Each Sunday morning my brother Ken and I walked from Ballyearl, through Upper Mossley and up the very steep Carnmoney Brae to Sunday School in the Lecture Hall.

William Lees was Superintendent then. After Sunday School, or Sabbath School as it was called, while waiting for dad to arrive on the church bus, we played around the gravestones of former ministers in the grounds and chased Jock McIlwaine's banties through the laurel bushes. Jock often threatened but never did tell our dad about our exploits.

Every Sunday morning, a few minutes before the service was due to begin, Jock appeared in the pulpit and deftly set the large Bible down on the velvet cushion. Before this he had been pulling the bell rope in the upstairs vestibule. On wet days we met our dad here and on one unhappy occasion my brother tampered with the rope, jiggling it until it came crashing down to the floor. It proved quite tricky responding to my dad's later observation that it was strange that he had not heard the bell ringing that morning.

Jock was fond of relating a story about a funeral he attended. The church building was being extended and it proved necessary to disinter a few minister's graves close to the building and reinter their remains in another part of the grounds. Jock was attending the committal of a particular minister. He turned to a friend and said: 'Do you know this is the second time I have been to this clergyman's funeral!'

Jock was usually gentle and understanding with youngsters but his wife Marty was a different story. As anyone who had ever kicked a ball in the Lecture Hall soon found out to his cost, her wrath did not always go down with the sun.

I can clearly picture Marty, summoned by noise to the Lecture Hall back door, in carpet slippers and arms akimbo, glaring at a ball smudge on the wall and lecturing a contrite brigade member on what the church committee would have to say about such a catastrophe.

In the 1950s the church chartered two buses to bring people from the outlying areas to the Sunday morning services. One came from Cloughfern Corner via Monkstown, Lower Mossley and Ballyearl and Bob Dunlop was conductor, opening the doors and lifting the money, a job my brother and I secretly envied. Tom Vint, I think, conducted on the other Ballyclare via Ballyrobert bus.

As we grew older we graduated to the Boys' Brigade Bible Class in the old upstairs committee room above the minister's quarters. It suffered from a terminal case of woodworm, a pest we were not unfamiliar with in Ballyearl, but had never seen before in such prodigious numbers. There were photographs on the walls of past dignitaries and behind the glass of each one could clearly see the bodies of insects that had tunnelled through to their deaths. The floor sloped perilously towards a small treadle organ in one corner, just about capable of wheezing out 'Will your anchor hold in the storms of life' for the croaky singers in the B.B. Bible class. This room became an important part of my young life in the church. Here the Dramatic Society met for play readings and later, following an extensive renovation during which the woodworm disappeared, I attended choir practices in the room.

The church committee met here too, and when I was elected at the early age, for those days, of 21, I attended the monthly meetings here. My contribution to the business was minimal because the chairman, Mr Sidney McC. Hamilton B.A., was the only person I feared more than Mrs Marty McIlwaine. Not too long before, he had been my venerable headmaster in Mossley Public Elementary School.

The early years of Rev. John C. Ferguson's ministry coincided with the change of Carnmoney from a quiet country congregation to that of a large suburban district. I remember Mr Ferguson as a handsome, cultured man. He often used a large white lavender-scented handkerchief. As a result of a childhood illness he had spent part of his life in Switzerland and spoke French fluently. I remember him telling us that he had preached a sermon in French on at least one occasion, not I feel sure, in Carnmoney. He went to camp with our B.B. company, bathing with us in the sea at Ayr and once wrote a sketch for the dramatic society. This was about a pianist performing at the BBC and not many of the members, and as it emerged later the audience, understood its subtle nuances. He had a yacht called Gossamer that he kept at Bangor and a little Ford Prefect car, registration number TZ160. He named it Dorcas that meant 'Full of Good Works' as we were told. The car, yacht and the manse pussies often featured in his children's sermons.

A distinct buzz of excitement was created in the congregation by the church tercentenary celebrations in 1957, especially the opportunities for serious eating at the many special suppers. For these Carnmoney and Mrs Ferguson were renowned. Renovations were carried out to the main church building at this time, much of the work being done by voluntary labour. Members of the local football team were prominent and the camaraderie that developed was special, trickling down even to teenagers like myself.

As part of these changes a velvet curtain and rail were removed from in front of the choir. I recall a subsequent debate of a very Presbyterian nature concerning the implications of this change for the modesty of the front row of sopranos.

One happy consequence of the new housing developments for the youth of the church was the appearance of fresh, young faces, especially girls. Suddenly the rather staid Girls' Auxiliary socials were not the only opportunity to meet 'talent'. In this respect my brother, Ken, was more successful than me.

Carnmoney church's link with the past was best illustrated by the old Stables building. I do not remember horses using it but when we changed here for the B.B. football matches in the mid 1950s the stalls and the square set floor were still intact. On Saturday afternoons we would see Jock wheeling barrow loads of coke over to the church boiler from the huge mound stored in the Stables. A Boys' Brigade club was held for a time in this cold, dank building until one day, fortunately when it was unoccupied, the back gable wall collapsed on top of the club snooker table. The Stables were eventually renovated and good use was made of the accommodation, particularly for indoor bowling but my most striking memory of 1960s building development at the church was of lively debates at committee and a series of subsequent plans for alterations to the church displayed in the upstairs vestibule. Not much progress was made on these plans in my time on the committee.

Another link with the past was the regular appearance at Sunday night worship of a charming old gentleman dressed in black suit, boots and high butterfly collar. He reminded me of what one of the old testament prophets might have looked like as he rode to church sedately on his tall, old-fashioned bicycle. To my everlasting shame, with an accomplice, I let his tyres down one night and after the service watched appalled as he trundled the bike down the road towards his home.

Around this time my brother and I met Mr Ferguson to discuss zipping up the activities for young people – probably in a cunning attempt to meet more girls. We got some things underway but eventually failed because, incredible as it may seem nowadays, there were not enough teenagers around to support the initiative. The area was developing rapidly and babies and baptisms were at a record level. Their time would come but for us it was still either the Floral Hall or Billy Twyford's chip shop in Glengormley on Saturday nights.

There were times when I found opportunities to become involved in entertainment on the Lecture Hall stage produced by the church Dramatic Society. I especially enjoyed playing a variety of roles in their kitchen comedies and pantomimes . Later when I was an indifferent tenor in the choir I took part in hilarious secular entertainments provided by the choir to the delight, if occasional embarrassment, of some members and the audiences.

The Sunday evening service was always my favourite. The church had a serenity and a tranquillity absent at the crowded Sunday morning worship. There were always the regulars sitting in the same seats every week. One of these was an old lady from Carntall who came on foot, topping Carnmoney Brae with breathless difficulty. My brothers and I sometimes caught up with her and accompanied her on the last bit of the journey.

Regularly on Sunday evening things would change when Reggie Magee, a former school friend, revved up his Nestles van and accelerated in a cloud of dust through the church grounds – much to the consternation of the older folk. The giggling girls, squeezed in beside the driver, obviously enjoyed the bravado while his male competitors stood by tut - tutting with jealousy.

All my formative years were centred on Carnmoney Presbyterian church. Here I forged many special friendships and there is not a corner of the old buildings and grounds that does not hold pleasant memories for me.

The McKinney Family in 1965 – Martha and boys, Edwin, Jackie, Ken, Wesley

Old Time Musical Hall Carnmoney Presbyterian Church Choir
Back row, standing (from left): Olga McKinney, Chris Forsythe, Iris Ross, Maureen Auld, Paul Hutchinson, Des Agnew, Andy Finney, Sydney Gillespie (Choir Master), Jim Coleman, John Jordan, David Boyd, Jack McKinney, Jim Price, Sammy Lewis, Campbell Johnston, Ena Rodgers, Robina Jackson. Middle row (from left): Laura Dyer, Ruth Anne White, Rosemary Walker, Alison Taylor. Front row (from left): Lila Finlay, Margaret Walker, Hazel Beattie, unknown, Rosemary White, Roberta Curran, Margaret McCracken

Chapter 11: College Boy

I have no idea when the idea of teaching as a career entered my head. I do remember that when I was about sixteen I wanted to follow my dad and become an electrician. I found so much pleasure in my spare time working on rough joinery or messy car maintenance. I think that, for whatever reason, my dad had earmarked my brother Ken as the future 'spark.' He was keen to get him started in the Post Office as an apprentice telephone engineer. He always thought this a better job with a brighter future than an electrician.

Stranmillis College, main building

In those days those seeking apprenticeships in the Post Office Engineering department often began as telegram boys delivering cables across Belfast. Alas brother Ken's only experience in riding a light motorcycle occurred after Uncle Alfie passed on to us his hopelessly underpowered French motor cycle, an Auto Vap. It hadn't the power to carry Alfie up the hill to his house in Lisnasharragh and only proved to be an embarrassment to us from the number of times it broke down, usually in the most awkward places.

In my last year at Ballyclare High School my dad was often ill, suffering the effects of his serious heart attack six years before, but he was instrumental in having me complete the application forms for a grant from the Ministry of Education to gain entry to Stranmillis Training College, Belfast in September 1958.

In those days I tended to go along with the career plans made by my parents.

At some point in 1958, Mrs Peggy Ferguson, the wife of our minister, Rev John C Ferguson in Carnmoney Presbyterian Church, took me to see her brother, Jack Quan, at that time a Ministry of Education senior civil servant in primary education. It was a very kind gesture but I remember being too overawed by the grandeur of the office at Massey Avenue, Stormont to gain much benefit from the visit. I doubt whether this interview had any bearing on an eventual offer of a place at Stranmillis Training College.

Later when I had qualified, Rev J.C. Ferguson, embarrassingly in my presence, often announced that he had always known that I was a natural teacher. I have no idea how he came to this conclusion. Mind you, when I was much younger, in the time of Rev Nicholson, his predecessor, I had spent a lot of time in the church pulpit on Children's Day Sundays reading out the hymn numbers and, in sandals and white shirt, acting as the junior assistant to the minister.

Although I surely must have had one, I do not recall much of my preliminary interview at Stranmillis. I have a vague feeling that my dad took some time off work and we went there together. I remember Mr Alex Keith, the principal, a tall, baldish Scot, but no details of the actual interview remain. I do know that when the results of my Senior Certificate exam together with an offer from Stranmillis arrived at Ballyearl in the post, probably some time in August 1958, my dad was determined that I should accept the offer.

He was ill by this time, indeed might even have been in hospital, but he told everyone from our family who visited him that he wanted me to go on to become a teacher.

My dad died on Friday, September 12 and his funeral was held on Sunday, September 14. Obviously at this time many things were happening in our house and we were confused and uncertain about what would happen to us as a family. We got advice from our relations but in the end we were the only people who could decide what direction our lives would take to cope with what was no less than a tragedy.

During August 1958, I had been working as a temporary postman doing holiday relief and the Carnmoney postmaster asked if I would consider resuming my round on the day after the funeral. Israel Abernethy was a kind and wise soul and I think he felt I would deal better with my grief being at work rather than moping at home. In this he was right. I would also earn some much needed cash.

My mum was in a delicate mental state and really struggled to come to terms with the sudden loss of her husband. My dad had always been the one to deal with financial and business matters and she just hadn't a notion how to proceed when he was gone. I was no great help except in a general, comforting role.

It was no great surprise that the letter from Stranmillis, telling me to report for the beginning of the term on Monday 15 September, was either mislaid or neglected. It only turned up when the college eventually wrote to ask why I had not appeared. Naturally this letter spurred us on and I eventually set off, some time around the end of September, on the 8.05am Belfast bus to begin my course at Stranmillis.

This was the beginning of a very tough year for me, indeed for the whole family.

Life at Stranmillis would always have been difficult without the complication of my dad's death and my mum's subsequent illness. I was essentially a country boy and, strange as it may seem now, very shy and introspective. I had no real experience of travelling to Belfast. I did not know my way around using the 'Red Buses' as we called the Belfast Corporation transport system. Eventually I became familiar with my well beaten path from Smithfield Bus Station to Royal Avenue and the Number 69 Red Bus to Broomhill Park and the college. I did not, so far as I remember, make the usual countryman's mistake of asking the Red Bus conductor for 'a return ticket' to Stranmillis' the normal request on the UTA Belfast via Mossley Green Bus service.

By the time I arrived at college the introductions for Freshers to the layout of the buildings and the way the seminars and lectures operated had already taken place and I had to discover this for myself. Each student had a personal tutor whose role was to provide some pastoral care to the group of students to whom he was assigned.

Mine was Mr Hickman, a music lecturer, and like many musicians he was somewhat eccentric. He played either the double bass or the cello, I am not sure which, a large, stringed instrument anyway. He cycled daily to the college from his home nearby with the instrument strapped to the back of his bike. It was a remarkable sight to see him struggling up the steep hill alongside the main college building. Small and wiry though he was he never needed to dismount. I did have several meetings with him and he was sensitive to my unusual position. He did his best to help me come to terms with the difficulties I encountered adapting to college life. On one occasion, following a tutorial session, he brought me all the way home in his car and listened sensitively to my account of our family's misfortunes.

One of the two groups of First Year Men Students, 1958
Back row (from left): Derek Loughlin, unknown, Ian Parke, Victor McKee, Derek Wilkins, David Wright, Gusty McCullough, David McCammond, Billy McFarlane, Jack McKinney, Edwin Mitchell.
Middle row (from left): Frank Martin, M McCullagh, Charlie McDonald, Morris McFarland, David McCreery, Billy Mc Sparran, Mervyn Kerr, Hugh Minnis, Reggie Patterson, Jack Pollock, Sammy McGrugan, George McCambley, John Ritchie, George Whitten, Maurice McAvoy, Michael Millar.
Front row, seated (from left): Unknown, Murray Lee, George Lyons, ? Wilkinson, Don McBride, Jimmy Kilpatrick, Robin McAfee, Billy Montgomery, John McKeown, Jim McDowell, Stuart Parker.
Seated on ground (from left): Jack Leathem, Charlie Leeke, Derek Patton.

He seemed genuinely concerned about my welfare and ability to cope with our domestic situation and concentrate on my college course.

What proved difficult in my first months was adapting to the change in how I was addressed as a student compared with the procedure in grammar school. Suddenly it was Mr McKinney and not the blunt McKinney. I was not expected to address the lecturers as Sir or Madam. School uniform was replaced by a much freer style of dress but I find it interesting now to look at a photograph I have of my group of first year men and note how different the dress style was from what would be normal, student attire today. In my year group there were no jeans and almost everyone was dressed in the standard blazer or sports coat with flannels or sensible trousers. Everyone wore a tie. College scarves were popular and when an aunt bought me one for Christmas I actually wore it often. This was in contrast to the black tie I had worn right through the first term as the traditional symbol of mourning for my father.

I had been fortunate that, because of the large intake of men in 1958, I was not eligible for a place in Balmoral Hall, the male students' hostel. This suited me because I was perfectly able to travel in and out on the bus and be there to support my mother at home. But I did miss out entirely on important aspects of the college experience.

The disadvantage of travelling daily to college was that I missed out on the camaraderie enjoyed by the students from Balmoral Hall. Often when I arrived at college for an early morning lecture and made my way up the hill to the lecture rooms, I met a company of young men approaching from the back entrance to the college. This was the Freshers' group making their way to college from the residential accommodation at Balmoral Hall about a mile away. Even on a Monday morning they would be chatting happily together or discussing and laughing at their weekend escapades and the battles with the warden there, Jock Murray. They always seemed able to commandeer the Common Room where the usual quota of extroverts engaged in brash and rowdy exchanges with the female students who had dared to use the room. I was just too overawed by this and in all my time at the college I did not spend more than a few hours in the Common Room feeling uncomfortable most of the time.

I gathered from remarks I overheard that a fair bit of the social life of the Balmoral Hall Brigade centred on 'The Egg', the colloquial term for The Eglinton Inn on the Malone Road. This was certainly not part of my scene.

The Freshers' parade reassembled at lunch times to return to Balmoral Hall for their meal. The break lasted for one and a half hours and 'day' boys had to eat in the refectory and visit the library or wander about the grounds until the afternoon lectures began. I always found this a difficult period especially in the early days of the first term when I knew few others at the college.

Soon I encountered Michael Millar who had been one year above me at Ballyclare High School. He, too, was travelling on the bus each day from Ballyrobert and we became friends. Indeed he proved to be very helpful by showing me some of the ropes and we stuck together at least for the first year.

The other person I became friendly with was Frank Martin. He cycled over to the college from his home in Cregagh and was a useful companion at break and lunch times in the refectory and on exploratory tours of the extensive Stranmillis grounds. He was an active Presbyterian, a stalwart in the Boys Brigade and his father had died prematurely too so we had a lot in common. My mother approved of this friendship mainly because she felt Frank would keep me on the straight and narrow amid all the temptations Stranmillis College might have to offer.

At this stage in my life I was really painfully shy and it took a great deal of courage to take the initiative and engage others in conversation. The refectory was indeed a nightmare. I would never have gone in there for meals on my own but always waited until I could attach myself to at least one or two others from my tutorial group. Even the thought of actually talking to an attractive young lady could bring me out in a nervous rash! In the three years I spent there I don't remember ever engaging in a one-to-one conversation with a female student let alone having a regular girl friend like many of the other young men.

When I arrived at college the clubs and societies were all well underway and, as they met in the evenings, the distance from the college and home made my attendance impracticable. Also, and perhaps more pertinently, the family responsibilities I had at home coping with my mother's illness meant I was not emotionally equipped to join in what I judged to be peripheral extras to the main college course.

Looking back now I realise that my first year at Stranmillis passed in a kind of dreamlike haze. I existed by sticking to regular routines, at home and at college – difficult as this was at times.

I just about managed to keep up with the course and scraped through the end-of-year assessments in Education Theory and Teaching Practice. Indeed, now I think I was a bit fortunate to survive the year without some kind of emotional breakdown.

In my second year, our domestic circumstances had improved and I was able to combine travelling to college by day with supporting my mother in the evenings and at weekends.

Eventually I got involved in the college football club and enjoyed playing regularly in the King's Scholars teams – usually the second 11. Sometimes, if my lectures finished early, I could even go home, have my tea and return to college for football training.

Occasionally I stayed over in the library after the last lecture finished at five-thirty until the training began in the gymnasium at seven. The facilities were excellent and the training, in circuits, was enjoyable and through the football club I made many new friends.

The home games were played on the college pitches at Balmoral where the facilities included hot showers and proper nets behind the goalposts – very different from my uncle George's field dotted with cowpats that I had been used to when playing for Mossley Young Men FC.

Every Saint Patrick's Day there was a match between the King's Scholars' current team and an Old Boys' Eleven. Few of the 'old boys' were more than thirty and it was always a jovial occasion. I played for the Scholars team in my third year and after the match a friend, Jimmy Hemphill from Coleraine, suggested I accompany him to the Schools Cup Final at Ravenhill Grounds that afternoon.

We walked there from the Balmoral pitch and on the way there he proposed that we call into a local pub for a drink. I immediately agreed. I believe this was my first visit to a pub and the glass of Guinness I ordered was the only time throughout my college career that I had an alcoholic drink! Wisely, I didn't mention such a sinful practice to my mother. These were happy days and I really liked the football training and the matches. I enjoyed being part of the team.

Kings Scholars football team
Back row (from left): Jack McKinney, Stanley French, David Walker, Alex McKee, Jim McFerran, Jimmy Hemphill. Front row (from left): Bert Robinson, Andy McWilliams, Clive McKnight (captain), Derek Nash, Murray Lee

Initially I found the formal lectures at Stranmillis rather daunting. I had been used to small class groups in the upper forms of Ballyclare High School and the formal relationship between teacher and pupil in this arrangement. There, pupils were addressed by their surnames but at Stranmillis the students were called Mr or Miss and did not put their hands up to indicate that they knew answers! In fact such questions were seldom posed. Lectures often comprised fifty to one hundred students and, depending on the style of the lecturer, the pervading atmosphere in the lecture theatre could range from noisy disrespect through acceptable repartee to a studious silence amid furious note taking.

In some lectures there were men only while others had men and women. The mixed sex lectures often encouraged a particular type of male student to draw attention to himself by 'smart alec' exhibitionism.

We had tutorials with no more than a dozen or so students and, as with most things at Stranmillis, these were formed from the larger groups using the initial letters of our surnames. In this way I was often lucky to be with my friends Michael Millar and Frank Martin. This arrangement was meant to stimulate discussion on the subjects covered in the lectures and in this respect the tutorials worked well. They also tended to bond a group of students and I found this helpful not only in gaining a better understanding of the content but in gradually losing some of my shyness. The bonding was further reinforced when we started to visit schools on teaching practice when we were again grouped according to our surname initial.

I found the structure and content of the curriculum of my course at Stranmillis peculiar and surprising. Sometimes the traditional university format of lectures for large groups in a theatre was followed. One subject covered in this way was entitled Education. At first I found this term puzzling. The word 'education' in my experience was an abstract concept. When the lectures commenced I discovered that it actually dealt with theories of education from the past and present and there was a strong element of psychology running through the theme. There were sections devoted to how children developed –physically, intellectually and socially and the relevance of such development to the type of education they should receive. I found this really interesting and pitched at an academic level that required thought and gave one something to study and pursue in depth.

The other subjects I found challenging and properly pitched at university level were English and history. I felt that, in these subjects, students were expected to develop perspectives and achieve new insights into the material, then to respond thoughtfully. I enjoyed the tutorials where these ideas were explored and discussed in our small groups. Mr Dicker proved an interesting lecturer on constitutional history while Roy Hawthorne introduced a little bit of controversy on aspects of Irish history. This was the first time I had had any in-depth study of the history of Ireland.

Although Mr Coombe was the lecturer in mathematics I only remember his lectures and tutorials dealing with arithmetic. Perhaps this is because I found the methodical way he explained the rules and processes to deal with arithmetic 'problems' so easy to understand. I had recently come from sixth form lessons on calculus and co-ordinate geometry and had had no experience of arithmetic since my primary school days. I had always struggled with the 'hard sums' we were given there to prepare us for the Qualifying Examination. I knew that I might soon be faced with the challenge of teaching arithmetic to the challenging Qualifying Examination standard in my primary school career so Mr Coombe's expertise was welcome and timely. Balding and severe of countenance he had no time for frivolity and his lectures were well planned and formal – he was a true professional. He gave the appearance of a middle aged clergyman and it came as no surprise when I found out that he was indeed a lay preacher. I remember he visited one of the schools where I was on teaching practice and he was equally thorough here but helpful and much less severe in a one-to- one discussion with his students.

Dr Mussen, a lecturer in English, similarly adopted a novel approach to literature. I have cause to remember him well because on one occasion he read out part of one of my assignments as an example of the kind of response he felt the question required. Later in my school career I tried to keep in mind how much my self-esteem had been enhanced by Dr Mussen's remarks and I always endeavoured to be just as positive when marking pupils' writing assignments.

His colleague in the English Department, Mrs Nancy Kincaid, brought a sparkle to her lectures and her remarks to the men were occasionally a little daring – even risqué. She was usually dressed in a skirt much too short for her years, had a blue rinse in her hair and used layers of make-up. She tottered into lectures on very high-heels.

She was also different in her approach to lecturing and one never knew what she would say or do. I liked her because she brought something special to what could otherwise have been terribly dull lectures.

My good friend, Michael Millar, a staunch Baptist and typical, unsophisticated country lad, was asked during a study of one of the poems of John Donne to outline what he felt Donne was expressing in a particular love sonnet. Much too shy to be forthright, Michael hedged about the meaning of the situation avoiding any reference to the erotic language Donne had used and the experience the lovers in the poem were enjoying. Nancy listened patiently for a time then broke into Michael's comments remarking sharply: 'Oh for God's sake, man can you not see it's about a man in bed with a woman?' Michael was truly shocked, indeed he took some time to recover from Mrs Kincaid's blunt remark. He said to me afterwards: 'Jack, how could she be so coarse?'

Some subjects were unusual if understandable on a course for future teachers. I found Speech Training more than a little trying. The rather prim lady who took my section was called Miss Annesley and I admit that I struggled to achieve any rapport with her. Her colleague in the Speech Department, Miss Kitty Abraham, was an elderly lady with a very posh accent, renowned for a method she employed to enable students to understand how voice projection operated in the human body. She would select a student, always a good looking man, from her tutorial group and invite him to come forward to assist her in a demonstration. Next, with arms out and breathing deeply while annunciating a line of a poem, she would ask the assistant to feel her diaphragm as she spoke and describe its movement in her chest. This always caused sharp intakes of breath from students and led to most sliding well down in their seats to avoid becoming the next victim! There were lecturers at the college with whom this could have been a pleasurable experience but Miss Kitty Abraham was not one of them.

As part of the Speech Training course we were expected to compile a personal poetry anthology adding poems of our choice over the first year of study.

Generally rather soppy poems chosen for their emphasis on the qualities of sound rather than sense were preferred. Examples of popular choices included 'The Sea is a Hungry Dog' and 'How now, Brown Cow'. Fine poems, perhaps, but not exactly what one would normally associate with strapping, nineteen year old males most of whom would have preferred a verse or two of John Donne's erotic sonnets.

Many students, like myself, had similar difficulties with the music course, especially as it was mainly practical. The policy of the college was that elementary music lessons in schools could be led by a teacher using the recorder to accompany the children's singing – no special musical expertise was required. We were expected to purchase recorders and begin the supposedly easy task of gaining proficiency inside a year. This proved a vain hope in many cases including my own.

Eventually it turned to complete farce when the music practical exams in singing and playing the recorder took place at the end of our first year. Some of us were able to loiter about the corridor outside the examination rooms and could barely contain our laughter at what we heard coming from inside. The process was cringingly embarrassing for the poorer performers, especially in the knowledge that an audience, not entirely appreciative, had formed within earshot of their attempts to sing or play a simple melody. To say that there were some false notes would be a serious understatement. The star failure in these tests was undoubtedly Jimmy Kilpatrick, who treated the episode as an opportunity to play for laughs and the range of strange sounds he produced from falsetto to basso profundo in his singing was remarkable. I remember he began the recorder playing assessment by inserting the wrong end of the instrument into his mouth. By this stage of the year Jimmy had realised that teaching was not for him and that a different career would be the better option so he had nothing to lose by failing gloriously in his music oral. He later joined the RUC and I used to see him often doing traffic duty at Shaftesbury Square in Belfast. I am confident that he did not make it into the RUC band!

At the end of the first year we were given options for our future courses depending on the type of school we preferred to teach in eventually. I chose the three year A Course that focussed on the primary school sector. My choice was decided by two considerations. From my experiences on Teaching Practice I found that I enjoyed dealing with 10-11 year old children. I found it easier to establish rapport with pupils in the upper primary classes.

The B course, designed for secondary school teachers, was spread over four years with the extra year devoted to the study of a specialist subject. Only one of these subject areas appealed to me. For a time I liked the idea of choosing Physical Education but eventually settled for the general subjects of the primary course. I realised that the perilous state of my family's financial situation meant that the shorter three-year course was the sensible option.

An interesting implication of my choice occurred when, in 2001, I was considering retirement after 40 years' service. I found that by starting my teaching career one year earlier than my secondary school colleagues I could claim my full pension one year before them. But young students did not usually consider such practical implications of their choice of courses on future retirement plans.

It is significant that in my time it was Stranmillis 'Training' College, not yet a university college of Queens as it would later become, so quite properly an important element of all the courses was Teaching Practice. This really did give students a clear idea of what their chosen career would entail – the daunting experience of standing up in front of a class of children and performing.

The experience could prove rewarding or unsettling often swinging from one to the other according to many factors – the discipline in the particular school, the depth of preparation for the lesson or the mood of the student on a particular day. Some students found their inability to create rapport with children sufficiently difficult to lead them to terminate their course and seek a different career.
In my case I liked teaching practice sessions simply for providing a break in the daily college routine. We went out to assigned schools in small groups, often comprising the same students, and, perhaps because we were facing the challenge of teaching together, we bonded happily and shared our experiences, good and bad, together.

First year students went out to schools in the autumn term. With my close friend, Frank Martin, I visited Beechfield PS in East Belfast. This was then a large inner-city school and, with my primary school background in a rural school of less than a hundred pupils, it was an eye-opener. The discipline in the rooms and outside in the playground was strict and the cane was used frequently, mainly on the boys. Everything was formal and, while there was respect towards pupils by the staff I found the children a bit too submissive and lacking in sparkle. The curriculum, as in other schools at this time, was traditional and focussed on text books, most of which were really dull.

On this first teaching practice session our role was simply classroom observation. The lectures prior to this spell of teaching practice had set out criteria in areas where we were asked to look out for and note signs of the stages the children had reached in their physical, social and intellectual development – their general 'maturation' was the term used. We were expected to include the observation notes together with those from further teaching practice sessions within a Child Study File. This dossier would become part of the end-of-year assessment. I can't recall anything about my file but, as I struggled successfully through my first year, it must have passed muster.

Following a number of visits my confidence in front of a class improved and I even enjoyed some lessons. The crucial factor in this was the atmosphere prevailing in each school. I remember with affection a visit to Ballygolan PS in North Belfast. I arrived at the school on the Whitewell Road by trolley bus. I was always fond of travelling on these fast, silent vehicles so this was good start to my day in the school.

The principal, Mr Moon, true to his name, was a rotund, jolly little man. On our first day there he escorted the three students around the premises and we all laughed at the humorous comments he made on various sections of the building. He was in good form describing the staff toilet facilities. He was obviously enjoying himself and I must confess that in later years as a school principal I did a little bit of showing off myself to students on their practice sessions in my school.

In many respects students brought a breath of fresh air into a school with their youthful vigour and innovatory approach to teaching. The student lessons helped to break up the daily grind of the normal curriculum and students' presence in a normally stuffy staffroom made for lively lunch breaks.

This was the period when all good lessons had to be supported with an array of 'visual aids'. Students were to be seen struggling in to their practice schools burdened by an assortment of charts, pictures, models and similar paraphernalia.

Much of this had been made or arranged the night before the visit, the women were by far the most

'A' Course students relax just before the final exams in 1961. The author is on the far left of the back row. His close friends John Beatty, Ian Dixon and Frank Martin are also in the back row

diligent in such preparation, well – with the exception of my good friend, Frank Martin, who never failed to astound colleagues and Stranmillis lecturers with the range and intricacy of aids to accompany his lessons. It was no great surprise to most when, at the end of his final year, Frank was awarded the McMahon prize as the top student in the year group. No doubt the quality of his visual aids for lessons contributed to this merited honour.

The curriculum in primary schools in those days was generally pretty dull with an emphasis on the use of set text books in each subject. Class teachers usually were quite happy to hand over the lessons in what were often seen as the fancy subjects – geography, history, nature study and physical education – to students. These subjects lent themselves to illustration by charts and diagrams hence the heavy load of preparation required.

Some student lessons appeared again and again and one wonders whether the children became a bit fed up with repeated versions of 'The Life Cycle of The Frog' or 'Farming in Northern Ireland.' In this latter category the most original lesson I encountered was taken by my colleague, Jimmy Kilpatrick, in Eden PS in my first year. Jimmy was always a bit light on preparation and the only written material I ever remember him bringing to school was a copy of the Daily Express. A Stranmillis lecturer arrived one day and announced that he intended to sit in on each of our planned lessons. Jimmy was unfazed and, with typical ingenuity, borrowed a pint of milk from the staffroom and delivered a good lesson on milk production. If he had had any written preparation to show to the lecturer he might even have earned a decent grade. My visual aids were rudimentary. Life at home left little time for anything but basic preparation for my next day's lessons. Going to some of my practice schools on my bike made it difficult to carry large charts slung over my back or jam jars of tadpoles strung from the handlebars.

In the early 1960s technology in schools was basic. In many cases the most recent gadget to be introduced was the mechanical pencil sharpener! Film strips were occasionally employed to illustrate geography and nature study lessons but they were cumbersome and most classrooms were not equipped with black-out curtains to make their use effective. Radio was generally available in schools and the quality of the BBC programmes was often excellent but television and video support was still some way off in the future.

In the absence of such equipment and with the pressure from the formal Qualifying Examination increasing in the last few years of primary school, lessons tended to be mainly 'talk and chalk' with reliance on some very dreary text books.

It was interesting to see the difference in pupils' experiences and the variety of teaching styles in the schools I visited as a student teacher.

I remember the beautiful handwriting, excellent discipline and the high academic standards in Skegoneill PS on Belfast's Antrim Road. The difficult social backgrounds of the children and the efforts of the teachers to surmount these impressed me in Edenderry PS just off the Crumlin Road in Belfast.

The school where I really got my teeth into the job of teaching was in Downey House Preparatory School on Belfast's Ravenhill Road. On my first morning there the Principal, Mr Fred Jeffrey, another jolly but astute eccentric, explained that a P5 teacher would be absent for the week I was due to be in her class and he asked me if I would consider taking over on my own for this week. I jumped at the chance!

Most students hated to teach lessons with the class teacher sitting 'on watch' in the back of the room or a Stranmillis lecturer trying to make himself invisible while taking notes on the student's performance. Here in Downey House I would have a whole five days to do things my own way and assess my performance. Marvellous!

The pupils were well-behaved and the class benefited from excellent planning and organisation from their teacher so this made my task much easier.

A good part of the work was pure routine, especially in English and maths, and my prepared 'fancy' lessons could be slotted in each day quite naturally. What I really enjoyed, though, was just talking to the children and thereby developing strategies, for example in questioning and allowing them to respond naturally without being overwhelmed by their eagerness to shout out answers. Achieving such control, even partially, proved to be a milestone in my development as a competent primary school teacher.

The school was set in expansive grounds and it was cricket season. I had a tremendous time taking the senior boys for cricket on their perfect wickets. This week was certainly the best teaching experience I had enjoyed since the start of my course at Stranmillis.

The third year of my course at college differed from the first two in that the whole of the spring term was taken up with teaching practice. We spent six weeks in each of two primary schools selected specially to be close to our homes. The idea, and it was a good one, was to give the student a long spell in one school where it was possible to get to know the pupils and staff well and feel a part of the establishment. In this way there was a better chance that we would teach lessons which dovetailed into the school curriculum and benefited the class teacher and the pupils.

When students returned to college for the summer term there was little time before we sat our final exams in June.

A fair bit of the timetable concerned general revision of the subjects covered on the three years of our course. We were also allotted time to complete and polish up our course work projects.

At the beginning of my final year I had no idea of the events which would make my last few weeks at Stranmillis almost as traumatic as those of my first term.

In my second year, and especially in my third year, the three-year primary schools' course students had many more tutorials together so we did get to know each other well. I even joined in the informal group discussions and almost became a normal student. In addition to Frank Martin, John Beatty, also on our course, became a close friend and joined in with Frank and myself at breaks and lunch times. This lasted until the end of our college careers.

There were only nine men completing the primary school course in 1961 so we all mixed in well together. This was in stark contrast to the four-year secondary schools' course where the groups were very much larger.

We all joined up for Education lectures, the relevance of which I now understood and enjoyed. The outstanding Education lecturer in my opinion was Mr Cameron, affectionately known to all as 'Bud'. In addition to explaining educational theory and psychology he gave some very sound, practical advice when he visited students in schools. Other Education lecturers, didn't have such charisma.

We had other sessions, they did not deserve to be called lectures or tutorials, that were not so effective in preparing us for teaching in primary schools. Art and Craft practical sessions proved particularly useful in honing skills that we could employ in our future teaching experience. The lecturer was friendly and approachable, but we were left a bit too much to our own devices in finishing the projects we pursued. Never a great artist or maker of models, I remember fiddling about with paint, paste, paper and cardboard but I cannot recall any project I carried out to completion. The problem arose when, at the end of the sessions in June, large squares were marked out on the Art Room floor where students were asked to display their finished creations for assessment. Frank Martin, of course, had supplemented his work during the sessions with many hours at home putting the finishing touches to what could only be described as spectacular models. He lived close to the Ulster Creameries Dairy and managed to obtain a large quantity of wooden lollypop sticks from a sympathetic manager. These formed the basis of several complicated models which he embellished with a masterly touch. His whole display was a sight to behold and his only problem was that the square he had been allocated was nowhere near large enough to display all his wondrous works. I came up with a solution by offering him space in my pitifully empty square.

In those days, craft lessons in primary schools were segregated – Handwork for boys and Needlework for girls. The women teachers seemed to have no problem coming up with enough knitting and needlecraft ideas to engage girls over a whole school year. While much of this work was repetitive and dull, the boys' handwork tasks were often not very creative. In my own primary school days I had been taught to knit and, while I think it had disappeared by the time I was teaching, another standby for boys' handwork periods certainly remained popular. This involved weaving strands of raffia on to a stringed cardboard base to produce a mat for a hotplate. As a change, four nails were driven into spent spools of thread and waste wool was twisted around the nails and down through the middle hole in the spool to become a woollen rope. Eventually these were long enough to be entwined on to cardboard mats to produce – hot plate mats.

These lessons were boring and often made worse when the teacher expected it all to be done in strict silence. It must have seemed like the school version of picking oakum.

Another weekly session we endured in our last two years of Craft included a topic called Toy Making. This took place in a workshop in the main college building. The lecturer was fondly known to all as 'Diesel'. The workshop was his den because he hardly ever seemed to leave it. He introduced us – I'm fairly sure it was men only on the sessions – to the useful art of making wooden toys. I presume that the relevance of this seemingly peripheral skill was that we could introduce this skill to craft lessons in our future primary schools. His attention was not always focussed on how we were progressing on these assignments because he often sidled off to a section of the workshop where he was constructing a large boat. He was an ex-navy man with a passionate interest in the sea and I always felt that, while he needed the job at the college, he considered the work he could squeeze in on his boat-building a greater priority than helping reluctant toymakers.

Our sessions fortunately, or perhaps unfortunately for maintaining a work ethic, were on a Friday afternoon. On a fine day there was a fearful temptation to register and then slip out and spend the time walking along the Lagan towpath, no more than a few hundred yards from the boat and toy workshop. I joined the escapees a number of times and there never seemed to be any questions asked about our absence. The fact that I joined the escapees demonstrates how I had changed over the three years from a shy introvert to one who was daring enough to break college rules with impunity.

Stranmillis College was bordered by an open area of trees and shrubs and I remember one science lecturer, Mr Bob Carlisle, using it to demonstrate to students how such a natural resource could be used in nature study lessons.

There was at least one badger sett inside this little wood and a large variety of trees and flora. Mr Carlisle was an interesting lecturer and got on very well with the small groups he led around the wood. Jimmy Kilpatrick, typically, used to run off at random in the wood and suddenly appear making animal noises from behind the trees.

Often Mr Carlisle's lectures focussed on specimens he had collected in the neighbourhood. I remember on one occasion we arrived in his laboratory and he was in the process of dissecting an otter. This became the basis of a fascinating demonstration although there was never any question that we would carry out such an exercise in a classroom.

I was fortunate that the first of my two long spells of third-year teaching practice was in Doagh Primary School. I could travel the five miles from home to the school on my bicycle and setting off on a bright winter morning was very pleasant.

This was easily the best experience of teaching I enjoyed over my three years at Stranmillis. The ethos of the school was caring and the atmosphere friendly while the pace of life there reflected that of the quiet, rural village. I sensed that I was making a useful contribution to the curriculum. The pupils were delightful – not shy and they were actually keen to talk to me. I could detect what I can best describe as a country innocence in their manner. They spoke with the accent and idiom of the Ulster-Scots dialect and I felt at home immediately.

The members of staff were helpful in a practical way and I picked up a variety of strategies on how to engage children in the subjects I taught. By this stage of my career I had learned how to gauge the ambience of a school, something one picked up almost by instinct. In Doagh I felt immediately at home and, not as often happened as a student, a different species from the regular teachers. The principal, Mr Cecil Kane was lively, witty in his remarks to children and staff and a very good class teacher. I benefited from being his student for three weeks. Last period on Friday afternoons I remember enjoying football games in the playground where he played with one group of senior boys and I joined in with the other. They were quite rough and I began to understand how Parkview, the local hockey team, had earned its reputation for robust play.

In the school with me was a woman student and I must confess that I had seen her at college and been attracted to her from a distance. In our free time in Doagh we engaged in what I judged as friendly conversation. Looking back now I reckon I might have had a decent chance of meeting in more congenial conditions if I had pursued the matter but, true to form, I missed the opportunity and once back in college we never met again. The dalliance, though, added to the allure of my happy time in Doagh.

On the last day of my spell in the school I said my farewells to the staff and made my way out to my bicycle in the playground. Attached to the seat of the bike was a charming note from some of the senior girls. I must have brought a bit of sunshine into their lives at least. Now if the note had been from my fellow woman student I would have been much more excited!

I had enjoyed my time in Doagh but my time at Kings Park PS in Newtownabbey proved very different. I was able to cycle to the school or take the bus so it was convenient but the set up was very different from what I had experienced at Doagh. I found this change difficult. The school was quite new and the buildings, grounds and the facilities were excellent. My problem stemmed from the management style of the principal. He had come to the school from a preparatory school and he ran Kings Park along the lines of such an establishment. Unlike other primary schools I had visited, the school day for P4 –P7 classes was divided into half- hour periods. Teachers were expected to change lessons when the bell rang. There were double periods but this system seemed to obstruct the degree of flexibility that was a positive feature of the traditional primary school curriculum.

The principal promoted a rather unusual approach to creative writing. From P4 there were lots of exercises for the pupils in joining sentences together using rather dull text books with little opportunities offered for free choice story writing.

The first class I was assigned to was a Primary 4. The teacher was co-operative and helpful in planning my lessons but I found it difficult to relate to this young age group. Throughout my teaching career I did not really enjoy working with year groups below P5. I was always much happier with the older children in P6 or P7.

I found the principal an eccentric figure and not easily approachable – his relations with his staff and certainly with students always appeared very formal. After a few days in the school I tended to avoid contact with him. He was very definitely not the type to join in Friday afternoon football matches with the senior boys.

In this respect I got off to a bad start with him. He called me into his office not long after I started my practice to tell me off for riding my bicycle across the playground. He was perfectly right to do this but somehow the manner in which he did so left a sour taste in my mouth.

As far as I can recall there were no other students with me in Kings Park and I took my packed lunch in the classroom at the midday break. In Doagh I had always managed to find a bottle of school milk to drink with my packed lunch. There were always plenty left over after this had been distributed to the children at morning break. Not long after I started in Kings Park I asked Mr Miller, the caretaker, if there happened to be any spare bottles that I could have with my lunch. He was taken aback and told me that the school had a strict rule that milk was not to be consumed by staff. Mr Miller was a really pleasant man and I remember talking to him often about the neighbourhood and the people we both knew from the district. I was having my lunch one day when there was a knock on the classroom door. There stood Mr Miller with a little brown paper bag in his hand. Inside was a bottle of milk and he pressed it on me with the instruction not to let anyone see or hear about his little present. From that day he somehow managed to bring me a daily bottle of milk for my lunch, always concealed in a brown paper bag! He was a proper gentleman and when my practice in the school

was over I waved a fond farewell to 'my milkman' as I carefully wheeled my bike across the playground for the last time..
Before I finished my practice in Kings Park School the principal told me that a teaching post in the school would be advertised sometime in the summer term. He also said that it would be a good opening for an enthusiastic young man and I do believe that he was inviting me to consider applying for the post. I did not need to think over this matter for long before deciding not to apply.

I returned to Stranmillis College following the six-week teaching practice just before Easter 1961. This, I hoped, would be my last term at the college. As things turned out it was to prove anything but a happy time for me.

One Saturday afternoon during the Easter break I was playing in a football match for local club, Mossley Young Men, when I injured my right knee. The joint jammed and I found it impossible to walk. A cartilage had been displaced. There followed a difficult period when attempts to straighten the leg under anaesthetic in the Casualty Department at the Royal Victoria Hospital failed. After a few weeks at home unable to attend college I was fortunate to be admitted to this hospital for surgery to remove the damaged cartilage. I made a speedy recovery from the operation and made it back to college by mid-May.

My final exams were due to be taken in June and I had an interview with Mr Keith the principal to discuss my situation. According to him I could forego the exams and return to the college to repeat my third year's study from September. My grant would be available under my unfortunate circumstances, he thought. Alternatively I could opt to take the exams but if I failed I would not be eligible for a grant to repeat my third year.

Deep down I realised that I really did not have a choice. Our finances at home were stretched to the limit and another year spent at college with no teacher's income from me would have put an unbearable strain on the family finances.

So I gambled and I won. I passed the exams, failing only in Toymaking but I expected that result. I had gained a certificate to teach and there were congratulations mixed with relief from all the family at Ballyearl.

From Easter 1961, lists of teaching appointments appeared regularly in the press. This was a boom time for prospective applicants for teaching posts especially in schools in the new housing estates then being built in the suburbs around Belfast. Many of my colleagues were sending off applications. I was held back from this on two counts.

In the first instance my period in hospital and the subsequent time I had spent at home recovering from the surgery presented an obstacle. Even when I became reasonably mobile and went back to college I found I was not fully aware of teaching appointment procedures. Another consideration held me back. The practice of interviewing candidates for teaching posts then was uncommon. Instead the applicants were expected to canvas members of the school management committee, usually in their homes. If this visit was not undertaken the applicant was seldom considered for the position. I hated this procedure and steadfastly refused to canvas for a post. I did apply for a few jobs that were advertised but I had a good idea that my applications would not succeed.

There are few things that I have done in my career that I am so proud of as my refusal to engage in this iniquitous canvassing. I heard stories regularly of colleagues who made visits to members of school committees involving journeys deep into the country and up long lanes often to be greeted there by savage dogs before being interviewed cursorily on the doorstep by a rather pompous committee member. Such visits were not unusual and the indifference and general nosiness experienced certainly did nothing for the dignity of the applicants or the teaching profession.

The Stranmillis graduation ceremony was held late in June but I did not attend. Instead I received my teaching certificate in the post. I could, of course, have gone there with my mother and I am not entirely sure now why this did not happen.

There is no doubt that my mother was proud of my achievement, especially in the light of the many trying times and difficulties we had encountered together over the three years, but she was never one for formal occasions. I did not express a strong desire to go to the Sir William Whitla Hall at Queens University for the ceremony.

In the end it wasn't an important decision for us and we carried on with keeping the wolf from the door at Ballyearl until the really big day arrived when my first pay cheque as a professional teacher would be paid into our bank account.

In June 1961 there was, sadly, no sign that this would happen soon or, indeed if I would ever find employment in a primary school.

Frank Martin was a student at Stranmillis Training College from 1958 to 1961

When I completed my education at Sullivan Upper School I applied for a job in the Civil Service. This was successful and I worked in the Local Government Branch. However, having experienced work with young boys in the Boys Brigade, I had this strong desire to teach. I applied for a place in Stranmillis Training College and although I was only nineteen years of age I was interviewed as a 'mature student'. I was delighted when I received an offer of a place in the College.

College was an extension of school but without uniform and in most cases the lectures were less formal. The Education Department lectures on Child Development were extremely interesting. As part of the course we had to compile a Child Study File based on our experiences during visits to schools. Sessions on Nature Study were mainly practical. Mr Bob Carlisle would often lead us around the extensive grounds of the college or along the Lagan towpath. The object of these exercises was to collect specimens of wild life. Speech and Drama lectures were of great interest to me as I had played a number of roles in school productions. One task was to select poems suitable to different age groups for inclusion in an Anthology of Poetry. I used these poems many times with the classes I taught on teaching Practice.

All other subjects were equally enjoyable with the exception of music! Singing is not my forte and my recorder playing could only be described as abysmal! At the end of the first year we were required to play a tune on the recorder and sing a song for the practical tests. As I expected, and to my great delight, I did not pass these tests and was allowed to select a second craft activity. In these practical classes I made several items including a wooden 'Woodpecker Door Knocker' which my nephews enjoyed using several years later. However my 'piece de resistance' was the construction of a large castle using lollipop sticks and UHU glue!

I had been looking forward to my first Teaching Practice session which was in Beechfield Primary School in East Belfast. The group included my very good friend, Jack McKinney and also Michael Millar and William Mc Sparran. As we entered the school gates on the first morning we were greeted with a loud roar from the children "Students! Students!". I think they were happy to see us! We were encouraged to use visual aids with our lessons and I remember travelling on a bus to Skegoniel Primary School carrying a stuffed owl which I had borrowed from the Ulster Museum. My most memorable practice was in Braniel Primary School in the Castlereagh area of East Belfast. This was a relatively new school still in the course of construction.

The principal was also a class teacher and I was assigned to his class. As he had to attend to a number of management issues during the day I was left on my own with the class for long periods. This gave me an opportunity to have rapport with the class and to teach more lessons than normal. It was a great experience. My third year 'six-week long' practice was in Carr Primary School, Drumbo which was a small school of principal and two assistant teachers. I spent the first part of the practice with the P3/4 class after which I was moved to the P4/5/7 group taught by the principal. He had undertaken a short post war course in teacher training and his views on many areas of the curriculum differed greatly from those presented to us at college. I was somewhat surprised and indeed horrified when he told me to prepare a series of lessons on 'The Growth of the City of London'.

After Easter we were back in college for the final term examinations and hopefully graduation. During this time teaching posts were advertised in the local press and I applied for one in Dundonald, a large primary school of over 800 pupils. I was both delighted and relieved when I was appointed. During the summer months I thought about the class for which I would have responsibility in September. It was exciting. I was now a teacher!

Chapter 12: A Novice at the Chalk Face

In June 1961 I received a letter telling me that I had passed my final exams at Stranmillis Training College. I had already sent off job applications for a position in a number of schools throughout Northern Ireland. The only one I remember now was to the Armstrong Primary School in Armagh. This, like the others I sent, was unsuccessful.

By the middle of August I was no nearer to securing a position and was becoming fed up with the process and desperate. One day a neighbour in Ballyearl, Mrs Rosemary Martin, suggested that I contact Mr Kennedy, principal of Abbots Cross P.S. She was an assistant teacher there and knew that in this growing school Mr Kennedy always used a number of temporary substitutes. Each year late in August, with the large Rathcoole Estate in the course of development close to the school, he was sure to find a queue of parents who had moved into the Rathcoole houses during the summer waiting to have their children enrolled for the Autumn term.

Consequently, at this late stage he was often looking for temporary teachers to deal with the influx. I gave him a call and he invited me to the school to talk to me and, I'm sure, to sound me out as a prospective teacher.

I hadn't had any experience of such an interview but I told him about my background and school and college experience. I did mention that I had done my last teaching practice, a six week spell, in a neighbouring school – Kings Park P.S. He seemed especially interested in this and said that he was aware that the school had recently advertised for a teacher. Had I applied for this position, he asked pointedly? I was perfectly frank. I told him that the principal, had asked me to apply but I declined because there was something about the ethos and atmosphere of this school which I found disconcerting and I knew I would not fit in there easily.

In my innocence I did not realise that the view I had expressed on Kings Park school clinched the job for me and there and then I was offered a temporary post in Abbots Cross starting around August 28, two days after my 21st birthday. I was unaware at the time that the naive expression of my views on Kings Park school, in the light of the rivalry existing between the two competing schools, had proved the deciding factor in Mr Kennedy's decision to offer me a position.

I was too delighted to ask Mr Kennedy about the class I would be assigned to and other details of my duties in the school. I walked out of the building on air and I rode my bicycle back up the Doagh Road driven by pure exhilaration knowing that there would be great rejoicing in Ballyearl when the news reached the McKinney household.

Abbots Cross Garden Village was a different and attractive development of houses and shops that had been built in the early 1950s. I was familiar with Abbots Cross because it was on the 156 bus route from Mossley to Belfast. Other Garden Villages had been built nearby at Fernagh and Merville and the distinctive, flat roofed properties were popular with young families.

Abbots Cross Primary school had opened in 1955 to cater for the children from this development. It consisted of prefabricated buildings supplied by Short Brothers and Harland, the wartime aeroplane constructors from Belfast. These were meant to provide temporary accommodation but the buildings, supplemented from time to time by a variety of temporary, wooden classrooms, remained in use until 1996.

When I began to teach there in 1961 the huge Rathcoole Housing Estate was continuing to be developed directly behind the school. This was soon to become the largest estate of its kind in the United Kingdom and, as the new residents were mainly newly married couples, children continued to pour into the school from the estate for many years. In 1961 the enrolment stood at just under 1200 making it one of the largest primary schools in County Antrim.

Aluminium houses – similar to the school, prefabs they were called – already existed along the southern boundary of the school. This street was called Rural Avenue and housed residents many of whom were from families in other neighbouring estates. The area was soon to lose its rural nature.

When I started at Abbots Cross there was a serious lack of accommodation in the main school and four classrooms in Whiteabbey Primary School and two others in the former Whiteabbey Technical School were in use as annexes. Pupils and teachers were transported each day to and from the annexes in three double-decker buses.

My first class assignment was through this arrangement and, after parking my bicycle in the shelters, I travelled down on one of the two double-decker buses to Whiteabbey Primary School.

Mr Kennedy, the principal, would pass messages to the teachers from his window as we went on our way down the path to the bus. Usually, Charlie McAuley, a senior teacher, acted as the person who received these and later passed the news on to the other three staff when we reached Whiteabbey Primary School. I thought it was a most unusual system of communication for a school staff. I was moved from the Whiteabbey annexe to the main school in April 1962. It was only then that I began to meet and get to know others on the large staff. Up until then I had difficulty distinguishing between the caretaker and teachers.

Mr J A Kennedy, Principal

I was in the Whiteabbey Primary School classroom until Easter 1962 and approaching the end of my first year's teaching service. I was rather unsettled but I got a lot of support from my colleagues. I have few memories of this time but a couple of things do stand out.

The classes in Abbots Cross were rigidly streamed by ability. In those days the class size was often over 40. Because of the transport difficulties I think the class sizes in the Whiteabbey annexe were under 40 but I did have a class of 48 while teaching in the main school. In Abbots Cross, with the constant enrolment of new pupils from the new housing developments in the area in the 1960s, it was always likely that the classes would be large. All our requisites had to be brought down on the buses with us to Whiteabbey and this obviously limited our resources.

We had few dealings with the principal there but I remember on wet lunch breaks he paraded all the senior children into the Assembly Hall and sat on a chair in the middle of the noisy throng playing his accordion. The children ran about and played – a bit like the Sunday School parties I remembered from Carnmoney Church – totally oblivious to the Scottish jigs and reels from their headmaster. Some years later when I was an established teacher in the main school Mr Kennedy told me that the Whiteabbey principal had held a low opinion of my performance as a teacher. I was then much more concerned about what James A. Kennedy thought of my proficiency as a class teacher. I was sure he had confidence in me from the promotion I quickly gained as I moved through the ranks in the school.

Occasionally my colleague Charlie McAuley felt obliged to follow the principal's example when he was on wet day duty in the hall. I think Charlie's abiding motto was 'Anything for a quiet life.' He played the piano in the hall and to much better effect. I discovered that he played regularly in a dance band in his spare time and had a better idea of how to produce the kind of music appreciated by his audience. A bit of excess noise did not disturb Charlie's natural calm.

The Head of Infants in Whiteabbey School, as she was titled then, was tall, grey-haired, very old fashioned and terribly formal in her teaching style. She often told her P1 class to 'go to sleep'. In this mode, with their heads flat on the desks and perfectly silent, she took some repose or the opportunity to do some chore at her desk. Another teacher was almost as formal and taught the middle or senior age range. She came from Ballyclare where her mother ran a small sweetie shop opposite the High School. I had been a regular customer there when I attended this school.

An elderly teacher of the senior classes was a dedicated musician who looked after the school orchestra and tutored the instrumentalists during his breaks and dinner times. He only appeared in the staffroom to fetch his cup of tea. He looked old to me but was probably in his fifties. He was slightly stooped and balding and wore his hair in a 'comb-over' style. He appeared shy and his rather serious demeanour reminded me of that of an elderly clergyman. He was rather eccentric, perhaps not surprising considering his obsession with music. I liked him, even though he was inclined to keep himself to himself and he was popular with his pupils. He taught me one very important lesson. His classroom was next to the staffroom. One afternoon I was passing along the corridor as the children were lining up outside his room waiting for his permission to enter. A number of the old fashioned, double desks had been stacked up against the wall and, as the class entered, I heard a bit of a commotion. A boy at the rear of the column must have tampered with the desks and one had slid down against him. He was alarmed rather than injured and I watched dumbfounded as Mr Gribben set about him, gently cuffing him with his copy of The New First Aid in English and berating him for, as he put it, his dangerous action. Later in the day he approached and told me that I was probably surprised at his treatment of the boy. He explained that he had recognised that the boy might have suffered a nasty injury from the heavy desk. He realised that this would have been entirely due to the inappropriate way the desks had been piled up there by the caretaker. He felt it was his duty to punish the boy to emphasise to him that the bump he had sustained had been entirely his fault, leaving him in no doubt that the school was blameless. I did admire his strategy and foresight even if I did feel the punishment a trifle harsh.

I clearly recall most of the other teachers who accompanied me down to Whiteabbey in that first term. Charlie McAuley was really my mentor but quickly became a friend. His unflappable manner in facing difficulties and his abiding humour were exactly right for a young, idealistic fellow who needed this kind of balance in dealing with the inevitable challenges of his first job. He often took me into Belfast after school in his little Ford Popular car and his casual conversation and commentary on the events of the day was hilarious. Such flippancy and his easy going attitude did a lot to help me keep any worries I had about teaching my class to a satisfactory level. A good laugh at the end of a trying day was the medicine I needed to remain on an even keel.

Sheila Fulton taught a P4 class next door to mine and was a sun worshipper. I vividly remember how, as soon as a blink of sun appeared, she had her shoulder, and sometimes a bit more, stuck out of the classroom window to catch every ray. She spent sunny lunchtimes in a chair out in the grounds, totally engrossed in her worship. Elizabeth Thompson worked here for at least part of the two terms I spent there and I knew her from Carnmoney Church where she was a fellow member of the Dramatic Society. I even got a bit sweet on her as a result of our association at the school and spent an occasional Sunday night after church service cuddling her in the back seat of her brother's car. He was always there at the time so the back seat affair soon withered on the vine.

I always felt that my P5 class in Whiteabbey was special being the first children I had ever taught. I got on very well with them all and I remember some names and personalities. Like the majority of the children I met in Abbots Cross they proved very responsive to attention and were extremely loyal, even affectionate and ever so co-operative in their dealings with me. I can picture a squat little girl, Patricia, rather sad at times and her bosom pal Ray, small and with a bow in her hair, usually wearing plimsoles. This pair often set each other off into fits of giggles.

There was Bill complete with a short crew cut hair style like that of an US Marine of this period. His older brother, Jim, was in Charlie McAuley's P7 class and obviously suffered serious learning and emotional difficulties. His behaviour was often strange and it never failed to amaze me how Charlie managed him so well and kept him occupied in class. Jim was confined to the lower deck of the bus to and from Whiteabbey on Charlie's orders. Previously he had sat upstairs with the other older boys but Charlie discovered from some of these boys that Jim's favourite trick was trying to extract liquid from the fire extinguisher by sucking it feverishly. After this incident Charlie always kept Jim close beside himself in the bus!

Quite recently I was approached in a local shopping centre by a middle-aged lady. This turned out to be a girl who I remembered as a tallish, shy pupil in one of my classes. She proudly told me that she had enjoyed a successful career in a solicitor's office. She had done very well to obtain and hold down such a position. I could have recognised her hidden talents at primary school. I was to meet Ian from another class when I served many years later as a parent governor in Ballyclare High School. He was interviewed and appointed as the school caretaker.

One of the cleverest pupil I remember was Gerald a neat, wee fellow, very alert and good at all his work. He soon became my 'right hand man' for all those low responsibility jobs that pupils love doing and are such a help to a teacher. He was exactly what I needed – a bright spark to lighten my life.

This situation was to change dramatically after the Easter holiday. Mr Kennedy assigned me to a P7 class in the main school. This proved a greater challenge than I could ever have imagined. By then the P7A stream had finished their work for the Qualifying Examination, the procedure used to determine the secondary level schools P7 children in primary school would attend. The exam had passed and they were 'freewheeling' until the end of their time at the school. They had been granted a few privileges including the freedom to spend a part of the day reading comics and generally relaxing. My role was to keep them busy and on a tight disciplinary rein until the end of June.

The A streams in Abbots Cross consisted of very bright and confident pupils and you had to be up very early in the morning to match their demands. This particular class contained Mr Kennedy's daughter and the son of Mrs Davison, soon to become Vice – Principal of the school.

I am convinced that I was given the class to demonstrate what I could do with this lively but sometimes unruly bunch. It was essentially a test of my teaching potential. I must have impressed because soon after I found my star was on the rise. I got on well with the class and, having decided to withdraw the comics for a week or two and resort to a bit of dull formal work, they discovered I was not an easy touch and buckled down, if not pleasantly but with resignation. In the end they proved a marvellous lot and we soon settled down to a series of projects at which they excelled. I also used the carrot of the abandonment of homework and this was a smart move that they appreciated. It only took a promise from me to include frequent rounders games on the timetable to gain their full co-operation.

Abbots Cross PS staff, c.1970
Back row (from left): Unknown, Rosemary Martin, Joyce Hunter, Joan McKinney, Zelda Wilson, Olive McMaster, Ida Littlewood, June Spiers Mavis Bell, Patricia Davidson, Ray Morgan, Ken Ruddock.
Front row (from left): Tom Adair, Desmond Ervine, Eileen Cairns, Paul Hutchinson, Joan Hutton, Jack McKinney, Mr James A Kennedy (Principal), Mrs Elsie Davison (Vice-Principal), Grace McKinstry, Eva Hall, Clarke Frampton, Sarah McIvor, Stewart McKinney

When I moved up to one of the ' hut type' extension classrooms ranged around the playground of the main school I began to meet and get to know many more members of staff than I had when based in Whiteabbey P.S. At this period there was usually a big turnover in the staff of the school – temporary and permanent – every year. This was a continuing feature of the school and I welcomed the new members as they arrived, often fresh from college. There was always a great sense of camaraderie and then I was one of the 'young' set.

I remember many of the teachers from my early days on the staff. Over the years there were some very distinctive characters.

There was Bert Colvin who taught in Extension 5, my eventual classroom base with a P6 class. He came from Ballyclare and, I think, emigrated to Australia soon after I moved to the main school. Wee Mrs Press, whose husband taught in the School for the Blind at Jordanstown, always carried a large granny – type leather bag with a metal rod handle in which she kept her knitting for the lunch break.

Mrs Glendinning looked after the tea for the staff. This was carried round by two senior girls – no thoughts of health and safety then! I think she came to the school having taught with Mr Kennedy in Glenwood Intermediate School in Belfast. I didn't have many dealings with Mr Wray, the Vice-Principal, but I remember he often took his lunch on foot in the dinner hall or in the playground. He told me this was an 'al fresco' lunch. I had no idea what this meant. He played up a bit to the senior girls who flocked round him. I knew that he used the cane but never on the girls.

Norman Priestley and Lindy Reid, another Ballyclare recruit, taught in a temporary building, a Nissen hut, in the grounds of the Congregational Church over the hedge behind the bicycle shelters. They sometimes had to set up the desks in the morning after their use by the church organisations the previous night. It was rumoured that Mr Priestley organised a game of British Bulldogs before formal lessons began – perhaps to warm the children up.

Accommodation was scarce and the dinner hall was used as a classroom with more than one class often based there. A very old lady, Miss McDowell, had her P3 class disrupted twice daily to allow the dinner ladies to set up and put away the tables for meals. I remember her as a friendly soul, frail and seemingly old enough to have earned a quieter time out at grass. A young teacher, Billy McCarroll, joked that if she passed on while in service she would be laid out in state in the dinner hall.

Miss McDowell's successor in the dinner hall for a time was Mr John White from Ballyclare who came to us having been made redundant elsewhere. He was a tall, quiet and inoffensive fellow and readily accepted his position with his P3 class and the disruption from the meals arrangement with quiet, good nature. He could have spent half an hour in conversation with me telling me how he had had his hair cut in Herbie Boyd's Barber Shop in Ballyclare at the weekend. He eventually transferred to Glengormley Primary School where he joined the little band of confirmed bachelors on the staff. Mr Kennedy, in the days before he took to playing golf there, often expressed his view that nothing good had ever come out of Ballyclare. I didn't mention that my mother had lived there before her marriage.

And then there was Gerald Meighan about whose characteristics and eccentric exploits a book could be written! He had been at Ballyclare High School when I was there though he was older than me by a few years. This fact meant that he went out of his way to befriend me. He did not make friends easily. For my part I refrained from becoming too familiar with him realising that his colourful life style was not to my taste. He expected favours, though. One day just after my brother and I had bought a little car, he persuaded me to drop him off at his house on my way home. He stressed that it would not be too far out of my way. Only when we had got underway did I discover that he lived in Straidhavern near Crumlin – a long way from Mossley and certainly not on my usual route!

Somewhat quick tempered, Gerry was always getting into arguments and scrapes with anyone who disagreed with his bizarre opinions. His 'extracurricular activities' in the evenings often conflicted with the responsibilities of a teacher. Nevertheless, while colourful, he was hardworking, conscientious and popular with his pupils.

Mr Kennedy got him out of trouble on at least one occasion when certain lady friends tracked him down to the school and tried to visit him. Once he was spared this embarrassment by being driven out of the school gate crouching down in the back seat of Mr Kennedy's car. More than once he came to school with a black eye and he gave us a colourful account of what had happened to him the previous night.

When he arrived in school he usually started the day off by drinking a bottle of the school milk – to settle the stomach, he said. This was when he wasn't late. Like some other teachers he caught the bus from Belfast to the school, arriving just before the school opened at 9.25am. Typically, Gerry missed the bus quite often but he was expert in cadging a lift out to Abbots Cross in a variety of vehicles. On one occasion he arrived in a coal lorry. On such mornings he would be seen hurrying up the path past Mr Kennedy's office, briefcase in hand and his coat tails flying out behind him in the wind. Mr Kennedy was always amazed at the range of excuses Gerry told him as the cause of his lateness.

His special responsibilities included daily duty in the dinner hall. One day he was patrolling the aisles between the tables when a boy approached him down the aisle with a plate rather too well filled with custard. As he drew level with Gerry another boy sitting close to the aisle raised his hand to ask Gerry a question. The plate of custard was instantly propelled by the boy's hand upwards in an arc to descend on Gerry's shoulder covering him with custard. He was always a natty dresser and was understandably upset at the state of his jacket but what really made him blow his top was Mr Kennedy's calm and tongue-in-cheek response to Gerry's predicament in telling him that he badly needed a wife to help him cope with such incidents.

I assisted Gerry Meighan in forming a football team and we had immediate success, remaining unbeaten in our first season in the local primary schools' league. We had no pitch for practice matches except the piece of green common in front of the houses of the Rathcoole estate. The difficulty of holding matches here was that play was regularly interrupted by ladies carrying bags of shopping across the pitch to their homes from the shops at Abbots Cross. Sometimes we played important matches at Macedon, the Dr Barnardo's Home on the Shore Road. We got to the final of the cup that year but Mr Kennedy withdrew the team when a teacher in a Carrickfergus school, made a terrible mess of the arrangements for this important game.

Our first match came before we had time to arrange a proper trial. Gerry's method of picking the team was unusual. He went round the senior classes selecting only those P7 Boys whose fathers played football regularly. This proved surprisingly effective and we only had to change a name or two during the whole of the first successful season. We had many fine players and at left back was Alan Green, the former celebrity radio commentator on English Premier League football matches with the BBC.

Abbots Cross PS trophy winning football team, 1960s
Back row (from left): Mr P Hutchinson, Jackie Vance, Richard Joss, Mr JA Kennedy (Principal), Wesley Currie, Alex Bothwell, Jim Richmond, Mr J McKinney. Front row (from left): John Corbett, Harry Gannon, Jim Scarborough, Stanley McKnight (Captain), Ivan Moore, John Brown

Gerry eventually met his match when Isaac Kerr joined the staff. They were direct opposites in their temperaments and approach to authority. Isaac Kerr kept to the rules in every detail and was utterly pedantic. Gerry liked to think of himself as above the rules, as a bohemian who would retain his individuality at any cost even when it brought him into conflict with colleagues and superiors. The difference between their temperaments was seen to best effect in the attitude of each to the completion of the monthly curriculum progress report. This was a book where each teacher was required to detail what had been covered in the various subject areas during the previous month. Circulating the book was Isaac's responsibility and he made sure that it reached each teacher promptly and returned to him completed and dated accurately.

Gerry abhorred what, in his view, was a useless bureaucratic chore, and when it reached him the book disappeared for days, even weeks, before Isaac, despite constant reminders, had it returned. One month the battle of wills heated up. The problem was that Gerry, irrespective of the actual day, always dated the return of the book as the day after he had received it. This made Isaac angry and he duly wrote on top of the incorrect date the exact date when it had come back to him. Not to be outdone, Gerry, furious by what he considered Isaac's pettiness, changed it again to his original date and sent it back to Isaac. This was now a real feud and the page in the fore leaf of the record was soon obliterated by messy alterations as it travelled back and forth between the two classrooms. Most of the other staff were aware of the ructions and found it all a great source of amusement.

Gerry Meighan eventually decided to take up a position in a school in South Africa and I always felt that dealing with Isaac was a factor in his resignation at Abbots Cross.

Part of Isaac Kerr's duties seemed to be the school's unofficial dog warden. He had had a farming background and prided himself on commanding unchallenged obedience from animals, just as he expected from his pupils. At this time there was what could only be described as a plague of dogs in the playgrounds, attracted no doubt by the children and the noise at playtime. Isaac set out on a personal crusade to clear the dogs off the premises, urging them towards the back gate once the bell had sounded. He was determined that stray dogs would not disrupt his playground duty. In a way I thought this was an appropriate task for Isaac because in some respects he resembled a fierce little Jack Russell terrier barking at the heels of those who dared challenge its authority. In the disputes with Gerald Meighan it was a case of the Jack Russell versus The British Bulldog!

While not entirely successful at break time in seeing off the many dogs from the senior playground, Isaac's shouting and flailing a rounders' bat did make some difference to the wild packs. Some proved more reluctant than others to leave so when he reached the relative privacy of the back gate Isaac reinforced his commands with a well-directed kick or two. Unfortunately for him but fortunately for the dogs, a lady in one of the houses opposite the back gate took exception to such treatment of the poor animals and telephoned Mr Kennedy to complain. She also threatened to report the school to the RSPCA. Isaac's campaign was put on hold and the dogs regained unchallenged supremacy. In no time the dog nuisance was as bad as ever. We really needed a full-time Dog Warden.

Although a distinctive character many would have considered Mr Kennedy much too conservative and traditional in his outlook to be termed eccentric. His ways sometimes were peculiar and occasionally quite mysterious. He had an inherent suspicion of parents especially when he felt they were trying to take liberties and score points over him. This applied to their presence in the playgrounds before and after school. His advice to remain outside the gates when they came to escort or collect their children often went unheeded. So, with the bit between his teeth, he set up a parental barrier made from a skipping rope and two stout poles across the main path to the senior playground. A large notice stating 'No Parents Beyond This Point' emphasised the message. This was strategically positioned just outside the window to his office and he regularly challenged offenders in his sternest headmaster voice, raised a decibel or two for effect. Not many turned the word with him when he was in such a determined mood and committed to one of his campaigns.

Staff meetings were not held frequently in my time at the school. In fact the staffroom could not have held a quarter of the staff. In my fifteen years in Abbots Cross I can recall two or three meetings at most. Later, when I became a member of what today would be called the Senior Management Team, I soon learnt Mr Kennedy's approach to planning. Mrs Davison, the Vice-Principal and I, as Senior Master sat round his desk and he scribbled notes in pencil on the formica top of his desk. Adjustments were made with a rubber and when the issues were settled everything was erased. I had the impression this was done to prevent Mrs Welch, the secretary, from getting her eyes on the details and broadcasting these round the staff on the school information grape vine. In particular the issue of deployment of teachers to classes for the following year was something that required confidentiality until each teacher heard this personally from the Principal.

It was often difficult to predict what J.A. Kennedy was going to do next. On Monday mornings he often came into my P7 Classroom and proceeded to tell me what he had been up to over the weekend. This was usually a stroke-by-stroke commentary on his game of golf at Ballyclare. The class were well used to this and knew better than to be restless so they kept their heads down and got on with some work while the golf post-mortem progressed.

On one occasion the subject was how he had constructed a fish pond in his garden. He got very excited about the project and suddenly said, "Come on down to the house with me and I'll show it to you." I mentioned a possible difficulty with the class supervision but he turned to them and, in his sternest voice told them that we were going out for a few minutes and that they were to get on with their work quietly until we returned. We set off to Dillons Avenue, Whiteabbey in his car, inspected the fish pond and came back to the room where I do believe there hadn't been a murmur since we left, half an hour before. That was the quality of discipline at Abbots Cross. It stood me in good stead when I later moved on to other schools and aimed to adopt the Abbots Cross standard of discipline. But I have to admit my home never had a fish pond!

Hockey team with Miss Carol Mitchell, Mr J A Kennedy and Mrs Joan McKinney, 1970s

I will never forget the Monday morning when we arrived at school to find that about eight classrooms had been vandalised over the weekend. The vandals had broken through the flimsy, interior classroom walls and systematically wreaked havoc by upsetting books, destroying the children's work displayed on the walls and breaking everything it was possible to break. My classroom had an aquarium which was smashed and the bodies of the fish and pond insects strewn about on the floor. The vandals had got access to the caretaker's cleaning materials and had spilt the noxious liquid he used to remove polish from the floors over the corridor ruining many of the tiles. Eventually a BBC television crew and a reporter arrived and we made the Northern Ireland evening news bulletin.

P7 class with Mr Jack McKinney and Mrs Elsie Davison, c.1975

Very soon the police apprehended the offenders – two boys from Tom Adair's P7 class. We were surprised as, prior to this incident, they had appeared to be quiet, well behaved pupils but they had spent a long time on the Sunday going from room to room on their mission of destruction.

The first Christmas Sale I remember was a truly momentous occasion. Possibly because we had not had one before, certainly not in my time there, the response of parents, when asked to donate items, was spectacular. There must have been a huge demand for sugar around then, possibly due to a national shortage or a strike, because it came in from the parents in vast quantities. I remember the Medical Room almost filled with two-pound bags prior to the Sale. It may have been this first sale or perhaps a later one when the crowds waiting outside the Assembly Hall became so dense about a quarter-of-an-hour before the official opening time that the double doors threatened to give way under the pressure and Mr Kennedy had to open up early. Even then, I believe, the ladies in the first surge from the queue were forced by the crush, large shopping bags in hand, into the hall backwards. Had they gone down there would have been serious injuries in the ensuing stampede. The melee around the various stalls was intense and, of course as usual, a number of items were swiftly swept unpaid from the tables into open bags by customers whose regular attendance at such events in the neighbourhood had honed their skills in the noble art of 'knuckery'.

When I started at the school I think there was a Parents' Association but I don't remember it being very active. I remember Mr Kennedy later explaining to me his policy on this matter. He was always wary of parents interfering in the running of the school so he said he liked to have a Parents' Association that was struggling to keep its head above water. This was preferable, he believed, to not having one at all because then there was a danger that a particularly assertive parent would start up an association that would be a nuisance rather than a support to the school. At this time such views were common in schools. Parents' Associations were often seen purely as forums where complaints about the school were aired. Mr Kennedy believed that a weak Parents' Association was a sign that the parents were satisfied with the school.

Football team in brand new strip, c.1970; Back room, from left: Mr J McKinney, Robert Scarborough, Unknown, Eddie Spiers, Mr J A Kennedy, Jim McLean, Alan Fawcett, Geoffrey Gleave, Mr P Hutchinson. Front row, from left: Unknown, Rodney Maule, Charlie Doyle, Paul Gallaher, Terry Maguire

Later in my career at the school the situation changed. With Mr Kennedy's approval it became a Parent Teacher Association with the aim of bringing parents and teachers together positively for the good of the school, particularly through raising money for extra equipment and resources. A teacher sat on the PTA Committee and I, along with younger staff members, found this role rewarding. Fortunately we never had any instances of negative discussion of school affairs and indeed I can say that in my case, I enjoyed working with the committee organising their activities. Very large sums were raised at Christmas Sales and such like and in, addition to useful items of small equipment, sectional stage units were bought for the school hall and a first class public address system supplied by Lloyd Sound, a reputable firm. This was quite the best sound system I ever experienced in any school and, with the stage units, transformed morning assembly and school productions. Football strips and hockey kits

Mrs J McKinney's class, c.1970

in their distinctive blue and yellow school colours, were also funded by the PTA. Our school teams were easily the smartest in their competitions.

A lot of time at PTA committee meetings was taken up with the catering arrangements for forthcoming events. The committee was a healthy mix of parents from different social backgrounds and this was sometimes evident from the suggestions for the snacks to accompany the cups of tea. Usually these were simply sandwiches, pastries or occasionally sausage rolls but one new member, a parent from Monkstown, did on numerous occasions suggest mushrooms pâtés. His idea was never taken up. I suspect that the group of ladies who dominated the discussions thought the pâtés were just a bit too posh. Then mushroom pates were a fashionable item at high class suppers. At a subsequent meeting the gentleman was absent and one lady piped up 'I say where is Mushroom Pâté tonight?' Comments like these enlivened an otherwise dull meeting!

I had a defining moment at a PTA Fashion Show in our school hall. The new stage units were ideal as a catwalk for the parent mannequins and the sound system gave the whole evening a professional touch. The Chairman of the PTA, Mr John Eaton, was a jolly, affable chap. He acted as announcer at the show and he and I connived in a little diversion at the end of the parade. At this time the church choir of which I was a member were staging an Old Time Music Hall event and my sister-in-law had acquired a splendid hat, gown and accessories for the show. I borrowed these and unwisely donned them. Then to the accompaniment of the chairman's spoof commentary, I tottered up the catwalk as best I could in my high heels. The reaction of the audience took me totally by surprise. Apparently my costume, mannequin's walk and the commentary were authentic enough to be accepted as a serious part of the show. Realising this, I quickly introduced a 'Dick Emery' type stumble before the whisper went round 'It's Mr McKinney!' I can only put this aberration down to my natural instinct to be in the limelight. It was certainly poor judgement on my part. The sequel occurred the next morning when I was called into Mr Kennedy's office to hear a stiff lecture on the 'Dignity of the Profession'. Thankfully he had not actually seen the performance but I soon gathered that a full report had reached headquarters. I had learnt a very important lesson and resolved to restrict my future stage appearances to church choir entertainment.

Chapter 13: Improving at the Chalk Face

There weren't many Christmas concerts in my time at Abbots Cross school. We did have an annual carol service that was sometimes held in Rathcoole Presbyterian Church. Usually it took place in the school assembly hall. Mrs Davison trained and conducted the choir, which was huge, there could have been up to 75 members. Other children read the lessons. The most impressive part for me was before the beginning when Mrs Davison raised her hand to command silence and attention. There was a total hush and seventy pairs of eyes became fixed on her raised hand. They breathed in as one and the first note of the first carol rang out, clear as a bell, throughout the crowded hall. It was an excellent performance. Mind you, the fact that James Kennedy often hovered in the background during the rehearsals had tended to concentrate the minds of the most boisterous boys into meek compliance. The most notorious rascals looked angelic for this occasion. Now, I just marvel that we were able to fit the vast crowd of parents and local dignitaries into the assembly hall. The carol service was certainly an enjoyable occasion in the school year.

The programme, in typical Abbots Cross style, ran through like clockwork but during one service a small hitch occurred in these careful arrangements. That year the art teacher had worked with some children to produce a rather large, life size model of Father Christmas. He had been designed with both arms held well out from his body in a kind of welcoming gesture. This merry fellow was placed in the main corridor beside the school hall and amused the classes as they passed that way. For the carol service Santa was given pride of place at the front of the hall supported somewhat precariously on a chair. With the audience respectfully silent and the choir awaiting the signal from Mrs Davison to begin their first carol, Mr Kennedy, vigilant as ever, noticed that Father Christmas had begun to slide from his chair. He realised that, left like this, he would soon end up on the floor. For members of staff, watching from the back of the hall, the way in which Father Christmas was gradually sliding, feet first, to the floor resembled someone who had had too much festive refreshment 'going under the table.' So, motioning to Mrs Davison to wait for a moment, Mr Kennedy approached the now almost recumbent figure and, putting his arms beneath Father Christmas's outstretched arms and around his body, bravely attempted to raise him up and prop him back again on the chair. This was a fearful duty and when so many eyes were watching it proved tricky. On the first few attempts Father Christmas refused to cooperate and each time slid forward almost as if he preferred, rather like the typical drunk, to remain on the floor.

In common with the rest of the audience the staff at the back of the hall felt for Mr Kennedy as he struggled to restore Father Christmas to his upright position. It was difficult to keep a straight face because, with the principal's arms round Father Christmas, it looked as if they were wrestling or engaged in some bizarre form of dancing. As ever, the total silence in which the ridiculous escapade took place, heightened the compulsion to snigger. Around this date the television talk show host, Michael Parkinson, had been involved in an involuntary wrestling match with the dummy of ventriloquist, Rod Hull. One could see an echo of this episode in Mr Kennedy's encounter with Father Christmas so the idea of finding this amusing was hard to suppress. Eventually Father Christmas was forced to his feet and, with the addition of a couple of improvised weights on his feet, remained there soberly until the end of the evening.

Towards the end of the Autumn term every year there was a special treat for the pupils, and enjoyed by many of the younger members of staff. During my fifteen years at the school in the days long before video and DVD, the Christmas Film Show was a popular annual treat for the children. A pleasant little man arrived at lunch time to set up his equipment in the hall. We had to wait until the bustle of serving dinners in the hall had ceased. News of his arrival soon spread throughout the school – no one ever got a gladder welcome to Abbots Cross. There were two shows, a short one of cartoons for the younger children and another of about an hour's duration for the senior classes. I remember when the classes all trooped down the corridors to the hall one could sense the air of excitement from the constant chatter and noise, the children totally unable to maintain the dignified decorum expected of Abbots Cross pupils on the march. On this occasion they didn't need to worry about too much noise and they knew it. Once everyone was assembled in the darkened hall and the projectionist had given the thumbs up Mr Kennedy addressed the merry throng.

'Now, Now, quieten down – I'm waiting for silence! Once the film begins you can shout your heads off!' And to the consternation of the reduced posse of supervising teachers they brought the roof down – well almost. The choice of films was excellent – a collage of slapstick comedy including Buster Keaton, Charlie Chaplin and The Keystone Cops. The staff, as well as enjoying the fun, found the dubbed sound commentary, delivered in the typical, exaggerated American style, hilarious. A supervision rota also allowed members of staff to enjoy a relaxing hour with an extra cup of tea in the staffroom while uproar continued in the hall.

On another occasion we did have considerably more difficulty in finding seats for the audience at a school event. Originally a school concert was to be held in the school hall with each senior class taking responsibility for one item in the programme. These, together with songs from the school choir, would provide enough material for an evening's entertainment for parents.

As was inevitable, teachers vied with each other, in a most civilised manner, of course, to ensure that each class's item would be up to the high standard expected in the school. Much time was spent in rehearsal and, as the date of the concert approached and costumes were finalised, it became obvious to everyone and to Mr Kennedy in particular that this event could be a major success. The staff were so busy with individual items that little thought was given to how all those who would certainly like to attend could be accommodated. At this time there were around 950 pupils on rolls, maybe 500 children in the classes involved in the concert. Even over two nights' performances the available space for the potential audiences in the assembly hall was never likely to be enough. Eventually Mr Kennedy took a hand in the proceedings and it was arranged to move the performances to The Rathcoole Youth Centre. Although this plan involved a number of trips by the various classes to the Centre for rehearsal it seemed the only way that the number expected to attend could be accommodated. As usual we all just got on with it and waited patiently for the big opening night. It was realised afterwards that the big mistake was not to have issued tickets to limit the number turning up for the performance.

Well, I can safely say that of all the shocks and surprises I had in my time at the school what I saw when I looked out of the first floor window of the Youth Centre about half an hour before the performance was due to begin, must figure near the top of the list. A long queue had formed along the side of the Centre and stretched past the Alpha Cinema some fifty yards distant. Even worse was the knowledge that the hall was by then already three-quarters full and we realised that many prospective members of the audience were bound to be disappointed. The concert eventually got underway following an announcement from Mr Kennedy that it would be repeated on two evenings in the school hall the following week. Nevertheless we knew that there had been a certain amount of 'muttering' from those forced to return home unable to see their children take part.

The performance was excellent only slightly marred by the timing. The business of squeezing in the maximum number and the explanatory announcements meant that the programme started late. It is fair to say also that the individual class items and the choir contributions over- ran by a considerable margin the time estimated for each. I don't remember a full dress rehearsal prior to this evening. The crucial point came about 11.40pm by which time one choir item and the item from Paul Hutchinson's P6 Class had still to take to the stage.

Amid a certain restlessness in the audience and the disruption caused by those making an early exit, Mr Kennedy, pulled the plug and the curtain came down on a marathon but outstanding event. Before the sudden ending I was assigned a difficult task. I was asked to inform Mr Paul Hutchinson that there was no time left for his class to appear on the stage to present their item. It would be an understatement to say he was distraught. He was livid. And I totally understood how he felt. In the school he was known as a perfectionist in all that he did. He and the class had rehearsed tirelessly for weeks before this big night. Words were polished, costumes obtained – many were made by parents – and make-up applied. They had waited patiently through the programme only to discover that on their big night they didn't even make it on to the stage. It was a big blow and we all shared their misery. Some consolation did come, however, at their performance in the school hall on the two evenings of the following week. They were magnificent and received well deserved acclaim.

My class's contribution to the evening was a stage version of The Christmas Rhymers, a mummers' verse play that folk in the country performed at Christmas, tramping around farmhouses and other dwellings. Among the list of strange characters in the play was one named 'Wee Johnny Funny.' He it was who, at the end, took round the hat to collect the money expected for the players' efforts. The day after the show Mr Kennedy told me he had particularly enjoyed this item as he had remembered the traditional play from his youth. However he said that what impressed

A section of the choir at the Concert and right, dancers from the Concert

him most was my casting of the characters from children in my class and in particular my choice of the little fellow who had the part of Johnny Funny. He then horrified me by explaining that a couple of weeks before the show he had caught 'Johnny Funny' going round the cloakrooms taking money from coat pockets. I had known nothing of this and was mortified. The following year I took the precaution of asking some questions about the behaviour record of prospective actors before casting the play.

Members of staff in the school were always a little anxious when they received a summons to see Mr Kennedy in his office. Usually one had a good idea what this was about but once in a while there was a surprise. This occurred to my colleague, Tom Adair, when he received a message from Mrs Welch, school secretary, to come down to see Mr Kennedy right away. Tom approached the door of the office and, while not exactly overcome with fear and trembling, he was certainly concerned that he might be about to hear bad news. Before knocking on the door he heard the sound of a recorder being played from inside the room. The rather hesitant and slightly off-key playing suggested that a child was in there perhaps showing Mr Kennedy the progress he was making in mastering the instrument. Tom took quite a lot to do with music in the school so was relieved to think that he was there to offer his advice on some aspect of learning to play the recorder. So he knocked and entered. To his bewilderment the only person in the room was Mr Kennedy himself who, seated behind his desk as usual, was tootling away on the instrument. The ensuing conversation, punctuated by a phrase or two on the recorder, centred on Mr Kennedy's decision to take up the recorder as a creative pastime. It was obvious that he was very proud of the progress he was making. Tom, of course, endorsed his enthusiasm but was hardly in a position to be entirely objective about the quality of the music played. The incident at least confirmed the opinion of the men on the staff that we never could be sure what would happen when we were invited into 'The Holy of Holies'.

The occurrence of the unexpected, especially from Mr Kennedy, was one of the endearing features of life at Abbots Cross and it contributed not a little to our enjoyment of teaching there.

I always counted imperturbability as an important feature of James Kennedy's leadership style. He always seemed ready to deal with situations which arose no matter how difficult or awkward they appeared.

I saw a good example of this quality one afternoon. Mr Kennedy was reprimanding a senior boy, for some misdemeanour. I recognised the miscreant as one of his regular customers. For some peculiar reason this encounter took place just inside the main entrance to the building. The reprimand took the usual form – a mixture of pushing and prodding accompanied by a recital in a very loud voice by Mr Kennedy of the boy's long record of poor behaviour and a desperately unflattering litany of the problems he often caused for the staff. As usual he finished off by outlining the likely future prospects for the boy in this school and beyond. Every so often he invited the boy to agree with this assessment and prediction. The lad, as many others had before and after him would do, reassured Mr Kennedy that he was accurate in his diagnosis. In the middle of this tirade Rev Harry Magill, a member of the school management committee, came through the door, saw was happening and tactfully sidled past with his head lowered and made his way quietly to the office. Not a bit put off, not to say embarrassed by this interruption, Mr Kennedy finished his harangue then dismissed the boy to his classroom.

When I later asked how Rev Magill had reacted to this incident Mr Kennedy told me that he was not in the least perturbed. Indeed he had said, 'I would have liked to ask you give that fellow one or two from me because he is the ruination of my Sunday School.'

Often on Monday mornings there would be a number of parents, usually ladies, waiting at Mr Kennedy's office door. With stout arms akimbo, wearing carpet slippers and with their hair curlers in place they were a formidable bunch indeed. They were generally there to take issue with the principal about some incident that had happened in a classroom or playground. Once inside the office battle was soon joined with the noise reverberating down the corridors. Following one such altercation I asked Mr Kennedy if he found this sort of thing stressful. 'Not a bit of it,' he replied 'a round or two of battle first thing in the morning just gets me warmed up for the rest of the day's work.'

Dealing with the hundreds who passed through the school meant that, over the years, the staff met a wide variety of pupils. Generally speaking the pupils were cheerful, relaxed and happy and building rapport with them was easy when one treated them with empathy and understanding. Thus the staff were able to concentrate on the business of teaching rather than on constantly reinforcing discipline. This led to an atmosphere in the classrooms conducive to enjoyable learning. There were few serious behavioural problems and, in the distinctive way he dealt with the pupils, the principal was able to create and maintain a balance between firm discipline and sympathetic support.

Then there were the characters, individuals with a way about them that has stuck in my memory – not always for their good points. It tends to be the boys I remember best.

Guy was serious in his demeanour, always very polite, mature and sophisticated for an eleven year old. He never got involved in mischief; for his sake I often wished that he would misbehave just a little. Somehow it would have been more normal for a lively boy to, maybe occasionally, get into a bit of minor trouble. Each morning before school began he would stand in his class line waiting patiently for the serious business of school to begin.

Andrew was a small ragamuffin who gained considerable notoriety by setting the Abbots Cross post box on fire. Mr Kennedy then banned children from visiting the shops at Abbots Cross Centre during the lunch break. Before long the postmaster came over to the school pleading with him to rescind the ban because he and the other shopkeepers were missing the dear little children so much. There was no reference, of course, to the loss of confectionery sales the ban had caused.

John, or as he was affectionately known, 'Wee' John, came to the school when family circumstances forced him to move from Belfast to stay with his granny in Rathcoole. She mollycoddled him terribly, forcing him to wear two pullovers in case he caught a cold. He was small and slight for his age and had apparently suffered from a number of ailments in his short life. None of these seemed terribly serious or unusual for a growing lad but his granny had helped John perfect a litany of these which he repeated at every possible opportunity. He was averse to PE or games – indeed to any physical activity – but he was bright and took part in the preparation for the 11-plus tests. One day Mr Kennedy chose to pounce on him to encourage him to improve his test scores. John's excited reaction was first to demand that he be allowed to visit the toilet and, when Mr Kennedy hesitated in giving his permission, he reinforced his request by a delivery of his catalogue of ailments quoting the authority and knowledge of his granny in these matters. The recital was as exaggerated as it was unnecessary and, as John rushed to the door, a smile appeared on Mr Kennedy's face and the class relaxed – not usually a feature of these test post-mortem sessions.

In those days children in the P7 year received a BCG inoculation. The pupils termed this the 'Six Needles' Injection because it was carried out by the school doctor with an instrument that had six very short prongs. It was not at all painful but its fearful reputation was gained more from the exaggerations of the first few in the queue outside the Medical Room than from reality. The others waiting in turn became more and more apprehensive as they listened to the descriptions and saw the grimaces of those coming out. Wee John was right at the back of the line and, just before his turn came, he slid to the floor in a faint, white as a ghost. Quite soon he recovered and bravely faced the terror of the six needles with fortitude.

Arthur was an entirely different kettle of fish from John. Apathy or indifference featured heavily in Arthur's natural approach to school work. In spite of this Mr Kennedy recognised the potential if Arthur could be cajoled into exerting himself consistently. He was obviously much more intelligent than his dozy outward appearance indicated. This was a condition that made Mr Kennedy see red and he took it as a challenge to push him, even against Arthur's natural instinct, to gain a place at a grammar school. Almost on a weekly basis Arthur endured the Kennedy treatment. This consisted of a bit of shoulder pummelling with glaring in the eyeballs accompanied by imprecations about 'Lazy Duffer' and 'Nimcompoop' directed at Arthur but it made no discernible impression on him whatsoever. The effect, strangely, was to create a rush to the toilets by various girls in the front seats whose performance was impeccable. It ran off Arthur like water off a duck's back. One afternoon, following a particularly heavy barrage on Arthur, Mr Kennedy had returned to his office and I was engaged on the difficult task of proceeding with the normal school work and breaking the trance-like atmosphere in the room. Suddenly the door burst open and Mr Kennedy made straight for Arthur's desk and recommenced the verbal assault tactics and shouting 'Every time I think of you, Arthur, it makes me angry!' He was obviously frustrated at not being able to disturb Arthur's stoic indifference to his test results. When the noise of the tirade subsided and Mr Kennedy had again returned to his office I read the class a funny story to lighten the atmosphere before home time.

In the P7 class I taught from Easter to June in my first year in the main school building there was a girl, Shirley, who was a superb, natural athlete. An aunt of mine was a colleague of her father in an office in Belfast. The summer game played in the large playground was Rounders and at this she excelled, much better indeed than all but two of the boys in that class. She had a remarkably lithe running style and a competitive streak that made her ideal as a team captain. It was no surprise to me to hear that eventually she became a P.E. teacher.

Then there was Stuart. When Stuart was in P1 he came over each day at 2pm to spend the last hour of the day with his sister, Audrey who was in my P7 class. Stuart and Audrey lived in Carnmoney and I knew both well from the time I had worked as a temporary postman in their father's post office. One Friday afternoon we were all busy tidying up after an Art lesson and, having just been assigned to this class, I asked if anyone knew how to dispose of the bucket of waste water. At this point the class was dumbfounded to hear Stuart chirp up from the back of the room 'Jack, you just throw it out of the window.' There spoke the authorative voice of experience! No one could imagine a P1 pupil calling a teacher by his Christian name, such familiarity was unthinkable in Abbots Cross School.

The administrative hub of the school, of course, was Mr Kennedy's office and to a much lesser extent the next door office of Mrs Welch, the school secretary. Her room doubled as a library and had a telephone that staff could use by arrangement to make personal calls. It was always busy at lunchtime and Mrs Welch was generally there to listen in to the calls. It wasn't a good place to make a call about a matter one wished to keep private. Mrs Welch was a friendly, decent soul but did rather enjoy picking up pieces of news concerning members of staff. She made no bones about referring to the subject of the telephone call with the aim of doing anything she could to help out.

During my fifteen years at the school the caretaker was Eddie Stallard. He combined his caretaking duties with that of school crossing patrol at the main gate. He was a friendly chap, a feature not usually associated with caretakers and he was popular with the children. He had settled in Northern Ireland following service with the army. Once, when he saw that I was setting up a little museum in my classroom, he gave me a wonderful collection of Second World War souvenir badges and emblems that he had kept from his service days. I have them still.

He often gave a hint of his military background when he was summoned by Mr Kennedy to carry out some duty. Mr Kennedy's shout would be heard echoing down the corridor, 'Stallard!' The reply would resound instantly, 'Yes, Sir! Certainly Sir, I'll do that straight away, Sir.' He always seemed a trifle overawed by Mr Kennedy's commands and I think he often had trouble stifling a salute as he took his orders. He had been a cobbler before he joined the army and I believe in his early days in Abbots Cross he did a little shoe repairing in his spare time. His room at the school was cluttered with bits and pieces of small equipment from around the building and it was the centre for lost property. He also acted as the School Crossing patrol. Each day he took his dinner in here before his lunchtime patrol duty but how he managed to find enough space to do this was a mystery. He and his wife lived for a time in Rural Avenue alongside the school. He liked fiddling at small jobs but he was not really very handy. Mr Kennedy found this out when he asked him to change the oil in his car. This proved an unsuccessful operation because afterwards the car leaked oil on the main Doagh Road and it had to be fixed at a garage. I think he washed Mr Kennedy's car regularly – a job it was not so easy to botch. His wife worked as a cleaner in the school. Mrs Stallard was not the most conscientious of workers and I can still picture her in classic pose leaning on her brush and taking any opportunity to break off for a smoke or to engage anyone nearby in conversation. This was a special hazard for teachers working in their rooms after school. Mrs Stallard was ever ready to interrupt her cleaning routine to begin a chat, allowing her further opportunities to adopt her characteristic pose of arms and chin resting on the brush. Her cleaning colleagues were certainly in awe of the caretaker's wife and they appeared to do most of the brushing. Their idea of cleaning consisted of moving the red, disinfectant sawdust- like material haphazardly around the parquet floors. They generally failed to pick up all of the smelly stuff and next morning teachers usually found stray piles of it under the furniture and in the corners of their rooms.

In the 1960s there were usually many younger members of staff and each year brought some fresh faces. I was young enough myself to be accepted into this friendly band. Soon opportunities for social events developed – weddings, parties and going out together for a meal. It was a happy time for all the young staff. I coached the school football team and was always looking out for teachers who would volunteer to take boys in their cars to away fixtures. One teacher appointed to the staff was Joan Milligan who, with Carol Mitchell, coached the school girls' hockey teams. Joan Milligan proved really co-operative and became an enthusiastic supporter of the school football team. The organisation of transport for the team meant that I had to consult with Joan regularly and it happened that I usually visited her P2 classroom after school and often remained there long after other members of staff had gone home. The upshot was that by the time the end of the Autumn term and various staff social events were arranged I was meeting her in rather more relaxed circumstances than her classroom.

Eventually one day in February I made my way down to Mr Kennedy's office to make an important announcement. With considerable embarrassment I told him and Mrs Davison who was in the office that I had become engaged to be married. They both expressed delight at my announcement. Mr Kennedy then said and I'll never forget his words, 'We are very pleased for you. Have you known the lucky lady for long? I'm sure we will not know her.' I replied rather shyly, 'Well I think you might. She teaches round in Room 4.' There was a stunned silence for a second or two, broken eventually by a whoop of surprise and genuine joy from Mrs Davison. It was not such a surprise to the cleaners who had obviously been monitoring the after school activities with interest. I was so much involved in the school that I had even managed to find a wife there. This added to the reputation of the school as an environment where staff related well in both the professional and the social spheres.

Walking back to my classroom that day I wondered how long it would be before my news would reach the ears of Mrs Welch and circulate around the rest of the staff.

Chapter 14: Managing at Abbots Cross

I think it is safe to say that the curriculum in Abbots Cross school was essentially traditional. The emphasis was on academic achievement across the full range of the subject areas covered. In my early days our guide was a Department of Education booklet 'The Programme for Primary Schools in Northern Ireland.' This set out the subjects and the time in hours to be spent on the subjects each week. I don't remember many policy documents, written plans or schemes created by the school to interpret the Department's booklet for teachers. I firmly believe this was all in Mr Kennedy's head but the staff seemed to know what he wanted and how this was to be carried out. To implement this teachers did write weekly teaching notes and also produced an annual scheme of work for their classes. He relied to a large extent, I'm sure, on trust though he did have a shrewd idea from the work produced in each classroom how the pupils were being taught. Again, he seldom visited classrooms specifically to examine workbooks and to judge a teacher's performance while teaching but he was good at assessing pupils' results set against his standards.

Together with most other teachers in the school I appreciated the trust he displayed in what we were doing and this gave us confidence to pursue our objectives without undue interference. He was blunt with staff and pupils when his standards were not met.

The school had an excellent reputation in the locality and beyond for the achievement of its pupils. This arose from the destination of pupils as they started off in secondary schools especially the percentage of those going on to grammar school. For most of my teaching service I was involved with other staff in the final year, with P7 pupils, extending and polishing their general attainment in English and maths. Alongside this, much time was taken up in the first term by practice on Verbal Reasoning tests of the type set by the Department of Education to help determine the secondary schools where pupils would be offered places.

This was one area where our principal did play an active role. He collected the scores of weekly tests, studied them and then visited classrooms to encourage those who had done well or to urge on any who had not produced the result he expected of them. These sessions were not for the faint hearted and the word 'duffer' did cross his lips regularly. These tactics worked and he took great pride in the number who progressed on to a grammar school – including a good proportion of the supposed 'duffers.' I found it remarkable that his tirades often reduced to tears those who had least reason to worry – typically meek, conscientious girls working at the top of the class - while the diehards who deserved Mr Kennedy's outbursts remained completely unaffected.

The practice tests used were copies of tests actually set in previous years and such copies were in use in any primary school in Northern Ireland that took the annual Transfer Procedure arrangements seriously. Raw scores in these were a useful indication of how pupils were progressing. Somehow or other Mr Kennedy had obtained a set of tables for four university research tests and these allowed us to convert the raw score into a quotient which took account of the age difference in months of those taking the tests. This information was very helpful and Mr Kennedy kept these conversion tables under lock and key in his office. I had nightmares about losing or misplacing the tables after I had used them and having to go to his office and make my confession. Fortunately, the nightmare never became a reality.

The text books we used to support the curriculum in the 1960s and 1970s now seem very dated but they were the standard fare in primary schools at the time. My favourite was The New First Aid in English, a kind of reference book listing synonyms, antonyms, group terms and other more unusual categories. It was a real curiosity. Here one could learn that a native African was a blackfellow, his wife a gin and his child a piccaninny. A Zulu apparently was at home in a kraal while Eskimos were cosy in their igloos. In the

General Knowledge section the Seven Wonders of the World were listed. All of this had very limited relevance to children growing up in Rathcoole.

Among other books in use was Effective Comprehension, comprising a number of extracts from various classic writers with questions based on the texts. Many books of this type were available from publishers. Another, '100 Exercises in English Usage', was dull in the extreme but was guaranteed to keep pupils' heads down while the class teacher got on with chores like marking the spelling books. Arithmetic text books were common and numerous such as Top Flight Arithmetic, Top of the Form Arithmetic and a book of fiendlishly difficult problems suitable only for the brightest pupils and a challenge even for many teachers called New Northern Arithmetic. The term 'mathematics' was not yet in common use in most primary schools although I did enjoy introducing my P7s in their last term to the mysteries of algebra. It was a bit of a novelty and, with a smattering of simple French conversation gave them, I hoped, a taste of the curriculum their secondary schools would provide.

We had television programmes but for, one reason or another, the television set was often unavailable and, anyway, I preferred the radio broadcasts. I think I used the programmes Singing Together and Rhythm and Melody on the BBC just as I had listened to these when I attended Mossley P.E.S. in the 1940s. Most of the songs included hadn't changed. I much preferred two other broadcasts on the National BBC Schools' Service – Living Language and Listening and Writing. These introduced older children, in P6 and P7, to imaginative writing from a range of authors. The poetry and prose excerpts were not only enjoyable in their own right but were excellent as a stimulus for the children's creative writing. Greek myths and legends often featured on the radio programmes and always engaged the pupils' interest.

Sometime in the 1960s the Northern Ireland BBC station began to broadcast programmes with a local focus and this proved a popular and exciting development. Eventually there would be locally produced television broadcasts by both the BBC and UTV but, in common with other colleagues, I preferred the good old 'Steam Radio'. As the BBC slogan said at the time 'Radio was best because the pictures were better.'

The Today and Yesterday in Northern Ireland Radio series concentrated on local geography and history topics with songs and music. This approach fitted well into a national policy in this period of opening up and making available to schools a range of sources for local studies. The museums and the Public Records Office for Northern Ireland were at the forefront of this development. They had Education Officers who liaised with teachers and held courses on material from their archives that could be used in schools. I was introduced to the photographs they had such as the Welch and Green national collections and I soon found out how interesting these could be for a local study. The Today and Yesterday in Northern Ireland programmes made regular use of such material and their published pamphlets for pupils and teaching notes for teachers were invaluable as background material in lesson preparation. The programme often featured snippets from Ulster authors and poets, introducing pupils and teachers to aspects of Ulster culture that had seldom been covered before, certainly not in the national school broadcasts.

A splendid series of programmes from Today and Yesterday in N.I. focussed on the linen mills and other factories in Belfast. Included were songs and games played by children from the streets and descriptions of conditions in the workplaces and the back-to-back terraces where the workers lived. This was especially interesting to pupils in Abbots Cross for two reasons. Firstly, the background of the parents and grandparents of most of our pupils was Belfast and the children were able to discuss at home what they had heard in the programme. Often in school we would be told further interesting details of life in Belfast streets that had been discovered by talking to parents and grandparents. This was a good way to learn the importance of oral history in finding out about the past.

Secondly we were fortunate to have in the school, Tom Adair, a teacher who wrote scripts for some of these programmes. His P7 classes enjoyed listening to him singing the street and mill songs and accompanying himself on the guitar. They, of course, joined in and a good time was had by all.

A high regard was held in Abbots Cross for neat presentation of written work and legible handwriting. Nothing set the principal off more quickly on one of his tirades than a piece of scribbled, grubby handwriting. The introduction of a modern script style was never contemplated. The school stuck to the tried and tested cursive method and the use of ball pens was discouraged. The children were taught to use nibbed pens using either liquid ink or ink cartridges. It was a source of pride to all staff to hear secondary schools complimenting the children who came from Abbots Cross on their good handwriting and presentation skills.

A good example of the quality of the work produced at Abbots Cross was seen in 1968. The Newtownabbey Urban District Council was inaugurated in 1958 and events and activities took place in 1968 to mark its first decade in existence. As part of the celebration schools were invited to engage in projects illustrating progress and development in the town and community since its foundation. The work from the project – in art, model making, and history and geography topics – and involving the full range of classes P1 to P7 – would be put on display in the schools and made available for viewing by the public. This was the first Open Day I remember being held in the school. The details of the work and projects we produced and displayed in the assembly hall are hazy in my memory now but I do recall how proud the staff were of our displays and pleased at the reaction of the members of the public who visited the school. I do remember the emphasis that was placed on the quality of the presentation of the written work.

Although the curriculum was traditional and the school was not always in the forefront of innovatory ideas there was freedom for staff to try out new ways of working especially in non-core areas like art, geography, history and nature study. Every year, once the stress of the Transfer Tests had passed, I enjoyed adopting a less formal approach with my P7 classes. I used a homemade formicarium to study the life of ants. The children were readily engaged in watching the ants develop through their life cycle. This proved as interesting as watching television. I had an aquarium in the classroom with a variety of pond insects and other fresh water creatures that were easily obtained from pools in the fields behind the Abbots Cross Shopping Centre. I was constantly amazed at the children's ability to track them down and bring them into our aquarium for inspection. Looking at the water beetles, water boatmen and even newts that we collected was fascinating. Many years later I met a past pupil who remembered above all else his delight in studying the ants.

After Easter I usually changed the lay-out of the desks from rows into a more informal arrangement by pushing them together to create maybe five groups. This allowed the pupils to work co-operatively on various art and nature study projects. The new seating plan was a very popular move with the children because at certain times they were encouraged to talk to each other and share ideas. Mr Kennedy had no difficulty approving such methods so long as he could see that the children were actively engaged in real learning tasks and that the teacher was still in control and could maintain good order in the room.

There was always a problem with Physical Education because the dinner hall was the only space suitable for indoor lessons. Even when there was not a class or two based here the preparation of the space for dinners limited the time when it could be available for P.E. Most classes used the playgrounds in the good weather months. I favoured rounders and the children loved the games organised in the summer term. The main playground was the perfect size and shape for rounders. This game suited boys and girls, indeed some of the best players were girls. Sometimes we had inter-class matches and the competition was fierce.

Over the course of my 15-year career at Abbot Cross School there must have been many incidents and accidents at break and lunch times. Fortunately most have faded from my memory but one, because of its unusual nature, will never be forgotten.

The scene in the senior playground every lunch break resembled organised chaos. The area was filled with shouts and laughter of the children and the racket was augmented by the barking of up to ten dogs, madly chasing playfully after the children who often seemed oblivious to their presence. They seemed to appear every day right on cue at break times. Some girls would be skipping others gossiping in little groups in the bicycle shelters while boys would be engaged in up to four rowdy, football games, arguing fiercely among themselves about refereeing decisions. Occasionally this ended in fisticuffs and the need for the supervising teacher to intervene but usually they just got on with the game, conforming to their own peculiar rules.

One particular day a crowd was seen to gather around one of the temporary classrooms bordering the play area. This large timber framed building was supported on concrete blocks and a football had gone underneath it. The enthusiasm of footballers is legendary and one little fellow had offered or, more likely, been coerced into crawling beneath the building to retrieve the ball. Though small, he was a tight fit and, once he had located the ball, found it impossible to squeeze himself out from underneath the classroom. It didn't take the teachers on duty long to realise that this was an emergency. Mrs Davison took charge and, once on the scene, managed to disperse some of the crowd that had gathered, curious to see what was going on. A few children had been shouting to the little fellow, some offering advice to stay calm, others foolishly telling him of the hazards below this room, including I remember, the presence of rats.

There was growing concern among Mrs Davison and the staff on the scene about how to tackle this problem. It seemed that the only course was to summon the Fire Brigade. They would certainly know what to do but, obviously speed was of the essence. At this point my namesake and rugby celebrity, Stewart McKinney, made a suggestion about how to extricate the captive. Acting on his initiative he rushed over to Mr Stallard's store and fetched a screwdriver. He then went into the classroom, and located the screws attaching the large plywood sheets forming the floor to the beams underneath. Fortunately these were not difficult to remove. The section of flooring above the wee fellow was raised and he was unearthed, popping up like a piece of bread from a toaster. Luckily he was quite unruffled by his bizarre experience and was able to resume his afternoon lessons as normal. For some time afterwards he became the hero of the senior school, the Houdini of Abbots Cross. Likewise, the reputation of Stewart McKinney was justifiably enhanced and I'm sure the incident gave him a good story to tell to his fellow rugby teammates.

The main after-school activities were football and hockey. I was a fervent football coach and my wife, Joan, helped with the hockey team. There were well organised football leagues and cup competitions in the area and we played against all the other local primary schools. The girls had weekly practices in the playground, had occasional games against other schools and took part in a special inter-schools tournament held in Larne in May. The boys' football comprised really competitive matches and not just the boys but many of the teachers were very keen, indeed sometimes too keen to win the various cups that were competed for each year. I must confess that, especially in my younger days at the school, I took the matches a little too seriously! Now I would rather forget the after match arguments that my competitive nature sometimes produced. Because we were the biggest school in the area we had an advantage and over the years often came out top in the leagues and cups. This did not always go down well with our rivals. The cup and league finals were big events usually played at one of the Irish League grounds in the area. One year we reached the final of the Belfast Telegraph Cup, a competition open to all the primary schools in Northern Ireland, but after a very close game at Solitude, Cliftonville FC's ground, we were beaten by a single goal to nil.

In my first years at the school we played our matches on a pitch on the large common green in Rathcoole Estate. A serious disadvantage here was that an unofficial path had been made from the houses nearby to the shops and ran right through the pitch. We got used to interruptions to the games to allow ladies with shopping bags a safe passage. Later we had the luxury of playing on the newly constructed Derryhill Playing Fields in Rathcoole Estate with no shoppers and the boys often had a hot shower after the games.

In the local matches the quality of refereeing often caused serious controversy. Teachers, of course, acted as referees and some were blatantly unfair in their bias towards their own teams. A teacher from a neighbouring school was notorious for such partisanship. One afternoon in a particularly tight encounter his performance was so biased that I took the issue up with him after the game as the players were changing in the dressing room. The discussion deteriorated and became hot and heavy as we addressed each other behind the pavilion. As the sound of battle reached top volume I had not noticed that one or two of our team had become interested spectators. Suddenly I heard one wee fellow shout 'Sir, Sir, Mr McKinney Sir! Go on Sir, Hit him!' This brought the two of us to our senses and we abandoned hostilities, accepting an impasse as the only satisfactory result. After this escapade I made up my mind to take a calmer attitude to future matches no matter how much I was riled by poor refereeing.

If this referee was a shade too officious the teacher who usually refereed at Glengormley PS was a complete contrast. He was the music teacher and it seemed from his attitude to football that he was a reluctant conscript to the role of coach. In spite of the custom that the home team provided the referee he often asked me to officiate when our two schools met. I was glad to take this on because, from my past experience when he was in charge, I knew how half-heartedly he carried out this duty. He had only a general grasp of the rules and seldom moved far outside the centre circle. From this distant vantage point he made his decisions. The school pitch was in an area behind the classrooms and I would not have been surprised if, on wet days, he had suggested refereeing from the comfort of one of these classrooms. Kitted out in galoshes and carrying an umbrella, his idea of what went on in either of the penalty areas remained sketchy but he regularly called out to some of his team to check on what was happening in the far off goal mouths. The touch and goal lines were never very clearly marked so the answers shouted back to him from either end of the pitch were arbitrary if not extremely doubtful. We listened from the touch lines as he bawled out ' Thompson, did that ball go over the line or not? ' Arguments soon raged all over the pitch and the whole game descended into chaos.

Because of the large enrolment at Abbots Cross the range of activities that could be offered to the pupils was restricted mainly to football and hockey.

For many of my first years there were no Sports Days and few educational visits were arranged. After the opening of Rathcoole Primary School some of the pressure on our enrolment eased and more such events became possible. I recall the first Sports Day organised by a few of the senior staff at the Derryhill Playing Fields. It was quite a scene to see the entire senior school march up through Rathcoole estate to these grounds. We had a small number of events but even then it proved a challenge to run off four sets of heats in each event before a Grand Final.

My memory of these days is hazy but I do recall a serious mistake we made in the organisation. To fund the events and provide medals for the winners we decided to set up a stall selling small bottles of lemonade. A stall was erected in the grounds and soon huge queues formed to buy drinks. This led to the race organisers calling out names of absent runners, many of whom were, of course, stuck in the lemonade queue. We learnt our lesson and the lemonade sales were discontinued in future years.

A popular event, as in all Sports Days, was the sack race. As I was from a farming background I always got the job of borrowing sacks from my farmer friends. On the day before one Sports Day a colleague, Grace McKinstry, shouted over to me in a crowded staffroom

'Mr McKinney, do you know anything about sacks?' Well, I knew what she was referring to but the others did not and their loud guffaws showed that they had misunderstood Grace's request. I, of course, retained a dignified silence.

In the 1960s educational visits to Britain became popular in primary schools. Unlike today, children did not have many opportunities to go abroad with their parents. I soon discovered that a big attraction was that the children loved to spend time with each other on overnight stays. The residential visits usually involved those in P7 who had spent seven years with class colleagues forming close friendships. The following year they would most likely be off to different secondary schools so the P7 visit was a fitting and enjoyable finale to their time at Abbots Cross. Our P7 residential often comprised a few days in Edinburgh visiting the Zoo, the Museum of Childhood and, of course, the Castle. Travelling by boat to Stranraer and then a long coach journey to Edinburgh required stamina. Such travelling followed by busy days spent visiting sites was tiring for both the children and the teachers supervising the party. Sleeping at night, especially on the first night of the trip, was difficult and the children seemed to drop off to sleep in a rota not allowing the staff very many hours of unbroken sleep.

On one occasion when we were travelling back to Stranraer in the coach the entire party dropped off to sleep soon after leaving Edinburgh. Approaching Stranraer teachers had to waken everyone up to prepare to board the ferry. One girl gave us some concern as, no matter what we tried, we could not rouse her. She seemed dead to the world. Eventually she surfaced, groggy and rather ill-tempered but perfectly well. She was just totally exhausted following the non-stop activity of the previous few days.

We also had day trips on the Larne-Stranraer boat to Ayr or Girvan and these usually involved large parties of up to 100 pupils. I remember one year going on holiday with my family from Larne not long after the July school holidays had begun. I found myself automatically counting the heads of the passengers going on board up the gang plank. I had been conditioned to do this from a series of recent trips to Scotland with large school parties.

In many ways, though, a favourite destination for residential visits was the NEE&LB Outdoor Pursuits Centre at Ballylough, near Bushmills. The buildings, a former school, were equipped with dormitories and a large dining room and, with its position so close to the tourist sites on the North Coast, was ideal for school visits. A minibus was based there to take the pupils round the sites and even wet weather clothing was available,

On our first visit not long after the centre opened, the toilet facilities were rudimentary and consisted of small Portacabin type cubicles outside the main building. One afternoon we lost track of a particular pupil. We could not find him anywhere on the premises. He was not the brightest fellow and we began to be a bit worried about what had happened to him. On a second prowl round the outside of the buildings a teacher spotted a length of toilet roll protruding from beneath the gap below a door of a cubicle. The door was opened and there sat the lad, scarcely discernible through a wreath of unrolled toilet paper. Apparently he had dropped the toilet paper and it had rolled outside beneath the door. He had pulled his end continuously trying, unsuccessfully, to pull it back into the cubicle. He was too shy to shout out and summon assistance to help him solve his problem. We rescued him unceremoniously from his confinement!

There was an open hearth fire in the large lounge when we first visited the Centre. Some evenings before bedtime we gathered the children round the fire and told ghost stories. This was done with only the light of the open fire to light the room. One night in the middle of a story the teacher, hoping to create a suitable effect, paused in her tale and, looking towards a dark corner of the room gasped, 'What's that black, furry thing creeping out from that corner?' With one accord the children made a mad dash for the door to escape from this supposed apparition. It proved more difficult than usual that night to settle the children into their bunk beds.

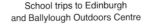
School trips to Edinburgh
and Ballylough Outdoors Centre

Around 1970 the Arts Council of Northern Ireland produced an anthology of poetry from primary schools in the province called 'Over the Moon, Under the Stars.' The school submitted several pieces of writing and the published book contained seven poems from Abbots Cross pupils out of a total of the seventy-two poems in the book. Everyone at the school was very proud of this achievement. At that time there was a team of teachers from the senior classes interested in children's creative writing. The entries in the Arts Council book fairly represented the quality of such writing being produced by our pupils.

Around then for a few years we produced a school magazine and this contained the usual reports on school activities but also outstanding written and art work from year groups P1-P7. Tom Adair, was editor of the magazine and was excellent at choosing the pieces for inclusion. The magazine was printed on the school ink duplicator, a temperamental piece of equipment, but Tom was a talented artist himself and somehow managed to reproduce the text and illustrations to a high standard. The publicity value to the school of this venture was recognised by all and the principal distributed copies to parents and gave one to every important visitor to the school. It really was a popular publication.

I always had a special interest in reading children's stories and over the years I spent at Abbots Cross I met many talented writers. I collected a selection of creative material from a range of classes. To my eternal regret I lent the folder to a student supervisor from Stranmillis College and sadly never saw it again. I do recall some of the writers and the subjects they wrote about. Edward Doggart, one of my P7 pupils, had an amazing ability and feeling for language. He was easily the most fluent writer I encountered in my teaching career. His sentences, superbly constructed, just flowed off his pen with scarcely a mistake in spelling or grammar. To a major extent this came from extensive reading. His favourite author in P7 was Rider Haggard whose books he devoured. One day the class began retelling the story of Captain Bligh and Fletcher Christian and the mutiny on the ship Bounty in the West Indies. There was a popular film on the mutiny showing at the time and the story had captured the imagination of my class, especially the boys. Edward began to write his story at 9.30am and I literally had to drag him off his work when school finished at 3.30pm. I think his story ran to just under twenty pages of his exercise book. There would not have been ten mistakes in the entire piece. His epic writing session coincided with a visit to my classroom of Mr Hoey, the district inspector, who was there to see me and check that I had reached the standard to have my first two probationary years in teaching confirmed. I have always recognised the contribution made to the award of my full teaching certificate by Edward Doggart and the others in that class of outstanding pupils.

Another piece I remember came from a nine-year-old child with learning difficulties. Sadly the original piece has disappeared. He had been asked by his teacher to describe what might happen if the Queen came on a visit to his house. He told of giving the Queen a seat by the fire and making Her Majesty a cup of tea, Along with the tea the Queen would be given a chicken's leg to eat. There were a number of other things that the Queen would be treated to but at the end of nearly every sentence he repeated 'and then I would give the Queen a chicken's leg.' After the Queen had gone he said that they would all sit down and, you have guessed it, have a chicken's leg. It was fascinating to see how, in this child's mind, a chicken's leg and luxury were connected. He may have had a leg of chicken for his dinner the previous night.

Mr Kennedy was good at finding perks for his staff. An opportunity to do this arose regularly when the school was used as a Polling Station. His influence as Senior Presiding Officer was instrumental in suggesting to the Polling officials that teachers be offered jobs as poll clerks or presiding officers at the elections. Not everyone wanted to take up such a position, preferring instead to have the election date as a holiday. I rather liked working at the elections because in addition to the extra cash, I enjoyed meeting the wide range of locals from the neighbourhood who came into the school to vote.

The hours were long – 7am until 10pm – but the chats with police on duty and the other officials at the station helped to relieve the tedium. Of all the spells I spent there on election duty the only disturbance to the peace occurred late one evening when a chap appeared who, from his stagger and slurred speech, it could be seen that he had indulged in too much 'refreshment'. He was noisy and argumentative when he obtained his voting paper and sought advice from the officials as to who he should vote for, all highly against the rules. An official managed with some difficulty to chaperone him into a booth where he somehow collapsed not only his booth but three others in the row. Mayhem ensued for a short time but eventually the police constable on duty conducted him safely outside the premises. A minor ruction such as this was sure to alleviate the boredom of a long day at the polls.

Mr Kennedy was excellent with the staff in two important areas. He supported teachers even when he, and often the teachers themselves, knew perfectly well that they had not been following correct etiquette or procedures. He always fought for his staff and they respected his loyalty and worked all the harder for the school because they knew that he was going to be behind them even when they had strayed from the narrow path. This particularly applied to disputes with parents or education officers.

The other area where he excelled in my view was that, provided you took a conscientious approach to your work with the children, he let you get on with your job. He seldom interfered unless he had major concerns about how things in a classroom were proceeding. He was also favourably disposed to the introduction of innovative or creative methods so long as these did not adversely affect the outcomes achieved by the children. He did not prowl the school looking for poor practice yet he kept an ear close to the ground. I was always surprised at how much he knew about exactly what was going on in the classrooms on a daily basis. His concern above all else was to ensure that the high standards he expected of the pupils and staff were maintained. His judgement was the main contributor to the reputation the school enjoyed for the consistently high standard of work and results produced by the pupils. He was very keen on firm discipline and the quality of the presentation of classwork, especially handwriting.

I started off in Abbots Cross School in August 1961 as a temporary assistant teacher. When I left in June 1976 I was Second Master, in effect a second Vice-Principal. My advance through the different posts of responsibility was achieved in part by good luck. I was in the right place at the right time. During my spell at the school the enrolment dropped from just under 1200 pupils in 1961 to about 850 in 1976. There was a large staff throughout my service and usually a significant turnover in teachers from year to year. I hung on! At one time indeed, albeit for a few months, I was the only male teacher in the school.

My final promotion to the Second Master post in 1969 came about partly because of two factors peculiar to Abbots Cross school. Such an appointment could only be made then in schools where the enrolment justified 1,000 points. At this time each child enrolled was worth 1.5 points to the school. Our enrolment exceeded 750 then so the appointment of a Second Master could be made. Strange as it may seem today, if the existing Vice-Principal was a woman the post had to be a Second Master and vice versa if it was held by a man. Elsie Davison was the Vice-Principal and I was the senior male post holder when I was appointed to the post.

My promotion was very satisfying and I was happy to be teaching in the school. There were many factors contributing to my pleasant experiences there. In the first instance I enjoyed being part of a large staff. There was always something going on, or so it seemed. This camaraderie led to excellent support for me from my more experienced colleagues and in later years I, in turn, enjoyed working with young enthusiastic teachers.

The pupils in Abbots Cross were invariably lively, co-operative and loyal to the school and to their teachers. We had few disciplinary problems. Parents too, were generally supportive of the school and interested in working positively with teachers for the benefit of their children. I feel that I could not have had better conditions anywhere else to begin my career and hone my teaching skills.

And then there was the contribution made to my development into a competent teacher by the principal, James A. Kennedy and indeed by Elsie Davison, his Vice-Principal. Mr Kennedy, most would admit, did have one or two idiosyncrasies but these were more than compensated for by his attributes. Although a man of robust health – he seldom had a day's absence – he did tend to talk quite a bit about various ailments – particularly his back. It usually improved magically when he was due to play golf at Ballyclare. The staff always lent a sympathetic ear.

I came to admire his directness. He was inclined to give frank if somewhat blunt answers especially if he thought someone was trying to put one over on him. I remember a teacher from another primary school asking him to allow his daughter, who was due to start the school in September in P1, if she could have a week there at the end of June to become accustomed to the routines. He ended up saying to Mr Kennedy 'I will leave it with you, you can think about it.' Mr K. responded immediately 'I have thought about it and the answer is no!' Not much room for further discussion there!

He frequently expressed his opinion that the secret of any good school was in the careful selection of staff. He used to boast that he had 'a hand-picked' staff. Over the years it could be said that there were some minor lapses in this principle but, generally, it held up well and was demonstrated by the reputation of the school.

Nowadays, I often receive reminders of my time at Abbots Cross School. I regularly meet former pupils in different locations. They turn up in the strangest places! One has a holiday home a few miles from mine and we visit each other there regularly. He was in the first P7 class I taught for a few months in the school in 1962. Another from my first year class is an avid reader of these scribblings before he passes them on to his mother, my former colleague in Abbots Cross, Elsie Davison. A former pupil, whom I taught through P6 and P7 in the school served as Vice-Principal of Whitehead PS when I was principal there. She has just recently retired.

One afternoon I was listening to the news on Downtown Radio and I thought I recognised the tone and inflection of the newsreader as that of a pupil I had taught in Abbots Cross. I remembered him as someone with a flair for creative writing. On the spur of the moment I wrote a short note to him care of the station. I received a prompt reply not only confirming that he was the former pupil but including a few reminiscences of his time in my class. He concluded by telling me that he was introducing his children to some of the books he had first read at Abbots Cross. A comment like this gives me a thrill and makes me realise how fortunate I was to have chosen teaching as a profession.

Although I was very happy in Abbots Cross school the time came when I realised that, if I wanted to reach the position of principal of a school, I would need some experience in the post of Vice-Principal. The problem was that unless I was prepared to take a cut in salary I would need to find such a position in a school with an enrolment of at least 750. Such posts did not come up very often. I really did not want to have to move house so I considered only Vice-Principal posts that appeared locally.

Then in 1976 the post of Vice-Principal in Ballyclare PS was advertised. I was immediately attracted to this position because it fitted exactly the criteria I had set myself before I applying for a Vice-Principal's post also my mother's family had attended the school in Ballyclare. I knew that its rural setting would make it different from Abbots Cross's suburban character but I felt that it would be an interesting challenge. So I applied and I was fortunate to be appointed to the post. I was delighted but my happiness was tinged with a feeling of sadness that my time at Abbots Cross would soon be over. Here I had been happy, had made many friends and the expertise I had gained in teaching and in the organisation of a successful primary school had been invaluable.

For such an experience I will always be grateful to the management and colleagues at Abbots Cross Primary School.

Chapter 15: Abbots Cross School – Other Voices

Guy Warner attended Abbots Cross PS from 1965-1972

"I was very happy at Abbots Cross. Looking back, Mrs Tease was a lovely P1 teacher. Years later I called to see her at Seaview Primary School and she recognised me straight away as did Mrs McKinstry, Mrs McAuley and Mrs Davison when I visited Abbots Cross in my twenties. I still have some notes from Mrs Tease and prize books from all of them. Our whole class moved up a year with Mrs McKinstry, we were P2 up to Christmas and P3 for the rest of the year. Steven McKinstry, her son, was in the same class and I remember him being taken into the store by his mum regularly to change his trousers.

I was very fond of Mrs Davison, she was very strict but fair. I remember one hot, sunny day she bought the whole class an ice cream. Mrs Press was a dear old lady, she took us for craft. One day she gave the whole class a slap, the lightest possible touch with a ruler and was almost in tears herself! On another occasion, P4 or P5, we had a student who had some difficulty in controlling the class and suggested that we should set upon the chief miscreant at break time for getting us into trouble. So we did and we all received a slap for our pains. I recall resenting this deeply as very unjust, after all we were only carrying out instructions! We made woollen mats with Mrs Press. It seemed to take all term threading the wool through the strings radiating from a circular wooden base. I found that my mum had kept it and I still have it.

With Mr McKinney in P6 we started the fish tank. Some of us visited local ponds at Nellie's Dam and Whiteabbey Bleach Green to collect specimens – usually tadpoles and occasionally, newts. One day I found what we all, including Mr McKinney, thought was a bit of stick. However, I had researched pond life and insisted that it was a caddis fly larva which it turned out to be.

I vividly remember posters of the four provinces of Ireland on the walls of Mr McKinney's classroom and listening to him reading from a book about the myths and legends of Ireland then reading the book myself.

My role with the football team was carrying the kit down to Macedon off the Shore Road. For some time we borrowed the pitch here from the Dr Barnardos Children's Home. I remember walking down with the rest of the senior school to the sea at Hazelbank to watch the Sea Quest Oil Rig being towed down Belfast Lough. One boy, out of sight of our teacher, entertained us by performing dangerous gymnastics hanging off the railing over the water.

In my P7 Year there was a display of military relics set up in our classroom but this was not without incident. Mr McKinney discovered that one of the objects on the table was a live round. There was also an inert hand grenade. My contribution was my great-grandfather and grandfather's medals from the Sudan, the Boer War and World War One.

A much coveted job was helping Mr Stallard, the caretaker, deliver the milk each morning. My youthful belief was that he was a big, powerful man which I later discovered was something of an exaggeration. On the subject of milk the boys had a daily competition to see who could knock it back quickest. Another nice job was being sent to fetch the radio speaker ready for the Time and Tune and Today and Yesterday in Northern Ireland broadcasts.

Mr McKinney ran a quiz competition in our P7 year. This required research in the classroom library, at home or in the Rathcoole Public Library. Bill Surgin and I vied to win a prize. I bought The Observer's Book of Aircraft (1966 edition) which I have still. I remember labouring long hours on a story of flying in World War One which owed much to extensive research in the popular W.E. Johns Biggles books.

I still remember many of the names of my classmates in Abbots Cross School – Bill Surgin, Sam French (the first person I heard use a four-letter word! I asked him what it meant, he said that he had no idea). Ned Doggart, Trevor McKeown, Jackie Walker, Andrew Armstrong, Andrew McCullough, Paul Gardner (a talented pianist who was regularly summoned to the hall to play the popular piece Rustle of Spring) Michael Bailey, Jack Arbuthnot, Ken Woods, Steven McKinstry, Stanley McKnight, Patricia Close (regarded by the boys as the best-looking girl), Karen Nixon, Jennifer Boyd, Jennifer Watson, Marian Richmond (who spoke with a Canadian accent), Elizabeth Millen, Sylvia Thompson.

I loved Abbots Cross and was very sad to leave, though I was looking forward to more history classes at Belfast High School.

Donna Kells (née Eaton) attended
Abbots Cross PS from 1961-1968

It was September 1961 and it was my very first day at Abbots Cross. We didn't wear a uniform back then but I was so proud to be carrying my new brown, leather schoolbag as I walked to school beside my mum. We were escorted across the road by the genial Mr Stallard, our caretaker and patrolman. My mum vividly recalls waiting in the assembly hall with all the other children and parents listening for their names to be called by Mrs Davison. There were lots of tears as some of the children cried or needed gentle persuasion to leave their parents. I think mum was a little put out that I just said a quick goodbye, gave her a wave and headed off happily to Mrs McIvor's P1 class.

Mrs McIvor was tall, elegant and had a beaming smile. I loved her and was fascinated that she often wore shoes that exactly matched the colour of her dresses. I then moved into Miss Cairns class for P2 (she later became Mrs Pollock). She was quiet-spoken and gentle. I remember writing a story about a dog show that she really enjoyed and shared with the class. When I was in the upper school some years later, she also took the girls for needlework and had endless practice threading umpteen needles. Petite Mrs Hall took my P3 class and she introduced us to multiplication. I remember she used a large felt board and small yellow felt squares to illustrate her teaching which made it more visual and fun.

Mrs McAuley took P4 and I particularly remember learning geography in her class. I loved to hear about people living in faraway lands. Sadly though, I am still not good at finding places on a map!

My P5 teacher was Mrs Davison and she was quite strict, you didn't misbehave in her class! She used to wear turtle-necked sweaters with matching coloured, beaded necklaces and as Vice-Principal she was second-in-command to the Principal, Mr Kennedy. He always looked stern and I was a little bit scared of him but he kept the school running smoothly. My dad, who was in the Parent Teacher Association, had great respect for him and all of the staff.

In P6, I had a male teacher for the first time, Mr Hutchinson, and he was lots of fun. When he took us for singing lessons he used to joke that he wanted to keep my friend, Helen Orr, in his pocket – well, she was tiny – because she was a great singer and he always relied on her to give us our starting note.

Next my P7 teacher, MrMcKinney, had the unenviable task of guiding us through the dreaded 11-plus exam. He was calm and understanding and he managed to turn a stressful year into a happy one. In Mr McKinney's class my friend, Catherine Frazer, won a national writing competition organised by the Cadbury / Bourneville company. This success helped to inspire her to write professionally some years later. She has gone on to become the accomplished author Catherine Campbell with seven books to her name. I remember winning a quiz in Mr McKinney's class and the prize was a tiny photo of Mr McKinney and Mr Hutchinson taken together in one of those little photo kiosks! I have kept it all these years.

It was lovely to be trusted to run errands for the staff, even over to the local shops on occasions. I loved helping to collect the dinner money and count it on Friday mornings under the watchful eye of Mrs Welch, the school secretary, with her bright lipstick.

I also really enjoyed helping to look after the younger children during wet playtimes. I remember, too, running round the school playground, skipping and playing rounders with the class. I have other happy memories of our school assemblies using our double-sided page of printed hymns and even now when I hear the hymn 'God who made the Earth' it reminds me of the school.

I also loved the art lessons taken by Mrs Herron, who taught us one afternoon each week. I was pleased to have a Red Indian Boy painting of mine placed on the display board beside Mr Kennedy's office.

I never cried when I started Abbots Cross School because I instantly felt part of a safe and caring family but I certainly did cry seven years later when I left! Fortunately, after all those years of good teaching, a large group of us moved on together to Belfast High School but I will always be thankful for my happy, primary school days.

Tom Adair was a teacher in Abbots Cross PS from 1965-1972

*A*s a rookie teacher at Abbots Cross, beginning in 1965, (my seven apprenticeship years) I inflicted collateral damage on the innocent lives of hundreds of P7 pupils. Each year I marvelled at how much they knew when they entered my classroom, (Room 13, unlucky kids) a tribute surely to the quality of the teaching that went before me. Those were years of lessons learned, mostly by me.*

Fifty years have passed and memory-loss has sifted all the forgettable stuff from the scene. I'm left with an 'Abbots Cross Greatest Hits', the fun, the petty tyranny, the vandalism, the 'characters'.

James Aiken Kennedy – "the Boss" – was self absorbed, a hypochondriac. The janitor, Mr Stallard, an ex-serviceman, was regarded by "the boss" as one from the lower ranks.

From behind his pristine, bum – polished, would be – presidential desk in a sterile office, 'JAK' would gulder "Stallard!" and from wherever he might have been loitering, Stallard, rushing, antennae twitching, came with unlikely Olympian sprint speed, wheezing, grovelling to the sanctum. Eveyln Welch, queen of knitting, and sometime school secretary, noted each passing morsel for her gossip-hoard. As a broadcaster, she could outdo the BBC with breaking news.

The fourth key member of the staff was 'Elsie,' Mrs Davison, renowned for her musical prowess conducting the choir. She was twice as capable as her errant boss, but being a woman, was fated to follow. She taught middle stages and somehow took me under her wing as a work in progress. From the cloakrooms outside her room I would often clandestinely stare towards the windows of my room, noting – unknown to them – the miscreants, the angels, the sluggards, the ever-diligent, returning minutes later to my abode with what they came to believe were spooky extraterrestrial powers of omniscience. I told them I was an Alien.

In 1968, one of those pupils broke into the premises with an accomplice, causing damage to several classrooms (including his own), ripping work from the walls, breaking furniture, pouring raw bleach over floors and walls, scrawling graffiti and drawing simplistic, crude cartoons of the head teacher, poorly depicted as a pig, on sheets of poster paper and pinboard. Mr Stallard discovered the crime on Monday morning. Ulster Television News arrived shortly after, just ahead of the BBC.

Appalled, James Kennedy closed the school while cleaners toiled to erase the damage. That night's local news showed in tell-tale close-up the chalk-written spelling list I had given my pupils that weekend. The camera zoomed. There, in my writing the words 'destruction' and 'destroy'. Had I unwittingly sown the subliminal seeds of rampage?

The pupils work-packed composition books gave the game away. The culprit's handwriting might as well have been his confession. I was shocked. He had been innocuous, almost invisible, never in trouble, not once punished by "the boss". In one of his essays, titled 'My Teacher', he had eulogised me as 'Mr Personality Man'. Confronted with the evidence, he confessed. We simultaneously sent for his parents and the police. He shopped his accomplice without a demur.

The lowest point in my seven years in Abbots Cross, this incident, (still bewildering 50 years later) was outweighed by soaring moments: taking my class to the BBC to record children's street songs and, along with senior teacher, Jack McKinney, conceiving the Abbots Cross School Magazine, showcasing work from every class. Standards were high. In an Arts Council poetry competition across Northern Ireland, edited by Ulster poet Michael Longley in 1970, Abbots Cross scored six inclusions, more than any other school in the land.

This engendered pride amongst staff, especially Paul Hutchinson (P6 teacher), Clarke Frampton (P7 teacher), Jack and myself, since those inclusions had come from our classes. We put on Christmas shows, took the kids on jaunts to Stranraer on the cross-channel ferry, had evening barbecues for staff – sunset-singalong affairs – at local beauty spots such as Brown's Bay on Islandmagee.

What it all added up to was a sense of professional pride, a realisation – in my case certainly – of privilege, most of all to have worked with colleagues who were gifted, committed and giving, not least , of friendship, along with an awareness that, by and large, the parent community and the children we served were appreciative too. Fifty years later, this is borne out by contacts sustained with former pupils, and by friendships continued with colleagues, bonds of connection among the closest I now possess.

In those mere seven years (the length of time it takes any human to shed a single layer of skin), I had learned a lot, not least how to grow and to pay attention to those who knew more. Like the best things in life, that time of begetting continues in memory, yet somehow, back in the day, it seemed it had ended in a blink.

Chapter 16: From Fractions to Fairview

I took up my appointment as Vice-Principal of Ballyclare Primary School on 1 September 1976. This would bring changes to many aspects of my life. On September 5 our first child, Ronan, was born. I seldom find transitions easy. Up to the present Joan and I had enjoyed a very settled domestic life, both teaching near each other. Our home life was orderly and had been so for ten years. Ronan was, of course, a perfect baby but his arrival did make a few adjustments essential.

Ballyclare Primary School shared many features with Abbots Cross. With over 750 pupils both were large schools with large staffs. Each year there was a considerable turnover of teachers with many young staff members making a lively contribution to the school. The two schools enjoyed an enviable academic record for their pupils and an excellent reputation with parents in their respective catchment areas. The school buildings had in common a number of temporary mobile classrooms ranged around the playgrounds. The Ballyclare school had recently acquired a minibus that was a valuable asset for extracurricular activities.

On the other hand there were significant differences between the two schools. Whereas in Abbots Cross the enrolment was in decline, due mainly to a settling of the school age population in the surrounding Rathcoole Estate. In Ballyclare the school was benefitting from its growth as a dormitory town with a regular influx of newcomers to the private and public housing schemes in the course of development in the 1970s.

The parents of the children in Abbots Cross who had settled in the area had come mostly from Belfast and they tended to retain some connection with the city, shopping and visiting relatives there regularly. When I taught local history in Abbots Cross the focus had to be Belfast to allow the pupils to relate to their past, by listening to their families' memories of life in the shipyard, mills and factories.

Ballyclare was distinctly different. A large proportion of the parents of children at the school had spent their lives in Ballyclare and their children could readily be engaged in the history and development of the market town.

I empathised with the accents and the Ulster-Scots speech of many of the children. My mother's family had farmed at Skilganaban near Ballynure and I could tune in and understand even the broadest form of the Ulster-Scots tongue. I particularly enjoyed listening to the children's conversations in the playground where it was the norm.

In my first year at Ballyclare I was assigned a P5 class that was meant 'to break me in.' Then in my second year I was given a P7 class next door to Samuel Stewart, a primary 7 teacher who had spent a lifetime as a pupil and teacher in the school.

As Vice-Principal I had certain managerial duties and these were made easier because I had met many of the staff in other contexts. I had been a pupil at Ballyclare High School with William Hoy who had a background in the local farming community. Willie sometimes spent his lunch breaks in the Ballyclare Auction Market keeping an eye on the current prices of livestock. He was a friendly conversationalist and our chats in the staffroom often centred on mutual friends we had when we were both at Ballyclare High School or members of the farming community that we both knew well. At times this ranged over a fair bit of the Ballyclare neighbourhood and its surrounding villages. It was not unusual for Willie to start off an anecdote in the pre-school gathering in the staff room, continue through the lunchbreak and not always finish in time for the end of school. I had also met Iain Hunter when we had played together at cricket and football on teams in Ballyclare.

The Principal, George Brown, was exceptional in giving me roles with real managerial responsibility. He was aware that my position and experience in my previous school could be drawn on in my responsibilities in Ballyclare and could make an important contribution to the policies and arrangements of the school. I had a role in requisitioning books and teaching materials and worked closely in this area with Nan Moore and Sylvia Auld.

In my first year I had some difficulty coping with the heavy double desks then in use in most senior classrooms. They were cumbersome and difficult to move into different formats for small group work. I had been used to the modern, light tubular steel desks but soon Mr Brown managed to have the older heavy double desks replaced with the modern single type. I was much more at home with these in my classroom. I did appreciate his thoughtfulness in making the alteration for me.

Ballyclare Primary School Staff 1980
Back row (from left): David McGeagh, Robert Hunter, Miss M McBride, Diane Girvan, Helen Armstrong, Valerie Campbell, Patricia Stevenson, Joyce Gray, Yvonne Dickey, Con Rooney, William Hoy.
Middle row (from left): Alma Cull, Pat Ferguson, Hilda Park, Joy Mawhinney, Moira Ervine, Rosemary Bell, Maybeth Ferguson, Valerie McAuley, Joan Millar, Jean Gowdy, Margaret Marcus, Lindy Reid.
Front row (from left): Manson Blair, Lydia Todd, Jack McKinney, Mr George Brown (Principal), Nan Moore, Jean Kirkpatrick, Sylvia Auld.

Mr Brown was an ardent football fan devoting a lot of his considerable energy to coaching the school teams. Assisted by Iain Hunter he coached the team to regular success in the leagues and cups of the district football competitions.

David McGeagh was another teacher I had got to know when his previous school, Glengormley Primary School, played football against Abbots Cross in the district competitions. I remembered David as a reluctant and rather indifferent referee. He had been appointed to Ballyclare Primary School essentially for his musical expertise and, with other staff, to establish a school orchestra. Although refereeing was decidedly not his speciality music certainly was and together with Samuel Stewart, Jean Gowdy and Sandra Ardill developed the music curriculum, choir and orchestra to a very high standard. The orchestra eventually comprised instrumentalists in all sections and attained remarkable success with primary school musicians. The reputation of this feature of the school was outstanding.

A curious incident occurred when I was enlisted in the musical activities of the school. Each year the choir and orchestra performed in Ballyclare Presbyterian Church just across the Doagh Road from the school. The piano in the church was not suitable and it was decided to move the school piano over to the church for the service. Mr Brown was expert at recruiting traders from the town to help out when the need arose. On this occasion he persuaded Sammy Kirk from Symington's furniture shop to employ his removal van to transport the piano from the school to the church. The men on the staff helped to load the piano on to the van parked in the playground beside the school hall and we climbed into the back to help unload it at the church. David McGeagh, always anxious not to strain his back at the heavy lifting, was there to ensure the careful treatment of his precious cargo. In jovial fashion, as Sammy Kirk headed the van across the playground to the Doagh Road entrance, David leant down at the keys and started to play 'Oh I do like to be beside the seaside'. The playground, though level for the most part, rose steeply towards the entrance to the road. Suddenly those in the back of the van realised that this incline had caused the piano to slide towards the rear door of the van that had been left open. The music stopped and , just in time, the men got their shoulders to the end of the instrument to hold it back sufficiently to stop it careering out the back door and down the hill towards the main entrance of the school. Someone later suggested that it would have been more appropriate for David McGeagh to have played the Laurel and Hardy theme tune. The service at the church passed off successfully and returning the piano to the school was trouble free.

When I began to teach a P7 transfer year class I worked very closely with Sam Stewart who also taught this year group. I enjoyed my P7 assignment enormously. The pupils were easily motivated and the parents were supportive of the initiatives introduced by the school. It would be fair to say that, while the teaching was mainly traditional, an openness to change was also present especially where it was felt that such changes did not affect the quality of the outcomes expected in the basic core subjects – what used to be termed the three ' Rs' – reading, writing and arithmetic .

In this context, mathematics was one area of the curriculum where change was happening. Molly Hunter, an experienced teacher from Olderfleet Primary School in Larne, was a pionéer of a practical, exploratory approach to mathematics right through the year groups in primary schools. She spent much time visiting other schools and promoting such an approach to the maths curriculum. I remember one course she led in Ballyclare Primary School on a Saturday morning. The ideas and teaching methods she endorsed were interesting and motivated staff to begin to integrate and develop these into classes in the school The new approach gradually merged successfully into the mathematics curriculum and new equipment, books and materials were ordered to support the initiative.

Ballyclare Primary – and when it was known as Ballyclare Public Elementary School – enjoyed a high reputation for football teams. Robert Gingles, principal of the school in the 1950s, had a keen interest in schools' football and was an official of the organisation of the school boy game at national level. Before the school reorganisation when Ballyclare Secondary School opened in 1963, the school team won many cups and competitions. Looking at the photographs of these teams I noticed how many of the boys shown became players I had played football with in the 1970s as a member of a local Amateur League side. I got used to remarks from boys in my classes, 'Sir, my dad says that he played football with you and he told me that you were often in trouble with referees.'

I remember some disruption to the normal school routine when an extension was being built to the staffroom. The construction involved building out into the closed quadrangle formed when the 1933 extension was constructed. A problem arose because there was no access to this area other than through a doorway in the main school corridor, opposite my P7 classroom. One day a load of blocks was delivered to the senior playground and a young labourer, whom I recognised as a supporter of the local football team, proceeded to transfer the blocks in a wheelbarrow, through the main school entrance and into the quadrangle via the door opposite my classroom. Labourers in Ballyclare in those days tended to work at a slow, steady pace, and I got used to greeting Wilbert as he and his barrow load of blocks nonchalantly passed along the corridor. The job inevitably took a considerable time but, soon after the last load was delivered, it was discovered that they were the wrong type for this work and Wilbert, totally unfazed by the change of plan, cheerfully reversed the process and wheeled the blocks back out to the playground. I think the completion of the work was done during the school holidays but I missed meeting Wilbert with his barrow load of bricks coming down the corridor. I did imagine the possibility of a collision of a pupil with the barrow leading to an unusual accident form stating 'the pupil was struck by a barrow load of blocks in the senior corridor.' I dare say it would have been no more bizarre than a report recording how a piano had crashed through the main entrance doorway! My good friend and colleague, Willie Hoy, found the episode of the wheelbarrow and the blocks a source of great amusement. I remember his loud laughs to this day.

One year he and I were in the party on the annual P7 educational visit to London. In those days we travelled by sea to Liverpool and then by coach to the capital. On this visit we were unfortunate to encounter one of the roughest crossings ever experienced on this route. Unwisely we had allowed the children to over indulge on chips and fizzy drinks not long after we had come on board. The consequences of this decision were unfortunate but predictable. As the wind rose in mid-channel most of the children and, it has to be said, many of the staff, found it necessary to relieve themselves of their meal. Willie and I struggled below deck coping with the misery of the seasickness suffered by most of the pupils. The other staff members bravely helped out but eventually had to retire to their cabins overcome by the conditions. Next day on the coach from Liverpool to London the entire party were untypically drowsy and some slept throughout the entire journey. In spite of such a difficult beginning everyone really enjoyed the trip.

In addition to his musical commitments at the school David McGeagh played in a small dance band most weekends. He had a standing Saturday night engagement to play the piano for diners at a popular Belfast hotel. One morning, I remember, while playing the piano for school assembly his two roles became a bit mixed up and he produced a rather jazzy accompaniment to the hymn 'What a Friend we Have in Jesus'. While the children seemed to enjoy this arrangement, I believe Mr Brown, had some concern and had a quiet word in David's ear and no future improvisations interrupted the traditional assembly hymn tunes.

One Christmas when I was at the school there was some vandalism to the civic Christmas tree in the town square. A large number of the coloured lights were smashed by a person or persons unknown. Mr Brown was contacted by the council and asked if he would mention the incident of vandalism in school assembly. He accordingly addressed the issue, stressing how this action was spoiling the pleasure of everyone in the town. He was really trying to involve the pupils in caring for the tree and at the same time gain inside information about a possible suspect for the damage.

The sequel to this was that the following weekend a vigilant reserve police officer discovered a young rascal making his way up the centre of the tree, climbing branch by branch. He was apprehended and on being asked what he was doing, replied that Mr Brown had put him in charge of guarding the Christmas tree and he was just endeavouring to carry out this duty! The officer did not need to have this story confirmed by Mr Brown to realise that the young lad was telling a tall tale. At times like this while one had to condemn the behaviour, one was forced to admire the ingenuity of the excuses offenders concoct!

Samuel Stewart had an interesting background to his position in the school. His father, Cooper Stewart, had been a teacher in the Boys' National School from the early 1900s and young Sam had been enrolled as a pupil. On his retirement he could claim over sixty years of connection with the Boys' National, Public Elementary and finally Primary School on this site. He was a talented musician and in addition to his contribution to the school music curriculum, he acted as accompanist to the Ballyclare Male Choir for many years. I found it fascinating to listen to him talk about his long connection with the school and hear him describe how conditions had changed and about some of the unusual tasks he had undertaken.

During the 1939-1945 war, children from Belfast came to Ballyclare to escape the air raids. They often spent some nights in the school corridor on camp beds while accommodation with families in the town was arranged. Sam Stewart and some colleagues took turns to sit on guard in deck chairs at the school entrance to ensure that none of the evacuees wandered off during the night.

Another of his wartime duties he related was to visit homes in the town, especially those with young children, and instruct them in the use of the gas masks issued by the authorities. He described how one mother of seven young children had listened to his instructions with growing impatience then burst out 'Och, away out of that, Mr Stewart, by the time I had gone through all that rigmarole with my weans, Hitler would be in on top of us!'

One day after school I was plundering in a cupboard searching for a set of text books when I made an interesting discovery. Stacked in a corner were the registers and report books of the school going back to the Boys' and Girls' National Schools that opened on this site in 1881. I also found similar records from Skilganaban National School that had closed in 1933. The registers had obviously been passed to the Ballyclare National School to which a number of the pupils had transferred. Using the Skilganaban registers it did

P7 Class in 1980: Back row, left to right: Mr David McGeagh, Roger Sherrard, Graham Hill, Stephen Halliday, Graham Cross, Alastair Hall, Trevor Brennan, Norman Todd, Stuart Parke, Geoffrey Dowden, Mr Jack McKinney. Middle row, left to right: Stephen McAlister, James Stewart, David Hoy, William Shaw, Ian Rutherford, Nicola Gibson, Karen McGladdery, Esther Wright, Christine Bingham, David Kyle, Ian Baxter, Sam Houston, Peter McDonald. Front row, left to right: Gillian McQuillan, Linda Longstaff, Carol McQuigan, Jane Magee, Tracey Ireland, Gillian Slane, Kerry-Ann Montgomery, Nicola McCune, Fiona Stewart, Heather Barkley, Doris McConkey.

not take me long to find entries for my Kennedy aunts and uncles who had attended Skilganaban School. This discovery proved a crucial event for me. Taken with other later discoveries, it kindled my interest, not just in the history of the school, but in the wider history of the market town of Ballyclare.

Robert T Grange

It was around this period that I took up an idea suggested to me by Nan Moore, my senior colleague. She recognised my interest in local history and introduced me to Mr Robert Grange the well-known authority on the history of Ballyclare. He was in his late eighties then but lively and alert. I began to make regular visits to his home on the Green Road and I know that he enjoyed sharing his knowledge of the town and locality with me. So began my long association with him. Over many years he had compiled a manuscript history of the town and the area in two large, bank ledgers complete with photographs and written in his immaculate copperplate handwriting. He was excellent as a source for the research I had begun on the history of the school and town.

It was a happy coincidence that, in 1978 the Northern Ireland Public Record Office introduced a programme and a conference intended to make teachers aware of the sources available to them from their archives to use in history lessons. Willie Hoy and I attended the conference and we were interested and inspired by this development. It prompted me to search for local history sources in and around Ballyclare. What I had already seen from the old school registers and heard from many former teachers and residents made me think that a good start would be to examine the background of the development of elementary schools in Ballyclare with specific reference to the history of Ballyclare Primary School.

In 1977 the Queen's Jubilee was celebrated in many parts of Northern Ireland by holding civic events. The prime minister, Sir Terence O'Neill, promoted a series of Civic Weeks in towns across the province. For a time it seemed that nothing along these lines would happen in Ballyclare but in good time Mr Brown and some local councillors were instrumental in forming a committee to organise a festival. With the close involvement of Mr Brown in the town initiative it was certain that the primary school would be taking part. The school's contribution was a Fancy Dress parade around the town. Parents and children really pulled out all the stops and suggested ideas for topics and costumes. I remember some boys and girls from my P7 class took up the theme of Bugsy Malone, then a popular film in the cinema. One teacher, Sylvia Auld even acquired a pony and trap for the procession with a group of pupils dressed in period costume. This event fitted in well with the history research I had begun on the school and the town.

Before the Boys' and Girls' National Schools were built in 1880 two very different schools catering separately for boys and girls existed in the town. One on Tow Loanin' (later called Foundry Lane) was a rudimentary edifice known as 'The Wudden Box.' The teacher was Robert Percy. The other school was situated at the east of the main square opposite the Market House and it was locally known as 'Fractions School'. The name referred to the Principal in the Boys' School, David John McCune, who had acquired the nickname 'Fractions' from his interest and ability in Arithmetic. Mr McCune retired in 1879. In addition to Robert Grange the main source for information on schools in the town in the 1870s is Archibald McIlroy, a banker and local author whose books include colourful descriptions of Fractions himself and the conditions in his school and in 'The Wudden Box' which he also attended for a time.

A new primary school was planned to open in Ballyclare in September 1980 to relieve the pressure on the increasing enrolment of the present school. Mr Brown suggested that it might be a good idea to mark the occasion by holding an exhibition of children's work focusing on the history of the school and the town. This was popular with the staff and plans for such an enterprise were drawn up allocating time to prepare projects and displays.

In June 1980 the school presented a range of class projects on aspects of Ballyclare's history. The material collected and the projects were displayed in the school hall and parents and others from the town community invited to inspect the displays. There were also some evenings for reunions of former pupils and staff.

The display of the pupils' work proved a great success and attracted large crowds each evening. A highlight was the number of former pupils of the National and Public Elementary Schools who attended. Many of these were able to see themselves or relatives in photographs ranging from the recent past to the first decade of the twentieth century. Others were able to recognise and greet colleagues who had attended the schools and who had been long forgotten.

Manson Blair and his P7 class constructed an excellent model of the school buildings on the present site. Copies of past work books and text books were discovered in odd cupboards around the school and in the homes of past pupils and placed on display.

On the week of the exhibition a social evening was held in the school when former members of the school's staff met the present staff over a meal and were entertained by the school orchestra. All in all, the week's activities proved a fitting way to celebrate the centenary of primary education on this school site and at the same time focus on the rich history of Ballyclare. The focus on the school centenary with the projects and photographs did create an interest in the town on the general history of Ballyclare. As a direct result of this and to maintain and develop this theme in the community a number of those interested got together in November 1980 to form the Ballyclare & District Historical Society. It is pleasing to note that the society remains active, 40 years after its inauguration.

A staff observer of the 'Swinging Seventies' writes:

"In 1970, George Brown (GB) became the new Principal of Ballyclare Primary School and introduced 'the Age of Enlightenment'. I can say this because shortly after his arrival a school inspector told him that 'shades of the Edwardian era permeated the school.'

G.B. was an innovator and encourager. Football, which had been neglected, was reintroduced and before long Ballyclare Primary dominated the Schools' League. Drama, Art and Music took pride of place and David McGeagh came from Glengormley Primary School to create an orchestra. Here we had an enigma – the best of company but a very eccentric character. The story goes that in Glengormley Primary School he was gazing into a mirror, either adjusting his toupee or admiring himself, when the young violinist by his side nearly poked out his eye with his bow.

He was a parsimonious gentleman. Sandra Ardill his colleague in the music department, was asked for her advice as to whether he should purchase a new suit. She told him to go ahead and spend his money. He replied that he might leave her some of it. She said 'Wear your velvet jacket – then play.'

On a school trip to Scotland, Davy's 'holiday canvas cap' blew off on to the railway line. Children were daily admonished not to go down to the railway line but Davy himself clambered down to retrieve his cap. Immediately a railway official appeared on the platform, bristling with the authority of his peaked hat. In a broad Scots accent he lacerated Davy for his behaviour by setting such a bad example to the children.

In the middle of the 1970s, Jack McKinney arrived as Vice-Principal to replace Miss Topping. Jack had just completed a university course in Education and was au fait with educational trends. His infectious enthusiasm and ability to motivate were of great benefit to the school.

The centenary of the school was on the horizon in 1980. A typescript magazine had been produced for the Queen's Jubilee but the school centenary needed full recognition. Jack produced an excellent history of the school entitled: 'Facts Figures and Fractions'. Simultaneously, a centenary exhibition was mounted by the staff and the old school registers from 1880 onwards were a focal point. Afterwards present and former staff held a celebration dinner. Entertainment was provided by the school orchestra and choir while later in the evening two senior members of the staff mounted the stage to give an unforgettable rendition of 'Oft in the Stilly Night' and Gilbert and Sullivan's popular duet 'The Two Gendarmes'.

One memorable school trip, organised by Mrs Sylvia Auld, was to London and we had one of the roughest cross channel crossings imaginable. Staff were all involved in dealing with sick children. Eventually when the trips to the basins cleared, Sylvia, Nan and Jack were on their own. Jack had propped himself against the wall and he had a smile playing about his lips. 'I wonder how the man we saw earlier eating the feed of sausages, beans and chips is getting on?' We were finished off by that and we left him to it to deal with any other casualties who arrived. I think Willie Hoy returned to keep him company.

Willie was a much-loved member of staff, an upright man who knew everything and everybody. He had gained a distinction in Senior Certificate Latin, no mean feat! Teacher Rosemary Bell's son who was a keen farmer like Willie so hero worshipped him that he asked his mother to buy him trousers like Mr Hoy's!"

With the preparation for the celebrations of the centenary of the school I knew that 1980 would be an especially busy time. As the year unfolded it soon became obvious that affairs would occur to make the year even more significant for my personal and professional life. On Monday, January 6, I was at home preparing to set out for school on the first day of the Spring term when I had a telephone call from my brother. Our mother who had been staying with him over the New Year holiday, had died suddenly early that morning. This was, of course, a dreadful way to begin a new year. In March a happier occasion occurred in the McKinney household when our daughter, Emma, was born.

Before we moved to live in Tildarg in 1978, I had travelled to Ballyclare from our home in Mossley, and approached the town down the Hillhead Road. From the steep incline of this road there was a clear view of the northern section of the town. One morning I noticed a new building had begun to appear off the Rashee Road just above

Mr George Brown (Principal, Ballyclare PS) making presentations to members of the first staff soon to take up positions in Fairview New PS in September 1980. All were previously members of staff in Ballyclare PS. From left: George Brown, Jack McKinney, Yvonne Dickey, Valerie Campbell, Patricia Stevenson, Robert Hunter

and west of Ballyclare High School. It transpired that this was the new primary school for Ballyclare planned to open on 1st September 1980. I must say that this information focussed my thoughts on my professional future. As Vice-Principal of the existing primary school I should be considering applying for the principalship of the new school when the post was advertised. The school was to be called Fairview Primary School and in March the advertisement appeared in the press.

Thus, began a dilemma for me. I had spent four happy years in my present role in Ballyclare Primary School. I really enjoyed the combination of managerial responsibilities and classroom teaching. Other positive features I enjoyed included my friendly, co-operative staff colleagues, the loyal support of parents, the rapport created with the pupils and the personal and professional relationship I had developed with the principal and others on the senior management team. All of these I recognised and appreciated. Therefore, I asked myself – did I really want to forego such a happy position to take on the difficult challenge of establishing a new school? Such feelings dominated my thoughts in the days before a decision had to be made. I completed the application form but, still undecided, left it on the top of a cupboard in our Tildarg home.

On the evening before the closing date for the application I met an old friend at a meeting in Ballyclare. He was familiar with my career and expressed disappointment that I was considering not applying for the job. His view was that if I did not apply this could affect my prospects of promotion in the future. I spent a disturbed night turning the options and their consequences over in my mind. Early next morning I took the completed form and handed it in to the Schools Department, County Hall, Ballymena.

I was appointed Principal of Fairview Primary School in April 1980 and from that date my life changed completely. Gone for ever was the advantage of passing the ultimate responsibility for decisions up the chain of command. It did take some time for this to settle comfortably on my feeble shoulders.

On September 1, 1980 I set out with four colleagues from Ballyclare Primary School, who had been appointed to the new staff, up the Rashee Road to welcome the first pupils in their brand new uniforms to the first day for all of us at the splendid new facilities in Fairview Primary School.

It would take too many more pages, I'm afraid to describe my future experiences teaching and managing in Ballyclare and eventually, Whitehead, the final assignment of my enjoyable 40-year career in the teaching profession.